CONTE]

Chapter 1

MARK and ANNIE

Owen's father, Mark, one of the Maginns of Kilcoo, could trace his family roots back to the 17th century in the Hillsborough area of Co Down. Records attest that, "Daniel Maginn of Kilwarlyn was possessed of the several townlands of Dromantanty and Clogher and the half town of Dromity in the townland of Dromatihugh in the civil parish of Blaris and of Hillsborough". Following the campaign of Cromwell's Parliamentary army, Daniel was dispossessed of his estate. The Maginns were forced to seek a new home and eke out a more difficult livelihood on the less favourable soil of Kilcoo.

Two of Daniel Maginn's sons, Patrick and Ronan, both priests, gained considerable importance in ecclesiastical affairs. Patrick, residing in London, enjoyed the favour of King Charles II and was confessor of his wife Queen Catherine of Braganza. In 1662, Patrick endeavoured in vain to win back his father's estate from the Downshire family. In 1677 in Paris he and another Irish priest, Malachy Kelly, succeeded in gaining permission from Louis XIV to occupy the abandoned *College des Lombards* as a place for training seminarians for the Irish mission. Thus began the distinguished Irish College in Paris. *Abbé* Maginn raised funds to restore the college, built a chapel, and established burses for students from Down and Dromore. After his death in 1683 at the age of sixty-five, a monument was erected to him by a relative, Arthur Magennis, over the spot in the college where his heart was buried.

Patrick's brother, Ronan, studied in the Irish College in Rome from where he graduated a Doctor of Theology. As Vicar General of

Dromore, he and seven of his priests were imprisoned by "heretical magistrates" in 1668. He suffered two more incarcerations, the most serious one occurring when he had been tricked into making a visitation of Derry to deprive and punish the scandalous Vicar Apostolic, Terence Kelly. Apprehended by Kelly's supporters, he was sent under guard to London where he might have forfeited his life had it not been for the influence his brother Patrick had with the King. In 1671, he was nominated Vicar Apostolic of Dromore; at this time he also had charge of the diocese of Down.

After being dispossessed, the Maginns established themselves in Fofanyreagh, Kilcoo. The name 'Kilcoo' comes from *Cill Chunaidhe,* meaning 'Church of Mourning' because, it was said, the body of St Patrick was waked there. In 1766, it was reported to the House of Lords that the parish of Kilcoo had 496 Protestants, 2,174 Papists, two Popish priests, and one 'fryar' (a Dominican). Tracing their Christianity back to St Patrick, the people persevered in their faith despite persecution. Well concealed Mass rocks and ruined churches bear witness to their trials and fidelity. Proudly Gaelic and nationalistic, Kilcoo was one of the last places in Co Down where Irish was spoken.

In *Griffith's Tenement Records* of 1834, the very old 'Chapman's Corn Mill', driven by the Muddock river, was owned by a 'Mark Maginn'. Believed to be the oldest and largest mill in the parish, it had a massive water wheel 13½ feet in diameter and 3½ feet wide. It was still owned and operated by Maginns in the 1920s. According to the *Valuation of Tenements* of 1863, Mark Maginn leased 2 acres 2 roods and 20 perches of land from John Fitzpatrick, the Earl of Roden. On it he had a house, corn mill, kiln, and a miller's house.

Another wealthy miller, Patrick Maginn, procured an imposing castellated tower-house on the shore of Strangford Lough at Kilclief. Known for generations as 'Maginn Castle', it had been first built for the Bishop of Dromore in the fifteenth century. A William Maginn lived there in the 1900s. Willed to a brother of Mark (Owen's father), it was sold and passed out of family hands. Now called 'Kilclief Castle', it stands resplendent as a Historic Monument in State care.

Maginn Castle

In a black notebook which Owen's father, Mark, kept for family history, he wrote about his uncle another 'Fr Patrick Maginn'. A native of Kilcoo, this Patrick studied at the Irish College founded by his relative two centuries earlier in Paris. Ordained by the Archbishop of Paris in 1834, on his return to Ireland he was appointed to the curacy of the united parish of Larne and Carrickfergus. In 1841, he was transferred as a curate to Bright, then to Belfast and, finally, to assist the ailing parish priest of Kilclief. On the latter's death he became parish priest. Dying in 1892 in Kilclief, he was buried near the church. Mark had a copy of Fr Patrick's will in which he left considerable property to his ecclesiastical superior and a farm in Kilclief to his brother, another 'Mark' Maginn.

It is said locally that Fr Charlie O'Neill, parish priest of Kilcoo, wrote the much loved republican song, *The Foggy Dew*. Another claim is that it was written by Peadar Kearney, author of *The Soldier's Song*. Whichever it was, it <u>was</u> the quick-witted Fr Charlie who paraphrased Prime Minister Winston Churchill's famous tribute to the men who fought in the 'Battle of Britain', "Never in the field of human conflict was so much owed by so many to so few". When promoting a parish sale of work in Kilcoo, he advertised it saying, "Never was so much offered to so many by so few for so little, coupon-free!"

Mark Maginn, Owen's father, was born in 1884, the eldest son of Owen and Bridget Maginn of Fofanyreagh, Kilcoo. In the 1901 Census of Ireland, Mark's father was described as a farmer and miller. Mark, then seventeen years old, worked with him. Mark had three brothers and two sisters: Bridget, thirteen, Willie, nine, Thomas, seven, Owen five, and Rosie, three. All, except Rosie, were described as 'scholars', meaning they were going to school.

With keen country intelligence and a great desire to learn, Mark did well in St Malachy's, the local primary school. He loved to read and liked to try his hand at writing verse. Grown tall and broad-shouldered, he had a well-merited reputation for hard work. Pleasant company and a good mixer, he was a popular man. A prominent member of the Kilcoo Flute Band, he proudly marched with thirty fellow bandsmen on patriotic occasions, wearing a uniform of jacket and cap with pike men at their side. He was also a member of the first Kilcoo tug-o-war team which, in 1908, competed against teams as far away as Newry and Newcastle and was never beaten. Later, he became the trainer of the Slieveniskey team whose members he drilled by getting them to raise a heavy boulder on a rope slung over the fork of a tree. He celebrated their victories in a poem, "The men who never knew defeat".

In 1917, at the age of thirty-three, he married Annie Mallon of Dromena, Kilcoo, an assistant teacher in Ballymoney girls' primary school and organist in the parish church. Fourth child of Thomas and Catherine Mallon, she was twenty-eight and had been teaching for nine years. Her parents at the time of the 1901 Census had eight children: Owen, Mary, Catherine, Annie, Thomas, Hugh, Patrick and Norah. All, except the last three, who were infants, were going to school. Even the oldest, Owen, who was twenty-one, was described as a 'scholar'; evidently education was highly valued in the family. The Mallons were noted for their staunch faith and commitment to nationalist aspirations.

Ironically, times were fairly good in Northern Ireland during the First World War. The British army was buying Irish beef and potatoes for the troops and flax for making linen bandages and aircraft wings. Land was relatively cheap and, the year before he married, Mark bought a forty-acre farm with a house on it at Drumanaghan near the village of Drumaroad in south Down. Though not the reason for buying it, he was pleased when he heard that it once belonged to a family called Rogans who had seven sons priests!

Annie and Mark's first child, Catherine, did not survive. In fact she died before she could be baptised. The second child was born on the 18th of October 1920 and baptised the same day with the name, 'Eoghan' or **Owen**', but it was 'Eugene' (the English form of 'Eugenius' the Latin for Eoghan) which was inscribed in the baptism register. The family never called him Eugene. As Owen, he was named after Mark's father. 'Owen' and 'Mark' were names that appeared in nearly every generation of Maginns. Owen's sponsors were Patrick Devlin, a neighbour, and Rosie, Mark's sister.

After the Great War, the economic situation in Northern Ireland declined; the sale of flax and potatoes fell; hard times set in. Emigration to America, already common in south Down, increased. Mark's brothers, Patrick, Willie, and Thomas, and Annie Mallon's brothers, Hugh, Patrick, James, and Tom, all left to seek a better life across the Atlantic. In 1923, Mark and Annie decided to go too. They booked passage on the White Star liner, the *Baltic*, sailing from Liverpool on 25 October.

Mark engaged a neighbour, Paddy Carlin, to keep an eye on the farm. The little family got the required inoculations and packed their bags. The last thing three-year-old Owen remembered was his grandparents from Kilcoo coming to say goodbye. The 'American Wake', the farewell party for departing kin, was his earliest childhood memory.

At sea, Mark admired the *Baltic*, the largest ship in the world when built by Harland and Wolff, Belfast, in 1903. At the ship's rail he struck up a conversation with a pipe-smoking sailor. Glad to air his knowledge, the 'old tar' proudly described the ship, "She's 24,000 tons, 709 feet from stern to bow, 75 feet in beam, and has a top speed of 17 knots; she can accommodate 425 first class passengers, 450 second and 2,000 third class". He spat in the water, "Too many, if you ask me. If she ever got holed, there'd be an awful loss of life, especially in third class!"[1] After a throaty cough, he went on to tell Mark how, in 1909, the *Baltic* had rescued survivors of the collision between the *Republic* and the *Florida* off the north east coast of the U.S. and, in April 1912, she sent ice warnings to the *Titanic*, but they were ignored.

It was cold at sea. Little Owen ran about the decks and asked his mother why his arm hurt where the doctor had stuck a pin in him. Neighbours, like Mr Laverty, relieving his parents, clutched him tightly by the hand for fear he'd jump overboard. He was learning to talk as fast as he could run. After mooring at Ellis Island, he ran ahead and shouted, "I'm the first man to land in America".

The Baltic

The new immigrants mounted the stairs to the Great Hall. They were scrutinised by a team of doctors standing above them. When they arrived at the top, the medics put chalk marks on the backs of some of the passengers. The marks indicated that possible weaknesses or disabilities had been detected: 'E' for eyes, 'H' for heart, 'S' for senility, 'X' for a mental defect. Mark nodded at the doctors, Annie looked them in the eye, and the small lad said, "I'm Owen".

It had been a fast voyage, the *Baltic* docked on the 2nd of November. According to its passenger list, the Maginns were bound for Albany in New York State, and their friend, or contact there, was registered as "H. Hanna". They stayed for some time in Albany but, as Mark didn't find employment, they moved on, finally settling in Detroit where he got a job in Henry Ford's motor works. Renting accommodation, first, in a district where, they discovered, everyone spoke Polish, they moved to an Irish district in the parish of St Vincent's near a big 'ball park'.

Detroit was a booming industrial city in the Twenties. Henry Ford's 'Model T' automobile, the famous "Tin Lizzie", was changing the face of transport in America and providing thousands with employment. Ford's revolutionary assembly line was capable of producing a car every ten seconds and earning Henry $25,000 a day! Intending to win loyalty and encourage his employees to become Ford car owners, the grandson of a West Cork immigrant, raised workers' wages to more than twice the national minimum and introduced a five-day working week.

Another phenomenon of the decade was the mushrooming illegal 'speakeasies' which dispensed liquor in that era of strict prohibition. Despite the laws against making and consuming alcohol, more of it appeared to be drunk than ever and control of its lucrative sale gave rise to gangs and vicious 'turf' wars. The 'Roaring Twenties', as the decade was called, was a time of quick money, loosening morals, and rising crime.

Work on the car assembly line was monotonous and stiflingly hot. Mark returned home every day drenched in sweat. He was made a section supervisor and entrusted with a key which gave him access to most of the factory floor. He rented a large house on Twelfth Street, Wayne and, to augment their income, Annie took in lodgers, mainly friends and relatives from home and a few Donegal men. Owen sold newspapers and, with the profits, paid to see his heroes, the Detroit Tigers, play baseball. When he and his friends had no money, they hung about the ball park entrance until a game was half over, then they got in free. At one memorable game, he saw Babe Ruth of the New York Yankees play.

Maginn's was like a 'céilinn house', where people frequently dropped in for conversation, a cup of tea or, maybe something stronger – the Donegal men were brewing beer in the cellar! Occasionally Mark and friends went across the Detroit River to Windsor on the Canadian side where there was no prohibition. Mark had a cousin in Windsor, Stephen McEleavey. Visiting him gave the men an excuse for crossing the border. Sometimes Mark brought Owen with him as Stephen had a son, Lochy, the same age as Owen.

Conversations in the house, no matter how they began, nearly always ended up about money, stocks and shares. People were investing heavily and the general expectation was that the good times would go on for ever. A second favourite subject was 'the old country', Ireland. Hearing his father speak often of a place called 'Shanbally', Owen imagined it must be a mighty city like Detroit and he hoped he'd see it one day.

Every now and then, sitting late in the kitchen, Mark wrote some verse. Motivated by yearning for home he wrote about Co Down as well as about contemporary events in Detroit. Some of his poems were published in the city's *Irish Weekly* including, 'The Man in Grey', 5 February 1927, and 'Neal Coll' (a Donegal man killed on Good Friday at a bridge construction site on the Detroit-Windsor highway, 19 May 1928). The poems reflected Mark's deep faith, patriotism, social conscience, and good humour. Other titles of his were: 'The Mass-Rock of Dunmore', 'Goward Hill', 'The Caraban Road', 'Roden's Castle', and 'Children at Play'. Among places mentioned were: Kilcoo, Moyadd, Slieveniskey, Attical, Cairn Brae, Spelga Pass, Bryansford, Hilltown, Loughinisland, Saul, Ballyculter, and Ballywillwill.[2]

Mark and Annie had six children but only two survived, Owen and Tom. Tom was born in Detroit, 25 September 1925. The high mortality was due to a gynaecological problem which Annie discovered, too late, could have been rectified. The deaths caused her and Mark great sorrow. Owen remembered going home one afternoon from school and, sensing gloom in the house, went straight to his parent's room. He found Annie in bed looking pale and distressed with Mark sitting beside her holding a dead baby in his arms. Mark was sobbing his

Owen and Tom

heart out. The scene gave Owen an inkling of how great parents' love for their children must be. He often wondered where Catherine, his sister, went after she died; he knew his mother worried a lot about her immortal soul as she had died before she could be baptised.

Two photographs, taken in Detroit, show Annie and Mark with the boys. In one, with a water fountain background Owen, dressed in knickerbockers, colourful knee length socks, high top shoes, white shirt and school tie, points a toy pistol at the photographer. Mark, wearing a fedora hat, stands behind him resting his hands on his shoulders. Tom, about three years of age, stands in front of his mother. Annie, wearing wire-rimmed spectacles and a dowdy pill box hat, looks all the part of a stern boarding mistress. The second photo shows the quartet on the sidewalk of a good-class residential area. In it, Mark holds the hand of Owen who

Mark and Annie,
Owen and Tom

is dressed in a smart check pullover, knickerbockers and, again, colourful knee length socks. Tom is rigged out in a white sailor suit while Annie, smiling this time, stands behind him hatless. A third photo from Detroit shows a plump-faced Owen arm around Tom with another boy who also has his arm around Tom. Owen, while

The Maginn family, Detroit, Mich., U.S.A.

looking alert and attentive, is not actually smiling in any of the three photos. Perhaps the last photograph was taken after his confirmation in St Vincent's on the 8th of January 1928.

He went to two schools, first to St Boniface's run by German Dominican nuns and then to the parish school of St Vincent's also run by nuns. The Sisters encouraged the pupils with 'modern' fear-free methods of teaching with lots of mind-stretching games and competitions. Owen was the fastest in his class at 'sums' but, one day, another boy beat him. Vexed, he went over the numbers again in his head and asked the Sister for another try. This time he demolished his rival.

A friend with Owen and Tom

Life in Detroit wasn't all fun and games. On the streets there were gangs like the Purple Gang who taxed legitimate businesses and ran illegal ones of their own. Teenagers and kids, aping the adults, formed gangs and fought off intruders in their 'turf'. Evenly matched, the youngsters didn't do much harm to one another but, sometimes, things got out of hand. Owen, leader of his gang, fancying himself as a champion pugilist, got into plenty of fights. One day outside a drug store, his mob was confronted by a Polish gang. Their leader, a wiry-looking gladiator, challenged Owen to 'single combat'. Supporters quickly formed a ring around them, one side shouting for Owen, the other for the Pole. Owen, no match for the bigger lad, was on the ground in no time getting pulverised. Unwilling to give in because of the crowd, a question kept running through his head, 'When will this beating stop?' It didn't stop until the Pole got tired. "I lost interest in fighting after that", said Owen.

When he was about eight, walking home from school one evening, he was set upon by a gang of Mexicans toughs. With his own gang, he had put them to flight on previous occasions but, this time, they had reinforcements and the bigger youths were carrying knives. They dragged him into a yard where they tied him, spread-eagled, to a wooden fence. Standing back, they took turns throwing their knives at him, sticking them in the wood closer and closer to him. It was a terrifying experience. After they left him, he made his way home, uninjured but in shock. Reaching his house, he went round the back, sat on a step and wept. Annie found him there and, between sobs, got from him what had happened. Furious, she went straight to the school. From then on, Owen was given a 'guard' to escort him home.

Along with the apparent prosperity, booming industries, and burgeoning cities of the U.S., the 'movie' business was also making rapid strides. 'Hollywood' and 'Metro-Goldwyn-Mayer' were becoming household words. 'Mickey Mouse' was a national hero. First appearing in 1928 as the star of *Steamboat Willie*, the mighty mouse was an immediate hit. Not the least of the fans was Owen Maginn.

One day, Mark came home from work agitated. The motor plant doctor, after a routine examination, informed him that he had a serious heart complaint, "You should put your affairs in order and make provision for your family!" he said. Annie and he were very upset but, strong believers in the efficacy of the Mass, they started to do a novena in the church of the Holy Redeemer, popular among the Irish. It was winter and bitterly cold. For nine consecutive mornings they walked early on the cold, icy streets to the church. Young as he was, Owen was impressed and thought, "If they can have such faith in

God, then so can I". Later, he joked, "The novena must have worked because my father lived to be eighty-four!"

Owen himself had a few unusual health setbacks while in Detroit. At one time, he went deaf. Nobody seemed to know why but, when he got his tonsils out, his hearing returned! Then he had an accident in which he broke both his legs.

Shortly before Christmas 1929, he received a hard-covered illustrated prayer book entitled *My Mass Book*. Inside the cover he wrote his name in a boyish hand, 'Owen McGinn' (not 'Maginn'). An adult hand also wrote his name in the same more 'Irish' manner, "Owen McGinn, St Vincent's School, 12-21-'29". The Mass book remained a lifelong treasure.

Recession 1930s
The New York Wall Street crash of October 1929 put an abrupt end to the gallop of the 'Roaring Twenties'. The Maginns, like everyone else, were badly hit. Mark, Annie and friends, with most of their earnings in stocks and shares, lost practically everything. A friend of theirs from Leitrim jumped to his death off the Detroit Bridge. Unemployment and poverty became the lot of thousands. Food was scarce, money scarcer, soup and bread lines grew. The production of motor cars dropped; factories closed; Mark was laid off. The misery surrounding him impelled him to write "The Cry of the Distressed", which was published in the *Detroit Irish Weekly*:

How long o Lord, how long / With hearts that are filled with woe,
In a land that is blest with plenty / Must the poor down-trodden go;
With the pangs of hunger gnawing / And hope but a dream that fled,
While the heart of the mother's breaking / As she wished her baby dead.

What need for this destitution / Or why must this trial be
And what hope for the suffering people / Is there o Lord but thee?

We know you are kind and loving / A friend to the poor and week
That you're always a willing giver / To those who your mercy seek.

Have pity then on thy people / As they suffer in dread and fear,
While the wolf in the guise of hunger / To the door is drawing near.
Yet blind for they will not see / The anguish that's being endured
Is known o Lord to thee.

Parents pinched and hungry / The future view with dread,
As they watch their children starving / And cannot give them bread.
O why must the children suffer? / O why this grievous wrong?
How long must the people bear it? / How long, o Lord, how long?

Keeping pace with hunger and unemployment, crime increased and gang wars escalated. Rivalling Chicago's 1929 Valentine's Day Massacre in which seven were murdered, Detroit, in 1930, saw the slaying of ten men in 'Bloody July'. The same month, an anti-mob radio commentator was gunned down in the lobby of the La Salle Hotel not far from Twelfth Street where the Maginns lived.

By the end of September 1930, only four days after Detroit authorities began registering the numbers of people out of work, 76,000 had submitted their names. As anger and frustration grew, the unemployed demonstrated in the streets and, eventually, clashed with police. People who could, returned to their home countries, but hundreds of thousands who lacked the means, roamed the streets homeless, hungry, and desperate. Annie's boarders left and, by the time of the Federal Census of 1930, only her younger brother, Hugh, remained.

Mark, fearing for his small family, decided to send them back to Ireland. He would remain himself for a time, hoping things would improve. Annie, Owen, and Tom, with heavy hearts, parted from him at the city railway station and boarded a train to Montreal. There they boarded ship for Ireland. Most of their fellow passengers were, like themselves, fleeing the slump. The mood was subdued. It was winter time and cold.

Mark traipsed about looking for work, taking on anything he could get, dangerous work, "on the roofs of skyscrapers and in the bowels of the earth". For years, Kilcoo men had gone west to the great mines in Montana. Mark need not have gone that far. Henry Ford, had mines near Detroit and the iron and steel industry of Pittsburgh always needed miners. Mark, working as a miner, one day saved his workmates from death or serious injury. After waiting a long time at the bottom of a shaft for the cage to come and lift them to the surface, Mark and those with him, believing something must have gone wrong with the cage mechanism, began to climb the shaft ladder. High in their ascent they heard the cage descending. It would have knocked them off the ladder but Mark, in the lead, grabbed and held it, allowing the others to pass. Exhausted when he finally got to the surface, he swore he'd never go underground again. Family lore has it that he took up other work on the railways and travelled as far as California as a locomotive stoker.

The dimensions of the economic catastrophe were beyond young Owen but, he sensed the despair of the adults and hated the idea of being separated from his father. On bidding his family goodbye, Mark had reminded him that he'd be seeing Shanbally soon. He looked forward to that but would have preferred if Mark was there to show him around.

It was cold and damp on deck as the big ship ploughed its way east across the Atlantic. Owen looked forward to his 'first' sight of Ireland and rushed to the rail when the cry went up, "Land ahoy!" Disappointingly, the 'Emerald Isle', looked grey and dreary in the mist. Annie, Tom and he disembarked at Belfast and stayed the night in a hotel. Next day Annie hired a taxi. As they neared home, Owen, with growing expectation, looked out for Shanbally but, to his utter stupefaction, they drove through it in less than a minute, "It's only a small wee wreck of a place", he complained. Annie defended it, "It was important enough at one time; even had its own fair". "That's our field there", she said pointing, "Shanbally field. We're home!"

Paddy Carlin, the man Mark had left looking after the farm, heard the taxi arrive and hurried to meet them. He had a good fire going in the hearth and the kettle on the hob was boiling. Owen was alarmed on seeing an open fire inside the house; he'd never seen the like in Detroit. Over a scalding cup of tea, Annie mentioned the whins and furze she'd seen in the fields, "Looks like the Wild West", she said disapprovingly.

The sudden transition from Detroit to Drumaroad for ten-year-old Owen and five-year-old Tom was difficult at first, especially in school. The primary school, St Francis', in the village a mile from home, had only one room. Therein, about sixty boys and girls, ranging from small children to big teenagers, were squeezed in. The master sitting at the top didn't look well. On his desk stood a teapot and cup from which, every now and then, he'd take a sup. Occasionally, he sent one of the bigger boys to replenish the 'tea'. Owen wondered why he went to a pub to get <u>tea</u>.

Fr Dan O'Reilly, about ninety years of age, parish priest and manager of the school since 1906, dropped in occasionally after late Mass. His customary greeting to the head was, "How are you today Master?" The latter invariably replied, "Ah, I'm not too well Father, something in my chest. I'm taking a drop of tea to clear it".

The two well-dressed 'Americans' when they first arrived caused quite a stir in the school. For a week or so, they were teased over their Yankee clothes and American accents but, as Owen was a big lad and protective of his small brother, the joking didn't go too far. Soon

Owen established himself as a leading prankster. Adept at provoking laughter, he got others into trouble but kept himself out of it.

The newcomers weren't long there when 'the tea pot master' was replaced by a young man, Daniel Fitzpatrick from Kilkeel, and Brigid Daly from Armagh, an assistant. Mr Fitzpatrick was a first rate teacher, very good at Irish, English, maths and indeed all subjects but, was unmerciful in his use of the cane. Miss Daly, a wee slip of a girl, was quiet and suffered at the hands of the bigger boys who locked her in the coal house whenever the Master was away.

One of the first things Mr Fitzpatrick taught them was that the word *droim* meant 'back' as in the back of an animal, or a 'ridge' on the land. There were plenty of hills and ridges around and many place names began with 'drum'. 'Drumaroad' meant the 'Ridge of the road' and, glancing at Owen he said, "'Drumanaghan', means the 'Ridge of the monastic land'." Franciscan friars took refuge there, at Drumnaquoile, during the Penal Laws; "'Drumnaquoile', means 'Ridge of the wood'". Branching into history, he explained that the Catholics were located in the hillier areas because they had been pushed out of better land around Drumcaw which meant 'Battle Ridge'. "But", he concluded, "there's been a school here and even a Mass house since long before the Great Famine".

It wasn't easy for Annie seeing to house and farm on her own. She knew only a few of the neighbours, like the Flanagans, Carlins, and Quinns; others, whom she had known before going to America, had moved. She was a hard worker, took no nonsense from anyone and kept a careful eye on her two boys.

Owen and Tom were very close. As young lads, after getting a new pair of boots they competed to see who could kick stones the farthest on the road home from school. Annie murdered them when she saw the cut of their boots. On another occasion, Fr Denis Cahill, Fr

Reilly's curate, gave them a small job in the presbytery garden. When they were finished, he put a few pennies in their fists. Sneaking into the house with their hard earned cash behind their backs, Annie accosted them, "What's that you're hiding?" On discovering the provenance of their wealth, she sent them straight back to the presbytery; no child of hers would take money from the church!

Drumaroad School 1933
Owen is first on left kneeling, next to him is Tom.
On extreme right is Mr Fitzpatrick and on left Miss Daly.
Annie Savage is standing in front row sixth from the left.

Owen found that things in school in Drumaroad were much different from what he had experienced in Detroit. There he had been encouraged to speak up, ask questions and be himself; it was not so anymore. One day, wishing to leave the room, he raised his hand. The Master, writing on the blackboard didn't notice but, when he turned, he caught Owen looking out the window. He snapped, "Can't you pay attention? Put out your hand". Owen stood up, but refused to offer his hand. Mr Fitzpatrick, dumbfounded, stared at him for what seemed "a full three minutes". Owen stared back unflinchingly. It was the Master who gave in, "He never tried to slap me after that!" said Owen.

One Friday morning he was ill so Annie kept him home from school. Friday was the day the Master gave the pupils a composition to write over the weekend. On Sunday, Owen found out from his fellow altar servers what composition they'd been given. He duly wrote two pages on the subject and handed up his essay with the others on Monday. Mr Fitzpatrick, when returning the exercise books, remembered that Owen had been absent and demanded, "How did you know what essay to write?" "I asked the altar boys, Sir". "In all my time teaching", expostulated Mr Fitz, "I have never come across the likes before". Apparently, Owen should not have written the essay and taken his punishment. Surprisingly, his classmates seemed to have the same idea. After school they collared Owen and threatened him, "If you ever do that again we'll thrash you!"

While Tom, in 'infants', was learning to sing "Birdie Birdie" and "My Grandfather's Clock" from Miss Daly, Owen in Standard 4 was being exposed to long poems like "The Deserted Village" and "Barbara Fritchie" from Mr Fitzpatrick. The Master loved poetry and sometimes recited humorous sagas like "The Cremation of Sam Magee" and "The shooting of dangerous Dan McGraw" to the delight of the class. But then, flexing his cane, he'd tell the scholars they'd better learn their poems properly or there'd be wigs on the green.

In school tests he did well, especially in arithmetic and composition in which he got full marks in 1931. He was near the top of the class, but not number one; Evelyn Boyd was. She got a total of 595 marks against Owen's 555! In the class below him, Annie Savage from Edendariff was also doing very well. Mr Fitzpatrick took special note of Annie, a well-mannered pretty girl, and married her in 1942.

The countryside that spread beneath Slieve Croob was more to Owen's liking than the concrete pavements of Detroit. He was growing well, but his strange health pattern followed him across the Atlantic. In 1932 (he remembered the year because of the Eucharistic Congress), he was detained in the Mater Hospital in Belfast; he couldn't remember for what. On another occasion, after receiving a scolding from his mother, he stayed out late and caught a cold. This, apparently, brought on some kind of tubercular swellings at the back of his neck. People said he might have caught tuberculosis from diseased cattle. Annie brought him to see Dr McDonald in Castlewellan. The doctor got Owen to lie face down on a table and, putting his hand on the swollen glands said, "Does that hurt?" "Yes", said Owen. The doctor lanced the swollen part. Owen squirmed. "Bring him back in nine days", the doctor instructed Annie. By that time the swelling was much worse and he had to be sent to Downpatrick Hospital. After some days, Annie visited him there and anxiously asked the doctor when she might take him home. The doctor replied, "You can take him any time, he's not going to get better". Shocked, she took him immediately.

They went home in a car driven by Mark's good friend, Johnny McGrady. Passing through Shanbally they ran over the favourite goose of Mary Ann Flanagan. She came after them with murder in her eye. Johnny thought it best to keep going. Owen, sick as he was, couldn't stop laughing.

Before reaching Drumanaghan, Johnny said, "We'll go up to Fr Reilly, he's said to have the power of curing". The old priest blessed Owen and told Annie not to worry. While grateful for the consolation, she sought further medical help, bringing Owen to a well-known herbalist, Mr McAlea. After examining him, McAlea clicked his tongue, "If you had come here first I could have cured him in a week". He applied some herbs and Owen was fine within a month.

In 1932, Annie, Owen and Tom were overjoyed when Mark returned from America. He told them that things had not improved in America. In January '31, Detroit city had been declared the hardest hit of nineteen big cities with over 223,000 people out of work. In

March '32, three thousand angry men marched from the city centre to Dearborn where the Ford headquarters were located. Rioting broke out when Dearborn police attempted to stop them. Four marchers were killed and hundreds injured. Huge crowds took part in the funeral procession of the deceased and some thirty thousand people gathered at the cemetery. With increasing unrest and little hope of employment, Mark decided it was time to go.

Owen loved being with his father ploughing, reaping, and seeing to the cattle. Mark appreciated the company and delighted in his son's quick intelligence. Owen was strong and a good worker. Without piped water in the house or on the farm, it fell to him to fetch water from the well in two big pails. He brought fodder to the cattle, groomed the horses, milked the cows and, when the fair in Castlewellan came round, helped herd the animals and look after them while Mark had a drink with his friends.

Mark increased his acreage of potatoes, flax, and oats. Summer was a busy time. In May the flax ripened. Pulling it was tough work, Owen proved good at it. He helped 'retting' the flax in the dam and joined in the filthy job of taking it out. No sooner was the hay saved and up in ricks than the corn needed to be cut. Then the potatoes had to be dug, picked, and put in pits.

Mark and Annie received good reports about him from school and, when the time came for him to begin secondary in 1934, they decided to send him to St Malachy's in Belfast as a boarder. But as fortune would have it, that very year the De la Salle Brothers, who had a primary school in Downpatrick since 1892, decided to open a secondary school there as well.

'St Patrick's', the new school in Downpatrick, though a lot nearer than Belfast was all of thirteen hilly miles from Drumaroad. Owen was given the choice, St Malachy's and board, or St Patrick's and cycle. He chose St Patrick's, and never missed a day, cycling the twenty-six mile round trip in all weathers. In the four years he spent there, he was late only twice, once because of a puncture and another time because he knocked into a motor van as he sped through a crossroads near Clough.

The school opened on the 4th of September 1934. Forty-three boys were enrolled that day, a few more turned up later. For the first week all were in the one class. Then the Brothers held a test and divided them into seniors and juniors. Not doing well in the test, Owen was put in the junior class but, before long, he was promoted to the seniors. By then, he had lost his American accent and had even acquired a broad 'Dromaroad accent'. His classmates laughed uproariously at the way he read a particular passage from their English Reader which ended with the words, "Miss Costello dear". Seventy-four years later, Des Egan, a classmate, still remembered the way Owen emphasised 'dear' at the end of the piece.[2] Not particularly worried about how he said it, Owen got a greater laugh out of another classmate's pronunciation of Napoleon's second name as "Bony-parts".

In the first week, a professional photograph was taken of pupils and staff. Missing from it was one who would become a great friend of Owen, Mick Toner from Portaferry. Arriving in Downpatrick with his mother a week after the school opened, he enquired of a young chap as to where the school might be. The young chap, Des Egan, brought him to number 116 Irish Street where the school was first located.

St Patrick's experienced all the usual difficulties of getting established but the Principal, Brother Alexis Galvin from Cork, made up for things. A man of vision and an educationalist of a very high standard he gave the school a great start and got the best from pupils and staff.

Opening St. Patrick's 1934

Front Row: (L-R): *Michael Sawey, Gerard Kelly, Kevin Bell, John Flynn, Francis Hanna, John Shields.*

Second Row: Pierce McConvey, Dan Smith, Fr Bradley, Bro. David, Canon McWilliams, Bro. Alexis - Headmaster, Fr Scullion, Teddy Egan, Michael J. Craig.

Third Row: Paddy Sheppard, Gerry Nolan, Johnny Blaney, Brian McManus, John J. Forde, Jimmy Irvine, Roddy Maguire, Joseph Darby, Tommy Skeffington, Seamus Croskerry, Bobby Bradley, Mickey King, Gerry Mulligan.

Fourth Row: Anthony Teague, Joe Watters, Desmond Egan, Vincent Teague, Fred Leathem, Donal O'Hare, Sean Savage, Maurice Devlin.

Fifth Row: Jackie Stewart, Derek King, Henry G. Fitzsimons, **Owen Maginn,** *Arthur McCavera, Mebride McGrady, Paddy Crangle, Ray Hayes, Jack Leathem, Benny Lynch, Vincent Bailie.*

Though St Patrick's did not have many pupils, it managed to raise quite a good Gaelic football team. Owen remembered playing an enjoyable game against an Armagh team but, in a game against St Mary's College, Belfast, one of the Belfast players suffered a broken leg. In the return game in Belfast, the St Mary's team were out for revenge. It was a cold wet day, the ground muddy, the game dirty, the language of the home team unprintable. After the game, no washing facilities or refreshments were offered. Brother Galvin was furious. There and then, he vowed to drop football and change to rugby. Previously, teaching in a 'rugby school' in England he had become an admirer of the game. Some staff members criticised him for abandoning football and some called him a snob but, he stuck to his guns and rugby prevailed as long as he was Principal.

The biggest lads in the school were press-ganged onto the rugby team. Owen, a big lad, playing in the back line proved to be difficult man to pass. An unusual feature for a Catholic – he kicked with his left foot! The St Patrick's team, new as it was to the game, did surprisingly well and managed to get into the semi-final of the Ulster Colleges' championship in Owen's final year.

In his last school rugby game, Owen was helping his team against strongly fancied 'Methody' College. Defending his line, he made a desperate bid to stop a big fellow heading for a try. The Methody man, with fist closed dealt Owen a stunning hand-off to the chin. Owen saw stars; it was the end of the game for him and the end of his rugby career, "I wasn't all that keen on rugby anyway", he said.

School uniforms became compulsory in the first year. As the blazer was red, the school became known as the 'Red High', distinguishing it from the 'Green High', the Protestant High School which had a green uniform. St Patrick's school blazer, actually 'maroon' in colour rather than 'red', was neatly trimmed with gold piping, and sported the La Salle badge on the breast pocket. The uniform was complete with matching cap and tie, white shirt and grey slacks. The boys liked it, it was smart and had lots of pockets for strings, penknives, chestnuts, dog-eared notebooks, and sticky buns.

One winter day, snow was falling as Owen set off for school. Progress on the bike became more and more difficult as snow thickened on the road. Arriving at Irish Street, he found the school closed because of the bad weather. Though tired, he thought it best to get home before roads became impassable. On an uphill stretch, he stopped to rest under the shelter of a tree. Out of the wind and snow, curled snug in a ditch, he fell asleep. Suddenly, something woke him. He didn't know how long he had been there but it seemed to be late afternoon. It was snowing hard like a blizzard and he was chilled to the bone. Rising stiffly, he trudged on pushing the bike through the driving snow. He feared that if he stopped again he'd freeze to death. As darkness was beginning to fall, he reached home. In the yard he found Mark organizing a search party to look for him. Exhausted, but none the worse for wear he wondered then, and often later, what had wakened him.

Cycling home from school, Owen and a few others became 'tight friends'. Often, one of the group, Gerry Nolan, raced off on his own "like the Divil". "What's up with him?" Owen asked. "He has a girl in Newcastle", his friends said, "and he's away to see her". The answer awakened in Owen awareness of the strange effect the fair sex can have on young men. But then he recalled that even in primary school in Detroit, he had been much attracted by a little girl called 'Griffin'. The Wall Street crash prevented the affair from blossoming!

As a teen-ager, coming from a farm, he knew well 'how things happened' biologically but he, and his pals, had little idea of how to deal with their own sexuality. The new stirrings in his life caused him a lot of bother when he was sixteen, especially after a preacher stressed the horror of sexual sins during a school retreat. Plagued with doubts, he went to his parish priest, Fr Dinny Cahill, who had succeeded Fr O'Reilly. The young priest told him to calm down and assured him that he was normal, but didn't enlighten him one bit as to how to deal with the sexual business.

His friend, Mick Toner, had the same distance to cycle to school as Owen, but from a different direction, Portaferry, on the eastern side of Strangford Lough. During school holidays, the two went on many cycling excursions together. Owen, in the senior section of the 1934 class, completed school a year before Mick. When Mick finished, he followed Owen into the African Missions. Another future African missionary, Paddy Jennings of Castlewellan, joined the Red High the year Owen left.

Boxing, a compulsory sport in the school, wasn't really Owen's cup of tea but, Toner, short, tough, and tenacious was good. Once, Des Egan had to get into the ring with him and got a bad mashing but, after it, the two became good friends. Toner succeeded in getting into the school's boxing final; in it, it was his turn to get a severe hiding. Owen, watching the defeat of his friend, felt very sorry for him. Since his own downfall as a street-fighter in Detroit, he had become more interested in books and study than fighting.

Owen and Gerry Nolan were among the best 'brains' in the class. Inevitably, there was some rivalry between them. On one occasion the Brothers put up a new bicycle as a prize for the best student in forthcoming tests. Owen, who had already come out on top in a prize essay, did not wish to beat Gerry again. He considered under-performing, but consulted his father first. Mark advised him to do his best always, adding, "Don't forget we're paying £10 a year for you in fees". This was no small sum in the 'Hungry Thirties'. Owen won the bicycle but, as fortune would have it, the Brothers decided to award a second bicycle to the runner-up. Gerry won it.

A few years after Owen, his brother Tom enrolled in the Red High. He also proved to be one of the best pupils but, before beginning his final year, Mark let him know that he could do with help on the farm. Tom fell in with his father's wish and left school. Annie was raging and refused to speak to Mark for a week. However, the choice was Tom's and he never regretted it. Both sons were like Mark in being 'gentlemen' in the best sense of the word. A measure of their closeness to their father was that they never called him anything but "Mark". Owen believed his special relationship with Mark helped him in relating with others throughout his life.

1. In 1927, the *Baltic's* passenger accommodation was reduced to 393 in cabin class, 339 in tourist class and 1,150 in third class. The ship made her final voyage in 1932 and, in 1933, sailed for Japan where she was scrapped.

2. Mark Maginn's poetry is not forgotten. Among other poems published, 'Cry of the Distressed', written during the Great Depression, was published in *Kilcoo, A Gaelic and Social Heritage; and* 'Andy's Mill' appeared in the *Down Democrat,* 3 July 2007.

3. I met Des, a pupil of the class of '34, at his home in Newcastle in the summer of 2008. He had just finished mowing the lawn and was thinking about cutting down some trees. A few months *older* than Owen, at eighty-eight years of age, he is one of the four survivors of the pioneering class of St Patrick's. He still plays golf but, only twelve holes "as my partner (a younger man) doesn't like eighteen"!

Chapter 2

MISSIONARY VOCATION

Owen thought of becoming a priest from an early age. Clergy were held in high esteem in the diocese of Down and Connor. Priests were a known and respected class who, with the same aspirations as the people, provided a benign and friendly kind of leadership. They were relatives, friends, and neighbours.

Fr Denis Cahill and altar servers, Drumaroad

Fr Denis Cahill became parish priest of Drumaroad and Clanvaraghan after the death of Fr Daniel O'Reilly on 25 September 1934. An energetic, go-ahead man, 'Fr Dinny', as he was known, began immediately to renovate the old church in Drumaroad and plan a new one for Clanvaraghan. Popular with the people he received generous support for his projects. At the collection during the inaugural Mass of the newly restored church in Drumaroad on Sunday 20 October '35, he received no less than £1,022. Sport-loving and sociable, he had everything going in the parish from tug-o-war competitions, to whist drives and gymkhanas. Prayerful too and a good preacher, his Sunday sermons were both edifying and instructive.

An ardent republican, Dinny had had many political arguments with his nonagenarian predecessor who was a firm believer in John Redmond and Home Rule. Age and hard times had prevented Fr O'Reilly from doing much in the parish in his later years and, when younger, he had devoted a lot of his time to cattle and farming in order to make ends meet.

Dinny hailed from Teconnaught, eight miles from Drumaroad. His father, as a young man, in order to prevent his nineteen-year-old sweetheart from emigrating to America when relatives sent her the fare, proposed marriage to her. She accepted. Their marriage was blessed with eleven children; four of them became nuns and two became priests. Dinny, the first born, went to the national seminary at Maynooth, where it required no less than half his father's salary as a primary school teacher to maintain him. One of Dinny's younger brothers, a twin called Sexton, joined the Society of African Missions and went to Nigeria in 1933.

To raise funds for the new church in Clanvaraghan, Dinny went to America in 1938. His missionary brother, home on his first leave from Nigeria, covered for him in the parish. In those days, missionaries spent five years in Africa and then got one year's leave. The American fundraising campaign was highly successful. One of the big attractions was Dinny's Irish linen table cloths embroidered with a picture of the new 'Queen of the Angels' church.

Nineteen thirty eight was Owen's last year in school. His desire to be a priest was inclining more and more to being a missionary. One of his teachers, Brother David, had been a missionary in Burma and, though he called the pupils "orang-utans" and made them learn the whole of Mark's gospel off by heart, they liked him and loved his adventurous stories of missions in the Far East. At Sunday Masses, the African missionary, Sexton Cahill, spoke enthusiastically of his mission in Nigeria. A Redemptorist, a former missionary in the Philippines, preached the annual retreat in the Red High in Owen's final year. By the end of the retreat, Owen had decided to be a missionary.

He told his father what he had in mind. Mark hesitated; he didn't want to oppose him, but neither did he want to lose him. After a long pause, he said, "Don't commit yourself to anything until you've finished school and seen your results".

In his final exams, Owen thought he could have done better, especially in English. *Hamlet* was on the course and he knew it almost off by heart but, in the exam, he chose to answer a question on a different play and, too late, he regretted it. However, when the results came out, he found that he had done quite well, getting credits in English, Latin, Irish, Geography, Botany, Maths, and History. Unlike Shakespeare's indecisive prince, he didn't waver about his vocation.

He went to the parish church to see Fr Dinny but, it was Dinny's brother, the missionary, whom he met. Sexton gave him a man-to-man talk about missionary life and a book entitled *Pioneers of the Faith* by Lt.Col.Francis Bowen.[1] The author, a British Army officer serving in Hong Kong, gave glowing accounts of the lives and deeds of missionaries in Asia and Africa. It impressed Owen that a <u>British</u> officer could praise Catholic missionaries so much. Bowen's concluding chapter began, "If anything I have written should inspire my young readers with a desire to help the great cause of the Foreign Missions, they may ask themselves, *how* and in what way can they do so? The first and best way of all, of course, is to become a missionary".

Owen wrote application letters immediately to the Columban missionaries, to St Patrick's missionaries, and to the Jesuits. None of them replied! Disappointed, he retraced his steps to the presbytery. Again he met Fr Sexton who (privately rather pleased) told him not to worry. Within a few days, Owen received an official invitation from the Society of African Missions to proceed to Cloughballymore, Co Galway, for the novitiate which would begin on the 15th of September.

Sensing that Mark wasn't too happy about his wanting to go to the African Missions, Owen wondered how to tell him that he had accepted to got to the novitiate. His brother, Tom, inadvertently helped him when Owen asked him casually, "What are you going to be?" Tom replied, "Ach, an ol' farmer like Mark; what about you?" "Well", said Owen, "I'm not going to be an 'old farmer'". "If you won't tell me, I'll tell Mark what you just said!" "Well, I want to be a priest" said Owen and, before Tom could let the cat out of the bag, he went to tell Mark himself. After hearing him out, Mark called Annie. When she came, he said, "Owen, tell your mother what you just told me". Owen, plucked up his courage and said, "I want to go to Galway to be a priest in the African Missions". To his relief, all she said was, "Good boy!" Mark shook his hand and turned away; his eyes had filled with tears.

With only a couple of days left before the start of the novitiate, Owen, a list of required clothing in hand, went to Belfast. At Kennedy's clerical outfitters he bought a black suit, black soutane, black shoes, Roman collar and stock, a soft black hat and a four-cornered biretta. He trudged home with his loads and dressed up for the family. Tom, seeing him in soutane and biretta, was highly amused and thought to himself that he'd prefer to be a farmer. There wasn't much time for banter; Owen had to begin his journey to Galway the next day.

Mark, Annie and Tom couldn't accompany him on the road as they wanted to finish cutting the corn and it was a good sunny morning. Before he left, Mark, mindful that his son was only seventeen, took him aside, "From what I hear, the training for priesthood is tough and people can be sent away for very little. If you don't like it, come home. No one will say a word to you". Owen felt lonesome as he turned his back on the farm and walked away. The words of a popular song kept running through his head, "They're cutting the corn around Creeslough today".

He took the train to Dublin where he stayed overnight with his cousins, the Breens. The next day he boarded the Galway train. Other lads about his own age entered the carriage. They were also going to the novitiate in Galway. Knowledgeable about what lay ahead, they pulled out packets of *Woodbines* and began to smoke furiously. "You're not allowed to smoke there", they warned Owen, offering him a cigarette, "This might be your last!" Owen, warming to their camaraderie, accepted one and helped fill the compartment with a thickening pall of blue smoke. The train rattled westwards, stopping frequently to let passengers on or off, or take on water until, eventually, it reached the small country station of Ardrahan where, on the platform waiting for them, was Fr Michael Mahony, the African Missions novice master.

Cloughballymore, 1938-1940

The 'novitiate' was located in a remote part of Co Galway, on the former property of Llewellyn Count Blake, a benefactor of the Irish Province of the African Missions and its first honorary member. It wasn't really a 'novitiate' such as

Cloughballymore

religious orders have but a place of probation, philosophical studies, and instruction on the spiritual life. Usually abbreviated to 'Clough', the property consisted of a 'Big House', a Blake castle, and over thirteen hundred acres of mixed land – grazing, tillage, great stretches of limestone rock, lakes which appeared in winter, and a forest of magnificent old trees.

Travelling in the car with Fr Mahony, Owen thought the countryside looked quite frightful. Wild and rocky, it was strewn with tumbledown stone walls, and had little sign of people. He wondered if he'd made a mistake in coming to such a place but, at the same time, he worried about being accepted. On arrival at the novitiate, the new candidates were brought to the refectory and given tea and 'shag' – fresh homemade bread – and delicious marrow jam. Twenty-four senior students were already there. Big men, they seemed very self-assured and evidently held very important offices. One called Anthony Glynn introduced himself as the 'Prefect', another, John Creaven, said he was the 'Magister Cantorum'. Owen felt like asking him what that was but, thinking it might be disrespectful, held his tongue. After due pause, John himself volunteered an explanation, "I'm in charge of singing". Another, Larry Carr, said, "I'm the Lector"

adding, "Reader". Despite their awesome responsibilities, they were kindly disposed and showed the newcomers to their quarters. The juniors, like Owen, numbered eighteen. Owen discovered with a shock that he was the only one from the North of Ireland. He found the accents of the southerners, especially Cork and Kerry lads, outlandish; he didn't know what they were saying and, worse, they didn't know what <u>he</u> was saying.

Clough Castle

The Prefect announced that the next day would be a free day and they wouldn't have to get up until 7 am. Normally, they'd be up "before the rooks at 6". Owen slept like a log until the insistent ringing of a bell woke him. They had Mass, housework, breakfast and then the seniors led them on a walk to a place called Tara on the coast about two miles from the novitiate. It was a small port where Connemara turf boats docked and was grand for swimming, especially when the tide was in. After swimming and walking back, they had a ravenous appetite. The rest of the weekend continued at a leisurely pace. On Sunday, they were allowed to listen to the All-Ireland football final between Galway and Kerry on the wireless. A new commentator made the game come alive – eighteen-year-old Michael O'Hehir on his first All-Ireland broadcast. The game ended in a draw, Galway 3-3, Kerry 2-6.

Owen expected that a study of Africa, missionary life, and priesthood would begin immediately but, to his surprise, such topics were hardly mentioned; instead they were given a lot of manual work to do. Threshing was in progress and all hands had to help. When the normal programme began, they were studying philosophy, Latin, English and the *Constitutions* of the Society. A German lay man came weekly on a motor bike to teach them 'Plain Chant' and German. As well as class, they spent a lot of time doing 'Propaganda' work – helping to raise money for the Society by filling envelopes with mission appeal literature, addressing them and, later, acknowledging the 'returns'.

Prayer, liturgy, and talks on the 'spiritual life' were central to the programme. They had to do a daily meditation of half an hour, spend another half hour in Spiritual Reading, give nearly fifteen minutes in thanksgiving after Communion, and visit the Blessed Sacrament before lunch and again after lunch. Silence was kept during meals while approved books like HV Morton's *In the steps of the Master* and biographies of the saints were read by the Lector.

Games, every Wednesday and Saturday, were eagerly looked forward to. Football, hurling, and soccer were the most popular and, in season, tennis, handball, and cross country running provided some variety. Indoor games and recreation comprised of table tennis, billiards, card games, impromptu *céilís*, concerts and stage plays. On Saturdays and on Sundays they swam at Tara or went for long walks. Owen, forgetting his early apprehensions about the place, began to enjoy it thoroughly.

The Superior was a Drogheda man, John Levins, called 'Da', because of the stress he put on the word '*Da*' when saying '*Oremus Da Nobis*' in the Mass which of course was always in Latin. Fr Levins spent a lot of his time in his room high up in the 'top corridor' where he pursued his hobby of painting rustic nature scenes on canvas. Particular about dress and punctilious in the way he said Mass, he was sometimes the butt of student jokes, but they liked him for his gentleness and sense of fair play.

Fr Mahony, "Mahocky" to the students, was Vice Superior as well as novice master. A quiet, even-tempered man from Galway, he had been a missionary in Liberia where many before him had died prematurely. He worried a lot about his health and, even in Ireland, went to great lengths to avoid extremes of heat or cold. The seniors alleged that when he'd been on the staff of Dromantine, the major seminary in Co Down, he used to close the window whenever he heard a train coming, for fear he'd catch a cold from the draught. The train passed half a mile away!

Owen liked the young Kerry man, Ned Harrington. Only twenty-three, as well as teaching philosophy, he was doing a degree in Galway University. Short in stature and hampered by a bad stammer he was, nevertheless, a very good teacher. On games days he was a courageous referee, unafraid to put to the sideline, not only students twice his size but even members of the staff who joined in the games.

The bursar was a Co Cork man, Nicholas Heffernan, whom the students for unknown reasons called 'Billy'. A late vocation, he had been an accountant before joining the African Missions. Popular with the students, his out-of-the-ordinary hobbies provoked much hilarity: astronomy, Connemara ponies, Celtic kilts, and boating. Occasionally, he dressed up in a kilt and explained the meaning of its colours and pattern. Hailing from the seaside port of Youghal, he loved boats and had two of his own at Tara. On free days he took the students on short 'voyages', insisting that, while on board, they use proper nautical terms like 'fore and aft', and 'port and starboard'. He also had a pony and side car and helped transport students in it from time to time.

Teaching English and elocution (with a strong West Cork accent), was another former missionary, Jerry Sheehan. At the end of his first missionary tour in Nigeria, he was given a lift on the back of a motor cycle to the 'mammy wagon' which would take him to the port of Lagos. On the bumpy road, his foot caught in the back wheel and he lost some of his toes.

Karl Wolff, the Plain Chant and German teacher, lived in Loughrea where he was the cathedral's organist. Though Owen was not really musically-minded or a singer, he learned to appreciate the beauty of Church music from Herr Wolff. A soldier in the Great War, Wolff often regaled the students with stories of life in the trenches. He left Germany after the War to seek a new life in Ireland.[2]

On the last Sunday in September, the drawn All-Ireland football final was re-played. Against the odds, Galway beat the Kingdom 2-4 to 7 points, the first time Kerry had ever been beaten in an All-Ireland replay. The Connacht students were ecstatic; the Kerry men went into mourning.

Owen turned eighteen on the 18th of October, no fuss was made. In Clough, it was Church holidays and saints' feast days that were marked in a special way. The old Celtic feast of Halloween was celebrated quietly with a long walk round 'Magánach' in the afternoon and a treat of nuts and apples at supper. The next day, 'All Saints' Day', was a first class feast, a 'Big Free', meaning a very special free day. For many the highlight was the rashers and eggs they got for breakfast, the first they'd tasted since leaving home.

Coming up to Christmas, Cloughballymore played host to the Knights of Columbanus, a lay group founded to counteract the influence of the Free Masons. The Knights liked to meet in quiet places like Clough. The students put on a play for them and, in turn, one of the visitors entertained them with an amazing show of card-conjuring tricks. A few students believed that Satan must have been involved in some of the tricks.

The weather turned cold, ponds, lakes, and even streams froze. Snow fell; it was a good time to be indoors. The house was appropriately decorated and a holiday timetable for Christmas and New Year began. Whist drives, comic plays like *Shivering Shocks* and *Professor Tim* were staged; *craic* abounded and Irish dancing flourished. Contrary to earlier fears, Owen thought that Christmas in Clough was one of the happiest of his life.

New Year 1939 was suitably celebrated but not long afterwards exams were held. More 'shivering shocks' were felt when the results were read out. Owen, not the fastest to pick up a new subject, didn't do well in Philosophy or in the History of Philosophy, getting only 49 and 57 marks respectively. He did well in English, 74, and Religious Instruction, 77. He attributed his good mark in the latter to the Sunday sermons of Fr Dinny Cahill.

Pope Pius XI died on the 10th of February. After the news was announced, a subdued air of grieving prevailed, prayers were offered for the deceased pontiff and the story of his life was read at mealtime. Mourning notwithstanding, the following day the students listened to an exciting international rugby game in which Ireland beat England 5 points to nil at Twikenham. On the 15th a solemn Requiem Mass was celebrated at which Herr Wolff played the organ.

On 2 March, Cardinal Eugenio Pacelli was elected Pope. Taking the name, Pius XII, he was the first Pope to give his inaugural blessing over the radio. His coronation took place on the 12th and, thanks to Herr Wolff's mediation, the students were allowed to listen to the radio broadcast.

April was a time for games against outside teams. Clough, wearing blue and gold jerseys, beat the local Ballindereen team in hurling, and the Galway University team in football. There were some excellent players in the novitiate at the time, especially among the seniors, men like – Larry Carr, Paddy Glynn, Frank McGovern, Leo McNeill and John Creaven and, among the juniors, Johnny Browne and Mick Maughan. Many of these would go on to play for their counties at senior level (though there was an ecclesiastical 'Maynooth' ban on doing so).

May, Mary's month, was celebrated with special devotions, ending every evening with a procession and Night Prayer at the large outdoor Marian grotto. As the weather improved, swimming at Tara re-commenced.

Coming up to the time of the Irish Derby, Jerry Cadogan, one of the seniors, received a telegram informing him that he had drawn a horse in the Irish Hospitals Sweepstake. Great hopes were entertained when it became known that the name of the horse was 'Bellman'! Despite the auspicious name, so appropriate in a place where everything was regulated by the bell, the much-prayed-for horse didn't win.

Towards the end of May, with the long evenings, practices for the Annual Sports were held after supper. It was also a time of 'stewing' for the June exams. Individuals and groups took to the woods to discuss Aristotle, Kant, and Suarez, beneath the shade of massive chestnut trees. Owen, who had worked hard at Philosophy, did much better this time, getting 69.

Exams over, the next big event was Sports Day, Thursday 22 June. It turned out to be a beautiful summer day. There were events to suit everyone, including comic ones like the egg and spoon race, sack race, and an obstacle race. Apart from Mick Maughan, the seniors dominated: Leo McNeill in the sprints, Larry Carr in the high jump and pole vault, John Creaven in the long jump. The seniors even collected most of the prizes in the novelty events: John Creaven and Frank McGovern winning the three-legged race, Paddy Glynn and Leo McNeill the jockey race, and McGovern and Carr the wheelbarrow race.

The same day, after dinner, a Question Time was won by Frank Hynes and John Creaven. After supper a farewell concert was staged for the seniors who, on the following day, would start a ten-day retreat prior to taking their first temporary oath of membership in the Society of African Missions – a major step on their path to the missions and the culmination of their two years in Clough. The concert ended an hour before midnight with a gusty rendering of the National Anthem.

The next day, the juniors took over responsibilities from the seniors. The names of the new office holders were announced after supper. Eliciting some surprise, because the two chosen were on the quiet side, John Moorhead and Owen Maginn were appointed Prefect and Vice Prefect. The juniors, released from 'senior control', and looking forward to completing their own two years in Clough, struck up a verse of a popular song:

> *In eleven more months and ten more days,*
> *They're going to set us loose.*
> *In eleven more months and ten more days,*
> *We'll be out of the calaboose.*

A damper on their high spirits was the fact that one of their class, Donal O'Sullivan from Cork, had departed that morning. The staff had decided that his health was not robust enough for Africa. Departures of friends always gave rise to some despondency. The seniors had lost four of their number. At the end of the retreat, only twenty of them took the oath. The next day, they departed for home holidays.

Feeling a little lonely, the juniors cleaned out the senior dormitory and moved into it themselves. Soon they would be facing the most serious exercise of the novitiate, the Thirty Day Retreat. Before it, they were treated to an excursion. After breakfast on the 4th of July, they boarded a bus at 'Mick the tailors cross' and, within an hour, were at Duras by the sea. After swimming, games, and a delicious picnic, they faced home and the Long Retreat.

The Retreat began after supper. Apart from three free days during it, they were expected to maintain absolute silence until it ended on the 4th of August – not an easy matter for a lively group whose average age was about eighteen. The 'Student Diarist' put away his diary and didn't open it again until after the retreat. He re-commenced with a cryptic reference to the retreat, *"Nothing, or, rather too much to report".*

The Thirty Day Retreat

Owen didn't enjoy it and he wasn't the only one. The retreat, a slightly modified version of the Spiritual Exercises of St Ignatius of Loyola, was intended by the author to be an aid for directors guiding individual souls on the way of spiritual perfection.

It wasn't the 'Exercises' that Owen disliked, but the style in which they were given. The retreat master, highly credited Tom Counihan sj, had for long been engaged by the SMA to direct this annual retreat. Owen thought he was good enough when speaking about the following of Christ, but not when preaching about sin. Then he seemed to think that his hearers were hardened reprobates who had no chance of entering Heaven unless they undertook extreme penances even to the extent of scourging themselves. Fr Counihan told the students that he was a regular user of the 'discipline' (as the scourge was called) "three times a week at midnight while reciting the *Miserere*", and he invited them to come individually to his room for a (bareback) demonstration of the art of self-flagellation. Each one would be provided with a whip to accompany the Master, blow for blow, on his own back. "It hurt!" said Owen and he didn't go again.

Fr Counihan also recommended the wearing of chains, hair shirts, and knotted chords, all designed to tame rebellious 'flesh'. He held up for emulation ascetical athletes like John Sullivan sj who practised jumping into icy ponds in winter to cool his passions, and Willie Doyle who recited 100,000 pious aspirations a day. The scriptural passages Fr Tom doled out were of the doomsday type, "Unless you do penance you will all perish". Owen found the emphasis on them depressing.

In the last week of the retreat they were instructed to write their own personal 'Rule of Life' which they should cherish and keep for the rest of their lives. Ideally, by the end of the thirty days, the retreat-maker, having trod with Jesus the *via crucis*, should rise with Him in Easter joy. All Owen felt was a great longing for the retreat to end. Eventually, it did, with Mass at the Grotto. Afterwards, they were given the mail that had accumulated for them over the month. Aided by the letters from home and a swim at Tara, they began to 'come down to earth' again.

A relaxed holiday rule commenced in which farm work and swimming featured a lot. When the students finished binding corn in Flaherty's field and in the '18-acres', they prepared for one of the great excursions of the holidays, a trip to the Aran Islands. On the 19th of August they were up before dawn and waiting for the bus to take them to the docks in Galway. Unfortunately, the bus didn't appear and they had to be satisfied with a less exciting excursion to New Quay.

The Aran Island trip was re-scheduled for the 22nd. This time, the bus did appear and brought them to the berth of the *Dún Aengus* in Galway. The sea was choppy but, on the three and a half hour voyage, no one was seasick thanks to the advice of the ancient mariner, 'Billy' Heffernan, who 'navigated' them away from eating at the wrong times or standing in the wrong places. They were famished by the time they got to St Kevin's Hotel on Inishmore. After dinner they roamed the island and visited the ancient fortress of Dún Aengus on the high cliff overlooking the foam-flecked Atlantic rollers. Back on board they steamed on to the two smaller islands. At Inisheer, the famous artist, John Keating RHA with his wife and children came on board. Wearing a traditional Aran *báinín* jacket and *crios,* he chatted and signed autographs. Homeward bound, the Clough lads started a sing-song and continued until their voices cracked. The *Dún Aengus* docked at 9.30 and, still buzzing with the excitement of the day, the students boarded the bus for home.

Meanwhile on mainland Europe, dark clouds of war were gathering. On the 31st of August 1939, the Clough diarist wrote, "War was the sole topic of conversation today". On the 1st of September, Hitler's army invaded Poland. The carefree lads in Clough were busy binding wheat and looking forward to hearing the All-Ireland hurling final on Sunday. Before the Final that day, 3 September, they heard a broadcast of the consecration of the new cathedral at Mullingar which had taken six years and £260,000 to build. In the hurling final, Kilkenny managed to beat Cork by the narrowest of margins, 1 point: Kilkenny 2 goals and 7 points, Cork 3 goals and 3 points. The game, called the 'Thunder and Lighting' final, because a horrendous storm broke out ten minutes before the end, had again as radio commentator the young Michael O'Hehir, this time making his debut in an All-Ireland hurling final. A broadcast the students didn't hear that morning was Winston Churchill's announcement that Britain and France had declared war on Germany. The Second World War had begun.

The students had one major excursion remaining before holidays ended – Kylemore Abbey, home of an old Irish congregation of Benedictine nuns. During Penal times the Sisters, forced to flee Ireland, established themselves in Ypres, Flanders. There they survived the French Revolution and the Napoleonic Wars but, during World War One, their convent was destroyed by German artillery and, subsequently, they returned to Ireland.

On the 11th of September, the students rose early and got ready for the bus. After a short delay in Leenane, they arrived before noon at Kylemore, 50 miles from Galway. The nuns, who ran a secondary boarding school for girls, served the would-be African missionaries with a fine dinner and spoke a bit about the strange history of their Abbey. They had bought the magnificent castle and property in 1920. Originally, belonging to the Blake family, it had been bought by a Mr Mitchell Henry who, at the time of his wedding in 1852 had lunched there with his young wife, Margaret Vaughan from Co Down. Captivated by the beauty of the place, they bought it. Henry built the castle, now the abbey, with its splendid white granite façade, towers and castellated parapets. After seven years of residence, Mrs Henry died of 'Nile Fever' while on holiday in Cairo. Eight years later, Henry's daughter was killed in a fall from a pony and trap. Devastated by his loss, Henry sold Kylemore. It fell into decline until the Sisters bought it.

After dinner, the 'missionaries' emerged to enjoy the wonderful surroundings. Some climbed the nearest mountain from where the views of the distant range of the Twelve Bens and nearby lakes and forests were spectacular. Others joined Billy Heffernan in a boat on the mirror-like Kylemore lake. Owen tarried in the Sisters' well-stocked bookshop and, after careful consideration, bought *A Treatise on the True Devotion to the Blessed Virgin* by Grignion de Montfort. The new edition of the classic work, took most of his savings but, he felt, he would use it a lot in the years to come. He inscribed his name and, "Bought at Kylemore, 11-9-'39", inside the cover. After tea, the students put on a concert for the Sisters, boarded the bus and returned to Clough by a different route via Clifden. As on the morning's journey, the Connemara scenery was magnificent.

On the 15th of September, the next set of 'juniors' arrived. Twenty-seven in all, a much bigger class than Owen's, it included five northerners, among whom was Mick Toner from Portaferry.

In keeping with the spirit of the times, the African Missions aspirants were cut off from 'the world'. They were not permitted newspapers and only got the radio on special occasions. Incoming mail was opened by staff and, sometimes, censored. Occasionally, a student might sneak a glance at a newspaper in one of the Fathers' rooms and glean a titbit of world news or the result of a big game; otherwise, they were in the dark as to what was going on outside.

Owen, curious about the progress of the war, occasionally distracted Herr Wolff in German class, with a carefully prepared question, "*Wie läust der Krieg?*" (How is the war going?) It usually worked. Herr

Wolff, who was probably anti-Hitler but had strong feelings for his fatherland, would spend the rest of the period bringing the students up to date and answering their questions.

Life as 'seniors' progressed much as it had done when they were juniors, except that now they were 'the big shots'. As well as being Vice Prefect, in October Owen was nominated 'Prefect of Propaganda' and 'Sub for Ulster' – the propaganda work was divided according to provinces.

At the end of October, some leaders of the Legion of Mary in Dublin came to start the movement in Clough. They explained its work and aims and on Sunday, 3 December, an auxiliary praesidium called "Our Lady of Africa" was founded. Owen didn't join as he thought the Legion couldn't function properly in a place where the members were not allowed out to do apostolic work. In Clough the Legionaries' work was restricted to study of the handbook and doing things like collecting used stamps and silver paper 'for the missions'. However, twenty-five students did join.

In November, Fr Counihan returned to see how his former retreatants were getting on. Some of them went to see him for confession or counsel on spiritual matters. On the 8th of December, the anniversary of the foundation of the Society by Bishop de Marion Brésillac in 1856, was celebrated. It was one of the biggest 'Big Free' days in Clough. The celebration helped usher in the Christmas holidays. As could be expected, the feast of Christ's nativity was solemnly and joyfully honoured in the novitiate. On the 30th of December a whist drive was won by one of the aspirant brothers, the popular Kerry man, Tom Fitzgerald. Two other notable aspirant brothers were Peter Houlihan from the Kerry gaeltacht and Jim Keane who, up to recently, had been in the British army in Norway.

Recreational activity in the New Year of 1940 began with the staging of two plays, *Eloquent Dempsey* and *Smuggling Cattle across the Border*. Performed twice for the public, a record crowd attended including the parish priest of Ballindereen. He was so pleased that he requested *three* free days for the students. Shortly afterwards the students staged a concert for the nuns in Oranmore. More whist drives and card games followed until, all too soon, on the 8th of January the decorations were taken down and the holidays came to an end.

The weather turned arctic, winter lakes froze and ice skating replaced field games. One exhilarated student, wearing soutane and hob-nailed boots, venturing too far on the ice, went through it. He had a cold underwater swim until he managed to find his way out. In the house it was freezing, the only heat generated was that of students 'stewing' for the exams to be held later in the month.

While the Fathers were busy marking exams, the students did a four-day retreat. Owen opened a new exercise book and on the first page wrote: 'Purpose of the retreat'

1. To renew fervour.
2. To see failings.
3. To provide against them.
4. To advance farther along the way of the Cross.
[He added some comments on how he thought he was doing.]
I know now:-
1. My lack of fervour causes failings.
2. I see this but, because the effort is too much, I just glide.
3. I lack perseverance.
4. I go to extremes, and this is the reason for n.3.
5. I don't pray as I ought, due chiefly to over indulging my appetite.
6. I am careless about my Particular Examen [a daily examination of   conscience].

I have written these things down before and yet failed to check them.

"First fervour" was typical and almost expected of novices. Time would tell if it was genuine or not. Obviously, Owen was conscientious and serious and, possibly more realistic than many of his peers. His 'confession' of previous failure would seem to indicate a realistic trait of humility and honesty.

In his notebook, he wrote up the lectures, evidently after the talks as his copy is too perfect to have been written as the director spoke. He did not mention who the latter was, but the themes were again heavy and fear-inspiring: the horror of dying unprepared for the Last Judgement, human weakness and eternal punishment "even for one sin".

By the time the students had finished the retreat, most of the Fathers had completed marking their examination papers. Whatever about slipping in spiritual fervour, Owen <u>had</u> slipped in academic results. This time he got only 62 in philosophy. It can't have diminished the staff's estimation of him for, at the beginning of February, he was appointed Prefect.

After the Retreat, the students returned to normal routine, glad especially to be able to talk again, except at meals of course. In the refectory, they all sat at specially allocated places, four to a table. The 'gods', as the priests were called, ate in the same hall but at their own table on a raised platform. To avoid the formation of cliques, student seating was changed every month. The very day the change was made in February, even the 'gods' smiled when the Lector, reading from the popular classic, *The Imitation of Christ,* announced that, "The imagination and the changing of places have deceived many".

Little was heard about the War in Europe, but news filtered through that two IRA men were hanged in Birmingham on the 7th of February. They had been convicted of a bombing in Coventry in which twenty-five people died.

That year, 1940, was a 'Leap Year', a year in which, according to tradition, on Valentine's Day a woman may ask a man to marry her. The students, never allowed to enter the domestic quarters run by the Sisters and lay staff, nor converse with females anywhere, were hopeful of, at least, a special smile but none of them got as much as a wink. Instead, the ladies made pancakes which, eaten on Shrove Tuesday, heralded the beginning of Lent.

Still in February, a great Gaelic match was played between Owen's team and that of the junior, Barney Cunningham. Maginn's team was beaten by one point. As Barney's went on to win the final, Owen's hadn't done so badly after all.

In the middle of March a doctor came to examine them. Good health was paramount in being accepted for the African Missions. The senior novices looked healthy, but one never knew. Time, as well as the doctor, would tell.

Lent passed at its own pace. Holy Week ceremonies, including *Tenebrae* on three evenings, were performed with due solemnity. Easter Sunday and Monday were celebrated as 'Big Free Days'. A missionary, JC O'Flaherty, gave a stimulating 'magic lantern' slide show and lecture on his work in Nigeria. The tennis season was declared open and the Bishop Elect of Western Nigeria, Patrick Joseph Kelly sma arrived. His interest was not in tennis but in prayer and reflection before his episcopal ordination in June.

After Winston Churchill's declaration of war at the beginning of September '39, nothing much had happened on the western front, in fact the stalemate, which lasted seven months, was called the 'Phoney War'. France, confident that its defensive Maginot line stretching the length of its border with Germany would keep the enemy out, didn't anticipate attack from another quarter. In May, the Germans invaded through Belgium and the Ardennes.

The Republic of Ireland prepared to defend its neutrality by increasing the numbers of its armed forces, building up local defence forces, and intensifying training. Army units from Galway's Renmore barracks and Local Defence Force men began training in the grounds of Clough. The friendly soldiers exchanged cigarettes with the novices and allowed them to dress up in their uniforms to have their photographs taken.

In June, with problems of philosophy pressing more on them than Hitler's advances, the students began cramming for their final exams. In the bright evenings, practice for the forthcoming annual sports was a welcome distraction. Another diversion was the hard-fought hurling final won by Jim McCarthy's team, despite the head injuries Jim received. After the match, Ned Harrington brought him to Kinvara to get stitched. Jim, a classmate of Owen, modestly gave credit for the win to the Novice Master, who had helped him pick and position the team.

The 1940 Sports Day was held on Friday 20 June under ideal weather conditions. Mick Maughan, the Mayo miler, and the ex-soldier Jim Keane, a champion runner in the Irish Guards, led the field in all races from the 100 yards to the mile. John Creaven (still in Clough as he was doing a degree in UCG) dominated the long and high jumps. Winding up practical business, the same day, new student office holders were appointed. Owen handed over the Prefect's job to Barney Cunningham; the new Vice Prefect was Mick Toner.

In the evening, the seniors began their ten-day 'oath' retreat directed by Phil Corish, a missionary not long back from Nigeria. The new student diarist began his script, "After two years the seniors fade away into the abyss of the ten-day retreat. The juniors, for the first time, marched down to Tara alone and in great spirits. The high tide and the choppy waves seemed to say 'Congratulations'". While the retreat was in progress, the juniors were warned <u>not</u> to "Whistle while you work", especially in the orchard near the oratory. The orchard was a favourite place for testing resolutions to abstain from forbidden fruits!

The retreat ended on Sunday 30th of June with Solemn High Mass and the oath ceremony. After the Gospel, twelve nervous aspirants, one by one, with hand on Bible swore in Latin to remain in the Society for a year and obey its rules. Five of their classmates had already departed, either of their own volition or that of the authorities. Owen, who by now could read Latin fairly well, took his turn and read confidently, "Ego Eugenius Maginn, Diocesis Dunensis et Connorensis …" After taking the oath, each one's form was carefully signed by the juror and two witnesses.

The new members of the African Missions, not quite sure whether they were supposed to be feeling superior to their junior brothers, risked having a cup of tea with them and graciously accepted their congratulations. Then, they accompanied them to Tara for a swim and a picnic. On arrival, Owen's attention was caught by a newspaper in a shop window. '**France Falls**' was its bold front page headline. This was the first the Clough boys knew of the invasion of France.
By now German soldiers were goose-stepping in the Champs Elysées and strolling on the banks of the River Seine. Paris had been taken on the 14th of June; on the 16th Marshall Pétain, handed over control of northern France to the Germans.

At the time, few in Ireland understood what the people 'on the Continent' were going through. Much Irish sympathy lay with

Germany, many were glad that Hitler was gaining victories over Britain. The allied troops at Dunkirk were fortunate to escape with their lives – over 300,000 were rescued – but equipment, artillery and transport had been destroyed or left behind. Hitler then turned his attention to the Atlantic and, with his U-Boats wreaking havoc on ships bringing food and supplies to England, he hoped to starve the British into submission. England was now the only country standing against the Nazi conquest of Western Europe.

Meanwhile, on the morning of the 1st of July, Owen and eleven classmates packed their bags and departed for summer holidays at home. In his final evaluation, he was graded 60% in Philosophy, and 71% in other subjects. Overall, he was thought to be "above average in intelligence", "very sound and practical" in judgement, "very good" in the exercise of prudence, "earnest and industrious in his spiritual exercises", and "very satisfactory" in discipline. He had maintained a "good observance of rule" and was "very respectful" to superiors. Regarding deportment and personality he was, "reserved and serious, but kind to others". In disposition he was, "energetic, persevering and steady" but, "inclined to over-exertion at his duties".

And so after two years absence, he returned to the farm at Drumanaghan. The first sight of the house took him aback; it seemed to have diminished, so small did it appear in comparison to the large buildings of Clough. Happy to be home, he fitted easily into the farm routine. Mark and Tom were glad of his help. He didn't feel special and certainly not 'holy'. He took part as before in the rosary and whatever other devotions the family went to; he didn't go to Mass except on Sundays and feast days and didn't do 'meditation' or any of the other pious exercises they'd practised in Clough. Like many of his peers, the novitiate was something he had floated through. He hadn't heard much about Africa or missionary work and, despite two years of study and prayer, he really didn't know where he was or where he was going. It didn't worry him, he had enjoyed Clough. Now, freedom and summer holidays lay before him.

1. Published in 1935, a copy of *Pioneers of the Faith*, now a rare book, was located on the internet by Yvonne McClean, Owen's niece, and purchased by her from a bookstore in Sydney, Australia.

2. Herr Wolff's son Benno, on holidays in Ireland when the Second World War broke out, being unable to return to Germany, continued his secondary education in the SMA Apostolic College of Ballinafad, Co Mayo. On finishing school, he joined the African Missions and was ordained in 1950. After serving in Nigeria and Zambia he took up appointments in Ireland and England and died in Cork in 1996.

Chapter 3

DROMANTINE 1940-1944

At home in the summer of 1940, Owen shared with Mark an interest in the progress of the war. An aerial bombardment, intended by Hitler to be a prelude to 'Operation Sealion' - his invasion of Britain by sea - began in July. At first, the German planes attacked harbours, shipping, and military installations but, in September, turned on London and other cities. The *Luftwaffe*, though outnumbering the RAF in planes by more than four to one, did not win what came to be known as the 'Battle of Britain'. The achievement of the RAF pilots and crews inspired Churchill's comment, "Never in the field of human conflict was so much owed by so many to so few".

On the 10th of September 1940, Owen proceeded to the African Missions Major Seminary, Dromantine. In times past it was the seat of the Magennis clan and, later, home of the Innes family. Lying seven miles from Newry, just off the main road to Belfast, it was only thirty miles from Drumaroad. Here, Owen faced four years of theological studies. What he noticed first on arrival was some senior students raiding the orchard!

His class of twelve from Clough, augmented by one candidate from the Dutch Province of the Society and two Irish

Dromantine

diocesan students, were allocated two to a room. Owen shared a room in the attic with Jim McCarthy. Their 'address' was "No. 23, The Castle". Apart from the risk of hitting one's head against a low rafter, the room was alright but, as winter set in, it became an ice box. There was no heating; in wartime everything, especially fuel, was rationed. Fortunately, having its own farm, Dromantine was able to feed its students reasonably well.

To help the newcomers settle in and redress loss of fervour among seniors, a retreat was laid on to open the term. Owen summarised the talks in his spiritual notebook, but not quite as perfectly as he had done in Clough. His notes indicate that the theme of the first lecture was again rather gloomy: sin, fall of the angels, and the terrible state of the world (a rare staff reference to the World War). The second lecture, on Christ's command, "Love one another", was more uplifting. Another day, the students were asked to reflect on their faults and make resolutions to amend them. Among Owen's resolutions were, "Always work hard at studies" and "Observe silence". Finally, they were exhorted to re-read the Rule of Life they had made at the end of the thirty day retreat in Clough. Number 6 of Owen's 12-point Rule was, "To be kind and charitable in word and deed" and, Number 7, "To see humour in irritable things". His 10th and 11th resolutions, may seem odd today but, were not at all odd in 1940: "To make 800 Aspirations [short pious sayings] each day" and, "To do 50 acts of mortification [penances] each week".

After the retreat, the first year students began to take stock of the staff. The Superior, Martin Lavelle from Inishbofin, off the Galway coast, was known as 'Auntie', his *nom de plume* for the children's column he wrote in the Society's periodical, the *African Missionary*. Students got into the habit of referring to 'Auntie' as 'she'; visitors sometimes exclaimed in surprise, "I didn't know there was a woman on the staff".

While Auntie's *African Missionary* articles were lively and full of fun, Owen thought his theology lectures were very dull.

John Cadogan from West Cork was Vice Superior. After ordination in 1921, he had been sent to Western Nigeria where he rose in the ranks until 1931 when he was spoken of as 'Bishop material' but, his appointment as superior of Dromantine put an end to episcopal possibilities. He lectured in moral theology; Owen noticed that he got quite confused with students' names.

Tom Hughes from Belfast was spiritual director. Ordained in 1931, he was sent to the 'Bight of Benin', as the Vicariate around Lagos was called. There, he taught in the prestigious SMA College of St Gregory's. After home leave in 1935, he studied in University College Cork and, on graduating, was appointed to Dromantine.

Two of the Dromantine lecturers were outstanding in Owen's estimation, John Flanagan and Thomas O'Shaughnessy. Flanagan, professor of canon law, had an absolute command of his subject and superb delivery. He was much in demand by the Bishop of Dromore, Edward Mulhern, who avowed, "He's the only canonist I know who will solve your problems over the phone and quote the correct canons word for word". Unfortunately, he voiced criticism of the men on the missions who, he claimed, were not following correct canonical procedures. This did not endear him to the missionaries, especially as he had never been in Africa. He had been appointed to Dromantine immediately after graduating with a licentiate in canon law. His attitude instilled in some students, including Owen, a critical view of what they thought was going on in the missions. Inevitably, he drew the censure of Society authorities on himself and had to leave Dromantine.[1]

Thomas O'Shaughnessy from Co Galway was professor of missiology and church history. In 1939, after mission work in Liberia, 'Shocks', as he was called, was sent to Rome to study the new subject called, 'Missiology', the science of mission. After attaining a doctorate in it in 1943 – the first man in Ireland or Britain to do so – he was appointed to Dromantine.

While in Rome, he interrupted his studies in response to a request from the German high command that he be chaplain to Irish prisoners of war in Friesach. He agreed but, after some time in the camp in 1941, realized he was being used by the Nazis in an effort to get Irish POWs to work for them against the British. After six months, he returned to Rome. In Dromantine, he wove into his lectures stories from his camp experience and tales of travels in war-torn Europe – including sleeping in Hitler's bed in a hotel in Austria! Owen admired his fresh approach and broad vision.

Teaching theology was a young man from Mayo, Bob Molloy. He had been with O'Shaughnessy in Rome but, after gaining his doctorate in canon law, he went on to do another one in moral theology. After completing in 1942, he was appointed to the staff in Dromantine.

The bursar, John Murphy, "a lovely character from the Kerry *gaeltacht*" said Owen, went to Nigeria after ordination. There he got cerebral malaria. After recovery, he was appointed to Dromantine. In Murphy's opinion Owen's class were, "the nicest group that ever passed through Dromantine".

Despite being back in Co Down, Owen felt unsettled and, for the first time, was troubled by serious doubts about his vocation. It wasn't unusual for first years to feel ill-at-ease after being transplanted from the relative simplicity of Clough to the more complicated life of the major seminary. A Dominican directed the customary pre-Christmas retreat. Owen thought it was very good; it helped him settle down and he remained relatively content for the rest of his time as a student. When he went home that Christmas for holidays, unlike the summer before, he began to attend daily Mass.

Though Dromantine, in its quiet rural setting, thirty miles south of Belfast, was removed from the theatre of war, there were ominous signs of its existence even within the seminary demesne. American soldiers, most of them black, occupied an extensive part of the grounds from the 'the pleasure garden' to the main gate. They were billeted in Nissen huts and were guarding large ammunition dumps hidden under green canvas sheets. Every now and then camouflaged trucks growled along the seminary avenue bringing in or removing boxes of the deadly munitions. If the Germans ever discovered what was hidden there, they would have blown the place sky high.

The *Luftwaffe* came near enough. Belfast was bombed on the nights of the 7th and 15th of April 1941 and again on the 5th of May. Over 1,000 people were killed and thousands of homes were destroyed, most of them in poor working class areas. The worst attack was on Easter Tuesday night the 15th of April. Then, 180 Heinkel and Junker planes bombed the hapless city, keeping up the bombardment from before midnight for about five hours. Over 800 people were killed and great damage was done to shipping and factories. Responding to an urgent request for assistance, Eamon de Valera called out units of the Fire Brigade in the south to help. Thirteen fire engines and seventy men from Dublin, Dun Laoghaire, Drogheda, and Dundalk rushed to Belfast. In retaliation, Hitler ordered a bombing raid on Dublin on the 30th of May in which thirty-four people were killed.

On the night of the 15th of April, Owen and colleagues were sleeping peacefully in their attic quarters when the alarm went off. Grabbing clothes, they made a hurried exit. Paddy Maher, formerly a sailor in the Mercantile Marine, got out through a window and shinned down a drainpipe. Runner, Mick Maughan, raced away and kept going until he found himself well on the road to Armagh. With so much explosive material in the grounds, Dromantine was not a safe place to be. On the seminary avenue, under a bright moon and stars, the students paced up and down trying to keep warm. With them was Stephen Harrington, the Provincial Superior, who had arrived the day before. On hearing the alarm, he thought it was the early rising bell. He rose immediately and began to shave. When he realized his mistake, he hurried out well-lathered and half-shaven.

The next evening, the Provincial spoke to the assembled students. He was an impressive orator even if his voice was a little nasal and his accent betrayed his West Cork origins. Owen listened spellbound as Harrington lectured, without a note, on the executed 1916 patriot Paraic Pearse's theory of education. After the talk, the Provincial mingled with the students. Owen, finding him friendly and easy to talk to, took a great liking to him. Holding him and his views in high respect, the students wondered how his view that mission in Africa would be more and more related to higher standards of education would affect them.

Despite the interest generated by the Provincial's talk, the students inevitably returned to discussing the bombing raids on Belfast as more news of death and destruction was reported. Brother Gerry Collins, the College 'Fire Warden', a quiet man enjoyed a little more than usual attention at this time. It was he who had set off the alarms on the nights of the bombings. Subsequently, he began to sound the alarm whenever "he heard something". Owls, winds, and tomcats were often responsible for his activation of the sleep-shattering siren.

Violent death was one sort of tragedy in the war years, premature deaths of young missionaries in Africa was another. The Society of African Missions, described by one historian[2] as "a Society engendered by death", experienced a high rate of premature deaths from its very beginnings in Africa when the Founder and all his companions died in Sierra Leone in 1859. Throughout the nineteenth century and well into the twentieth, the mortality rate continued to be alarmingly high.

Some of those who died prematurely in Nigeria were known to the students: John Marren, Achonry, 29, died 28 September 1937 of yellow fever; Tony O'Dwyer, 27, Clonfert, died a week later; Florrie O'Driscoll, 30, Ross, had died two years previously of typhus. The death that touched Owen most must have been that of Sexton Cahill, the man who had facilitated his entrance into the Society. Struck down by yellow fever during his second tour in Nigeria, Sexton died on the 7th of September 1942 at the age of thirty-five. His death, or the deaths of the others, did not cause the students in Dromantine to falter one bit. "The deaths didn't affect me in the slightest", said Owen.

Owen became friendly with six diocesan students who were studying in the college: James Fitzpatrick from Hilltown, Bertie McGovern from Newry; and three Traynor brothers from Burren near Warrenpoint, Barney, John, and Frank. In the three brothers' early years in Maynooth seminary, two of them contracted tuberculosis and were sent to Switzerland for treatment. When the War started they were repatriated but, unable to continue in the national seminary, they were sent to Dromantine. The sixth student was Owen's own cousin, Lochy McEleavy, the young lad he used to visit in Windsor on the Canadian side of the Detroit River.

In Dromantine, the students had a better chance of keeping abreast of world affairs than in Clough. Naturally, they were particularly interested in how their older brothers, who had recently departed for Africa, were faring. At this time there were serious delays in getting to Africa because of the danger from German submarines in the Atlantic.

Passenger ships were not allowed to travel except, on an odd occasion, in convoy, accompanied by navy warships. On these occasions, the Elder Dempster shipping line, would announce that a ship would soon attempt the voyage and passengers should be ready for embarkation at Liverpool. Among those waiting for passage was the new Bishop of Western Nigeria, Patrick Joseph Kelly, and Dromantine's ordination class of 1939. Early in May 1941, they received word that a convoy would sail within a few days. They rushed to Liverpool and embarked on the steam ship *Abossa* bound for Lagos. Not long at sea, they were attacked by a German plane. One of its bombs apparently entered the ship's funnel and immobilised the engine. Separated from the convoy, a sitting duck for enemy plane or submarine, the *Abossa's* engineers worked feverishly while the Bishop and the missionaries stormed heaven. After a few hours, the engine came to life; the *Abossa* got under way and rejoined the fleet. After more scares and long delays, the ship docked in Nigeria having taken more than twice the normal time for the voyage.

In the New Year of '42, another convoy sailed. Among the passengers this time were about forty missionaries, fifteen of them members of the SMA. On the 2nd of February, the Dromantine diarist noted with relief that they arrived safely, "Their ship had not even once been attacked, a rare thing for the times".

In the seminary, Owen felt frustrated by the dry theology they were being taught, "Dinny Cahill's Sunday sermons were more meaningful!" he said. He appreciated one volume of Hieronymus Noldin's moral theology books called *De Principiis,* not because of its content but, because Fr Dinny had given it to him as a gift. What inspired Owen and his classmates more than theology was the spirit of Paraic Pearse and the Easter Rising of 1916. The post-Rising and post Independence period in Ireland was a time of growing patriotism and willingness to make sacrifices for a cause. The idealism of Pearse and his colleagues found expression in numerous cultural and altruistic organizations. One in Dromantine, called *Cumann an Phiarsaig*, aimed at promoting all things Irish, especially by serving God as <u>Irish</u> missionaries". Another was an Irish language movement which Owen joined, signing himself as 'Eoghan Mac Fhinn'.

This was the period in which a number of new missionary congregations were founded: the Maynooth Mission to China, 1916; the Missionary Sisters of St Columban 1922; the Missionary Sisters of the Holy Rosary 1924; St Patrick's Missionary Society, 1932; and the Medical Missionaries of Mary, 1937. Already existing congregations, including the SMA, its 'sister' order, the Missionary Sisters of Our Lady of Apostles, the Holy Ghost Fathers and the Vincentians, experienced a marked increase in numbers of applicants.

The first Mother General of the Holy Rosary Sisters was none other than Fr Dinny Cahill's sister, Anastasia. As a young woman doing teacher training in Belfast, she heard the appeal of Bishop Shanahan cssp who was trying to found an order of Sisters for his Vicariate of 'Southern Nigeria'. Becoming one of its first members, after profession she was appointed Mother General.   .

The rising spiritual dynamism was felt among Irish laity too. Foremost among new apostolic groups was the Legion of Mary founded by Frank Duff in 1921. During this period, the rosary took on new nationalistic and missionary overtones. The 'Annunciation' was interpreted as St Patrick's announcing of the faith; the 'Visitation' as its extension to the Continent by Irish monks; the Sorrowful Mysteries were associated with persecution under the Penal Laws; and the Glorious Mysteries were seen as the contemporary era of Church growth and missionary flourishing.

Dromantine, established as a major seminary in 1926, was the first Irish seminary to host and promote the Legion within its walls. Frank Duff visited it on a number of occasions and two Praesidia were founded, "Our Lady Queen of Apostles" and "Queen of All Saints". Though Owen was still critical of its limited apostolate (as in Clough the students were not permitted to go out), he admitted that it produced some great Legion men, one of them being his friend, Mick Toner. Marian spirituality spread with the growth of the Legion. One of the most widely read spiritual books of the time was de Montfort's, *True Devotion to the Blessed Virgin*, the book Owen had bought at Kylemore. Other popular spiritual books which he liked were those of the Irish Benedictine, Dom Marmion: *Christ, the Life of the Soul; Christ in the Mysteries;* and *Christ, the Ideal of the Monk.*

It goes without saying that games played a very large part in student life. When Owen first arrived in Dromantine there were over seventy students in four classes of theology. Great rivalry was exhibited when inter-class games were played or, rather, 'fought'. So many injuries occurred during these games that they became prohibited. A number of the students played for their counties at senior level, but under assumed names due to the 'Maynooth ban'. Owen had been asked to play for Down but, obedient to rules, he explained that he couldn't because of the ban. Modestly he admitted, "Down wasn't so good then!"

"The best brother one could have".
Tom and Owen.

The road to Holy Orders

Owen and his classmates took their second 'temporary oath' in June 1941, the third the following year, and the permanent one in '43. Since June '41, they had been conferred in stages with the minor orders of tonsure, porter, lector, exorcist, and acolyte. 'Tonsure', the symbolic act of cutting off a lock of hair, was the ceremony which had the greatest impact on Owen. He took to heart its invocation, "Lord, you are my portion and cup". On that day, 14 June 1941, he committed himself firmly to missionary priesthood and to a celibate life. During the retreat before it, he wrote in his spiritual notebook, "What is the purpose of this Retreat?" and answered, "To conform myself more and more with the perfection of Christ; to acquire His virtues, to put them into practice; to view His life more closely so that I may be enabled to imitate Him, to love Him and to see how far short I am of the ideal that is expected of me. To contemplate how I must prepare for the great gift of the priesthood".

He also wrote some practical points for the coming summer holidays: "Do at least a half-hour meditation; put away uncharitable thoughts; try little chats with family and be a source of edification to all". For the next term in the seminary, he wrote, "Put time you would spend at cards to typing or something useful; don't 'cod' at table; and get rid of 'damns', 'hells' et cetera".

At the end of his third year in Dromantine, June 1943, he was ordained sub-deacon. Quick to see humour in things, especially in pomposity and solemnity, he was feeling skittish by the end of the ceremony. When a new man on the staff, Alfie Glynn, not a great singer, bravely attempted to sing the final dismissal, '*Benedicamus Domino*', Owen got a fit of laughing. It didn't help Alfie and, as soon as he got a chance, he hissed at Owen, "You bloody man, could you not control your risibility".

In September 1943, at the beginning of their fourth and last year, Owen and eleven classmates were ordained deacons. In December, they began a special retreat before their priestly ordination scheduled for Sunday the 19th. Owen remembered little of the retreat, except the last conference which took place on the night before the ordination, a wild and windy night. The preacher, an octogenarian Vincentian, glared at the fiercely rattling windows of the oratory, then, fixing his eyes on the *ordinandi*, cried out in a loud voice, "Gentlemen, take no notice, it's only the devil trying to put you off course, pay no attention to him!"

Snow fell heavily that night. The mountain roads between Drumaroad and Newry became impassable. Next morning, Mark, Annie, Tom, a few relatives and friends (numbers restricted because of the war) unable to get to Newry by the normal route had to make a long detour by bus around the coast via Kilkeel.

In St Colman's and St Patrick's cathedral, the ordaining prelate was not the Bishop of Dromore, Edward Mulhern, but Daniel Mageean of Down and Connor. Mgr Mulhern, who had welcomed the SMA to his diocese in 1926, had died on the 12th of August, and a successor had not yet been named.[3] After the ceremony and 'first blessings' by the new priests, Owen's 'ordination breakfast' took place in a nearby restaurant. Jim McCarthy and his people, with nowhere else to go, joined them. Mark and Annie seemed happy; Owen himself felt no great elation.

The following day, he celebrated his first Mass in the cold and dimly lit Drumaroad church, assisted by Fr Cahill who had not gone to the ordination in Newry as he was still grieving over the death of his missionary brother the year before, but he tried to add a bit of solemnity to the Mass by singing a *Te Deum*. Only he and Owen knew the words and Owen's efforts to join in knocked him off key. Once again Owen became unable "to restrain his risibility".

1943 Ordination Class

Seated: H. Conlon, M. Conlon, J. Moorhead, T. Lennon, J. McCarthy
Standing: M. White, PG Scanlan, J. Browne, M. Maughan,
P. Fitzsimons, O. Maginn, P. Clancy

For his ordination card, Owen chose a 'Brian O'Higgins' one with a Eucharistic theme. Written within a tracery of Celtic designs were the words 'Do this in commemoration of me' and, in smaller letters, a prayer:

> *For strength and grace to God I pray,*
> *That I may bravely serve His cause;*
> *That I may praise by night and day*
> *The freedom of His binding Laws.*
> *That I may ease the soul in pain;*
> *That I may hear the sinner's call;*
> *And garner many a golden grain*
> *For Him the First Great Priest of all.*

On the other side of the card, he made a request to Mary the 'Mother of priests', "that I may present myself approved unto God, a workman that needeth not to be ashamed, rightly handling the Word of Truth" (a quotation from St Paul, 2 Tm 2,15).

Nearing Christmas the weather improved. Christmas Eve turned out to be a beautiful, clear day. Fr Dinny gave Owen the privilege of saying the Midnight Mass in Drumaroad. As Owen walked up the hill to the church that evening, he could see people ahead of him carrying lighted lamps and lanterns. It was like a biblical scene. During the celebration, he felt more emotion and joy than he had at his ordination or first Mass. The crib, the candles, decorations, and the prayerful congregation, most of whom he knew well, evoked an atmosphere of deep Christmas peace.

After Mass, he spent some time in thanksgiving. On the way home, he marvelled at the beauty of the starry night and the moonlit countryside. Able to see Newcastle and beyond out to sea, he tarried, breathing in the crisp air and the peace. Next morning, there was snow on the ground two feet deep, and he was down with a bad dose of 'flu which kept him in bed for the rest of the holidays! Otherwise, in these years of theological studies, he enjoyed good health. In the Dromantine "Infirmarian's Register" there was no record of a visit or medication in the blank column under the name of 'Owen Maginn'.

Owen

The seminary re-opened on 14 January 1944. The young priests returned for their final six months of theology. In this term, much to the envy of the other students, the newly-ordained got 'a fry' for breakfast and sported smart 'wings' on the shoulders of their soutanes. A decisive flicking back of a 'wing' came in handy when emphasising a weighty opinion, or, if out of doors on a windy day, it was a great help in lighting a cigarette. On weekends, the new Fathers helped in the local churches, especially nearby Glen and Barr.

On the 20ᵗʰ of January, two interesting Polish visitors arrived, Fr Nowiecki sma, a chaplain in the RAF and Mr Belacki a pilot. That evening, Nowiecki gave a talk about the persecution of the church in Poland, and Belacki gave an exciting account of the life of a Spitfire fighter pilot, including tales of thrilling aerial 'dog fights' which he described as "great fun".

Early in February, an auction of old books was held in Dromantine. Some of the tomes had been gathering dust in the old house since the Inneses lived there. Knowing how much Mark would appreciate them, Owen bought a few old volumes of the works of Bobbie Burns, Alfred Tennyson, and Lord Byron.

Patrick's Day 1944 was celebrated in style. *Cumann an Phiarsaig* staged two plays, "St Patrick's Day in the African Bush" and "Breaking Day" a play about St Patrick himself. Also staged was a variety concert for "our coloured friends in the U.S. forces stationed in Dromantine". The programme opened with a lusty rendering of 'The Star Spangled Banner' and ended with an even more lusty rendering of the 'Soldier's Song'. During the concert, the American soldiers sang a selection of Negro spirituals.

Two weeks later, the 'Yanks' installed a telephone in Father Superior's room so that the sentries at the gate could more easily check the credentials of visitors. The army did not want unauthorised people becoming aware of what was hidden in the grounds. Some of the soldiers were impressed by the spiritual life of the seminary and one, an officer, was received into the Church and baptised by the Superior in May.

Owen was president of the Literary and Debating Society and, rarely stuck for a word himself, was showing great ability in leading it with common sense and good judgement. In mid April, a debate was held on the motion that "Clerics should not attend Pictures (cinema)"; the voting resulted in a draw. Another motion was, "There are too many organizations in the house". Legion of Mary members, like Mick Toner, felt attacked and stoutly defended their burgeoning praesidia. Owen maintained his stance that the Legion apostolate could not be properly pursued unless the members were allowed out.

At the beginning of April, Owen's classmate, Johnny Browne, was withdrawn from the office of Lector (reader) as all his teeth had been extracted! Sad news was received towards the end of the month. A recently departed staff member, Belfast man Joe Donaghy aged forty-five, scarcely five months in his new mission in Egypt, had died there of smallpox on the 23rd. Previously, he had worked in Liberia and Western Nigeria and had been teaching in Dromantine since 1939.

Throughout Owen's four years in the seminary, the war continued. Interested in Irish attitudes to it, he found that the majority of Northern Catholics were pro-German. Occasionally, he attended diocesan meetings. One of them happened to be held at the time the Germans were advancing into Russia. A priest sitting next to him said, with evident satisfaction, that the Germans would be in Moscow in fifteen days. They weren't, but the statement, Owen thought, was fairly typical of the pro-German sentiment in the country. There were exceptions of course, the parish priest of Banbridge, Dr O'Hare, made a contribution towards the purchase of a Spitfire for the RAF; the majority of his parishioners were not pleased. As the war went on, the pro-German stance waned and increasing numbers of northern

Catholics joined the armed forces, not because they had become pro-British but because, economically, times were very bad.

Owen knew a number of men who enlisted. Of his former classmates in the Red High, Jim Hanna from Strangford, "the quietest fellow imaginable", joined the RAF and won a number of awards for bravery. Four more, Arthur McCavera, John Flynn, Michael Craig, and Joe Darby also joined the Air Force. Pat Sheppard joined the Royal Navy, Bobbie Bradley, the British Army, and Anthony Teague the Irish army.

The first pupils of the Red High were an impressive group who distinguished themselves, not only in the armed services but, in teaching, civil service, and in business. In sporting circles they also excelled. Four of them, Michael King, Pearse McConvey, John Shields, and Tom Skeffington played senior football for Down. Apart from Owen, two became missionary priests: Henry Flynn was ordained for the diocese of Port Elizabeth, South Africa, and Seán Savage became a Columban and worked in Korea.

As the months were passing quickly, the young priests became anxious to know their mission appointments. Most would be going to Nigeria or Liberia – the Irish Province's main mission fields. On Tuesday the 23rd of May, the appointments were posted:

> Asaba: John Browne, Hugh Conlon, Michael Maughan.
> Ondo: Paddy Clancy, Michael Conway.
> Kaduna: John Moorhead, Gerry Scanlan.
> Jos: Tommy Lennon.
> Lagos: Pat Fitzsimons.
> Liberia: Martin Whyte.

With sinking hearts, Owen and Jim McCarthy looked for their names. At the bottom of the notice they found, "Frs McCarthy and Maginn are being detained for study purposes".

When the initial excitement about the appointments died down, the 'detained pair' learned that they were going to be sent to Cambridge University. As well as a disappointment, this was a surprise; no one before them had been sent there. Their superiors explained that the Society was becoming more and more involved in secondary and third level education in Africa and missionaries with degrees from Cambridge would be most acceptable, and even necessary, in British colonies like Nigeria.

Owen, despite his criticism of the kind of theology prevailing in Dromantine, had done well academically and otherwise. In his final evaluation by the staff, they said his deportment was fair and his intelligence, excellent. They commended his aptitude as an organiser and credited him with initiative and practicality. His manners were pleasing and his observance of the rule excellent. His general disposition was that of one who was willing and obedient, but, he was *inclined to argue the point!* His outstanding trait was practicality. Under the heading of 'Misdemeanours', they wrote, 'None'.

On the 18th of June, the young priests went home to enjoy their last holiday before going to Africa (or Cambridge).

At home, Owen gladly helped with the harvest at Drumanaghan. A charming story tells us something about him at this time. A little girl, Una Toman, used to walk to and from school at Drumaroad bare-footed. One day council workers tarred the road. Finding her way home covered with tar, she feared to step on it. Owen happened to come along on his bicycle. Seeing her predicament, he put her on his bike and, carrying her over the offending portion, brought her home. Now, a married woman in South Carolina, Una never forgot his simple act of kindness.

On the feast of the Assumption, 15th of August, Fr Cahill organized a fund-raising gymkhana at Edendariff. More than 3,000 people, Protestants as well as Catholics, attended; over £500 was raised for the parish. Owen, enjoying the day immensely, regretted that his holidays were passing so quickly, soon it would be time to be getting ready for Cambridge.

Even on holidays, one couldn't forget the war. Every now and then someone received news of a relative, neighbour, or friend 'killed in action'. Pat Nolan, a brother of Owen's friend, Gerry, in the Red High, was a flight engineer in the RAF. In August, his plane was shot down over Germany. The Nolans were informed that, as other crew members' remains had been found, he had been posted 'missing and presumed dead'. Pat's mother requested Owen to say a Mass for him. Before departing for Cambridge, Owen went to the Nolan's home and said, "Mrs Nolan, I just want to tell you that I believe Pat is alive as I could not say a Mass for the dead". They did not really know what he meant but it gave them hope. Three months later, a letter arrived from Pat via the Red Cross. He had survived the crash and was a prisoner-of-war in a camp near the Polish border.

1. Fr Flanagan took up parish work in England and attained a high profile among clergy and laity there. Incardinated in Southwark diocese, he died in his parish, Polegate in Sussex, 27 March 1977.

2. Leon Leloir gave as subtitle to his book *Marion Brésillac*, *"Un Ordre qu'engendra la mort"* meaning an Order engendered by death or, an Order which engenders death, (Namur 1939). Leloir gave a series of talks, about missionary societies and their founders, on Belgian radio in 1939.

3. Mgr Eugene O'Doherty, the president of St Columba's College, Derry, was nominated bishop of Dromore on 19 March 1944.

Chapter 4

CAMBRIDGE

In August 1944, Owen completed his Cambridge application forms and sent them off along with his Public Examination Certificates. A few weeks later he applied for a Travel Permit. Duly processed, the travel permit obliged him to arrive at his destination not later than 10 October, the day the 'Michaelmas term' began. He and Jim McCarthy arrived in the university town a few days in advance and were directed to St Edmund's House, Mount Pleasant, where Catholic priests attending Downing College resided.

At first they found things very strange. "We are rather bewildered" Owen confided to his Provincial Superior, Stephen Harrington, in his first letter to him from Cambridge. There was too much to do and too little time to do it but, "I expect we will soon become accustomed to our new mode of life. I wouldn't be surprised if we even came to like it". He qualified this by saying it was a big 'if', "Because, from what we have heard and seen, work is hard".

Harrington was in his second term as Provincial Superior. Quite a prodigy, he had been too young to be ordained with his class in 1921. Even the following year he was still eighteen months below the canonical age but, with a dispensation, he was ordained. Owen, having been impressed by his friendliness in Dromantine, wrote him quite long letters almost every month. The Provincial advised him to aim high. Academically ambitious, Owen had little need of such encouragement and felt that, with hard work and God's help, he would do reasonably well.

Life in the University proved to be a culture shock for the two Irishmen. Their English colleagues appeared to have a much broader outlook on things and to be far less submissive to rules and regulations than they were. Owen felt that he and Jim were ill-prepared for undergraduate work. Their peers had been educated in the English school system up to 'A levels' and, having been taught by Cambridge graduates, needed little orientation in the University. The Provincial took note and, subsequently, men appointed to Cambridge were given a year to adapt. Owen and Jim 'thrown in at the deep end' had to make the best of it.

In Downing College, one of the twenty-five attached to the University, Owen registered to study history for his "tripos" as the honours BA examination was called. 'Tripos' was the name of the three-legged stool examiners used to sit on in days gone by. Owen's history course was wide-ranging, covering ancient, medieval, modern, social, and constitutional history. Jim registered for economics. In contrast to the strict regimentation in Irish seminary life, Owen reported that "Here, time is absolutely at our own disposal. We can follow whatever activities we wish and, if we are so inclined, we need not do a scrap of work. There is no compulsion to attend lectures, but it is highly recommended".

In his first year, Owen's impression of his lecturers was unfavourable. While acknowledging them as masters of rhetoric, he thought they were shallow in content. The few with good content, he judged, were not as articulate as the ones with indifferent matter. The best of them he thought was Dr Postan, but he lectured only on certain aspects of Economic History; "first class" were Professor Brooke on medieval European history and Dr Picthorn on Constitutional English History. Owen appreciated the great sense of humour of Picthorn, a Member of Parliament for the University.

The college appointed the benign and helpful Mr Whalley-Tooker as Owen's tutor. But the one he had most to do with was his director of studies, Mr Goulding-Brown MA. He gave his students topics and a bibliography and, later, discussed their essays with them. In the first term, Goulding-Brown did not rate Owen highly, "Mr Maginn seems to me an ordinary II, ii (2nd class, division 2); but he finds Mr Salter's lectures on Economic History too elementary to be worth his while to attend regularly, so, perhaps, he may be better than I see him. Or it may be Irish caprice. I have told him that it is useless to go to lectures irregularly, and have given him permission to cease to attend Mr Salter's".

In the 'Lenten Term' of 1945, Goulding-Brown, warmed a little in his estimation of Owen, "He works quite well, but I do not see more than a moderate B in him. II, ii probable". In the Easter Term, 'GB' was not happy, "Mr Maginn having complained of the elementary nature of Mr Salter's lectures, I gave him leave to cease attendance. But I was not pleased to receive Dr Picthorn's notice of 16 May, showing that Mr Maginn had 'cut' 3 lectures out of 8. I do not think that Mr Maginn has any interest in History except Medieval. And if it be possible for him to be transferred at once to Anthropology, it would, I think, be better than reading History half-heartedly, and despising (quite unnecessarily, for he has no great ability or knowledge) and cutting his lectures. One might expect a priest to know some Latin, but 'seperate' is not a spelling which inspires confidence".

It was hardly surprising that in his first year, Owen, was a bit negative about his director, describing him as "a rather eccentric, moody, old Victorian type". Owen suspected that he was prejudiced against the Irish, especially Irish Catholics, "because his daughter married one and became a Catholic herself".

One day, after reading an essay of Owen's, Goulding-Brown exploded, "You god-dammed Irish! Why are you so stubborn?" Owen never discovered what he had written which so provoked him. In fairness, Owen admitted that Goulding-Brown was very thorough and could be extremely nice. On another occasion, he professed, "You Catholic priests have a big advantage in your training. You have a good philosophical background which gives you a different attitude towards life from the rest of us".

Senior students advised Owen that his director worked according to a plan "which should be followed blindly, keeping one eye open at the same time!" Owen worked on his rapport with Goulding-Brown and, in the Michaelmas report of 1945, GB said, "Maginn seems to be more interested. Some of his essays on early modern history have been good". But he drew back again in the Lenten Term of '46 commenting, "Industrious, but not an historical mind". In the Easter Term he reported, "Better than II, ii, but is unlikely to reach II, i. A central Second Class candidate". In his second year at the University, Owen was happy to be able to say, "We have got on extremely well together this year, which is more than most of his students can say".

It wasn't all work and no play. In front of St Edmund's one could play bowls or skittles, nearby there was a football pitch. Farther away was the legendary River Cam. Owen went along with Jim one day to try his hand at rowing. Jim, from Haulbowline in the port of Cork, knew well how to row but, even he found that rowing in Cambridge was 'something else'. After their first session on the river, both agreed that it was too strenuous for 'ageing missionaries'.

Owen liked to walk and, curious about the old town and the other colleges, he found plenty to interest him. Fascinated by the historic buildings like the tenth century Church of St Bene't, King's College Chapel, and the Norman Church of the Holy Sepulchre, he determined to follow a course in architecture if ever one was offered in Downing. He appreciated also the beautiful setting of Cambridge. The Fens, on which the town was built, was quite unlike the hill

Student priests at St. Edmund's, Cambridge. Owen is standing, third row, seventh from the left. Jim McCarthy is in front, first on the left.

country of home but, in winter, bone-chilling winds from the Continent swept in unchecked over the flat land.

He and Jim ate, studied and slept in St Edmund's where nearly forty priest-students resided. Most of them were friendly, especially members of the English Mill Hill missionary congregation. A few residents were anti-Irish because of Ireland's neutrality. As the war was still going on, food was not as plentiful as it might have been. Each student got a Government ration book, which he handed up to the house bursar who, with a large number of books, was able to buy quite a lot of rationed food. The house had a large kitchen garden and the gardener, a refugee from eastern Europe, succeeded in providing a good supply of fresh vegetables. On special feasts the students were treated to a modicum of wine or beer. The University chaplain, one of the famous Gilbey distillers family, was a most hospitable host in his chaplaincy, 'Fisher House'.

St Edmund's residence had been established in the mid nineteenth century when the proposal to send Catholics to Cambridge was first passed. Initially, the idea had been opposed by the Catholic hierarchy because of the University's anti-Roman bias. Eventually, the bishops acquiesced provided priest-students reside in a separate hostel under a strict rector who would see that they were not 'contaminated' by reformation heresies. In Owen's time Fr Petit was rector. To the Irish he seemed a bit aloof. He scolded Jim McCarthy for not taking enough exercise, "Get out there and play football!" he admonished. But Jim, a very keen footballer, had hurt his ankle and was only temporarily off the game. When his ankle got better, Petit began scolding him for playing too much. In 1945, Petit was nominated bishop of Minevea in Wales. He was replaced in St Edmund's by Fr Corboy, an English diocesan priest and a graduate of Cambridge.

According to university rule, residents of St Edmund's had to dine in Downing College Hall at least twice a week. At it, all had to wear the academic gown – a black garment falling loosely from shoulder to knee. Dining in Downing Hall made quite an impression on Owen and Jim and brought them into contact with students from many parts of the world, including many students from West Africa. These were delighted to speak about SMA Fathers and Brothers they knew at home. Owen met only two or three Irishmen in Cambridge; one was Brother Baptist, superior of the De la Salle community.

College debates and extra-curricular activities were many and varied. One could go to a different society meeting practically every evening of a whole term. Owen liked to dip into them all especially the 'Irish Club' which, he found, was dominated by Trinity College (Dublin) graduates of a distinctly Anglo-Irish persuasion. He got a kick out of winding them up, and doggedly defended his point of view even when it was clearly dubious. Variety, in the daily lecture schedule, was provided by visiting lecturers, many of whom were American. Owen thought the 'Yanks' were a breath of fresh air in the self-centred atmosphere of Cambridge.

On weekends, Jim, wearing football togs beneath his soutane, cycled off to play for Cambridge's second team, the 'Falklands'. Owen, now that he was free to go out, used to go to London on Legion of Mary work. In Soho, he sought out the 'ladies of the night', endeavouring to engage them in heavenly conversations, which of course, drew the rancour of the pimps, but didn't stop him.

Jim returned to Ireland for the Christmas holidays bringing some heavy books on economics with him. At the port of Heysham he was stopped by customs men who, thinking he might be spying for the Germans, confiscated the books. Owen remained in England and, wishing to combine serious reading with a bit of priestly ministry, found a post as temporary chaplain in a convent in Chilton near Thame.

There were soldiers everywhere in Cambridgeshire. Highly visible were Americans in 'snazzy' uniforms. With friendly faces, chocolate bars and cigarettes, they were popular with the local girls. Overhead at night, bomber planes droned on deadly missions. One week-end Owen went to Norwich to assist an Irish priest with Sunday Masses. On Saturday night the town was bombed. Near the presbytery anti-aircraft guns began firing; the noise was terrible and the house shook.

Another week-end on a similar errand, he stayed in a small hotel in London. Next day, shortly after he had left the hotel, a German 'Flying Bomb', a V1 or a V2, demolished it. He went back to look, but all that was left was a huge crater. It was the nearest he had come to being a war casualty. Walking the streets of bomb-damaged London, he felt a rising admiration for the English, their resilience and determination to carry on.

At midnight on the 8th of May 1945, the World War came to an end in Europe. The following day, 'Victory Day', tumultuous celebrations were held all over England. Winston Churchill visited Cambridge.

Owen went to hear him speak. In the course of his speech, he criticised Eamon de Valera and the Irish for remaining neutral. Owen was angry and not at all impressed by the speaker who, he noted, was inebriated. However, it was not the Prime Minister's remarks that stayed in his mind, but the sight of three lorry loads of German prisoners who, on being driven past, were jeered by the crowd.

The June '45 exams were Owen's first big academic test. He had worked hard throughout the year and thought he did reasonably well but, he was disappointed with the grades he received believing they were not a fair return for the effort he had put in. He concluded that there was a large element of chance in the way papers were marked, "I do not think the Cambridge system is all that it is cracked up to be … In most cases there is 75% bluff. The brilliant student would shine anywhere". Continuing in this critical vein, he complained about the social, moral, and religious dangers for Catholic students at the University, "I would not advise an Irish parent to send a child there, unless he had a good knowledge of the Faith".

He resented the negative attitude to the Catholic Church and its teaching that he perceived among the Cambridge professors. Stephen Harrington reminded him that we can be blind to our own short-comings and can learn a lot from non-Catholics. Owen hastened to assure him that it was not intelligent criticism he minded but the deep-seated assumption that Catholic doctrine was erroneous and that in the 'Church of Rome' there was no more unity than in the Protestant church.

He was also critical of 'The Sword of the Spirit Movement', a Catholic social movement founded during the war to combat secularism and to unite Christians against Nazism. Owen found it too liberal and thought its protagonists, "many of them converts from Protestantism", diluted Catholic doctrine too much, "Apart from F.S. Gregory [one of the leaders of the movement], there is not one of them who could not pass for a respectable Protestant any day".

While Owen defended the Church when others criticised it, he was not averse to criticising aspects of it himself. Writing to Harrington, he said the Church was tackling mission unwisely. Harrington was intrigued as he had just written a booklet entitled *Our Missions,* and was soliciting reactions to it. In a rather advanced statement for the Forties, Owen said, "The native outlook has not been sufficiently considered or thoroughly investigated. The European missionary has condemned native customs, irrespective of their true significance, simply because they have not been in conformity with his preconceived notions. Moreover, the missionary has too often been a tool of imperialism". Owen's ideas partly stemmed from Thomas O'Shaughnessy's missiology lectures in Dromantine, but also from a Dutch missionary Fr Henry Van Straelen[1] who studied philosophy and comparative religion at Cambridge 1942-1944 and gained a doctorate on the "Yoshid Meiji Restoration" of Japan. Owen struck up a friendship with Van Straelen who, among other avant-garde ideas, believed that a new Christian civilization would develop in Asia, or in Africa which would surpass 'super-civilized' Western Christianity. Owen observed that, "Although Van Straelen appears to be a heretic, he is receiving every encouragement from Rome".

Contrary to his first year in Cambridge, in his second Owen found a lot to be commended, "I believe there is a great deal to be said in favour of the training here". In November, he and Jim received the sad news that their classmate, Fr Paddy Clancy from Limerick, had died of blackwater fever in Ondo, Nigeria, just six months after arriving in his mission. The first of the class of '43 to die, Paddy was only twenty-seven years of age.

Owen spent Christmas 1945 at home in Drumaroad and in Dromantine. Although he found the seminary an excellent place for study, he admitted "doing precious little work".

Though a prolific letter-writer, Owen rarely wrote articles for 'publication'. One of his rare essays in print appeared in the *Dromantine Annual 1946*. No doubt the editor had put a little pressure on him to write something. In his article, "The Sixteenth Century and Western Europe", Owen manifested a rather flamboyant style of writing. Describing that century as "A notable period for the formation of various States, religion, politics and their economic future", he said, "It closed in an atmosphere of gloom … chilled by a cold blast of heresy that threatened for a moment to freeze the heart's blood of the Church itself; and ancient Europe, Medieval Europe, passed in a mutilated form into the homogeneous, dismembered, conglomerated set of States that threaten to destroy one another today".

At Easter, he and Jim went again to Dromantine. For the last two weeks of the holiday, he assisted in Gunnersbury parish, London, from where, with tongue in cheek, he wrote home saying, "I'm here at the nerve centre of the Empire". In the exams of June '46, he thought he did better than in his first year; at least he was sure he did well in five of his six papers. Goulding-Brown thought so too and said he expected him to move up a grade that year. Owen arranged a busy summer for himself doing pastoral supply work in Edinburgh, Chester, and London, followed by a stint in Paris to improve his French.

The summer work turned out to be more strenuous than he had bargained for. Apart from routine week-day activities, he had to say two Masses on Sundays and preach at three. It was a good experience, he said, but he would not recommend it to anyone looking for rest and quiet. Working in three different places in Britain, he hadn't a chance to settle in any of them, "Nevertheless, it was a cheap way of seeing a bit of Scotland, and too much of England".

For his sojourn in France, he contacted the SMA in Paris seeking accommodation. Its procurator advised him to try the Society's novitiate in Belgium. Feeling put off, he was about to drop the whole idea when he got an offer as temporary chaplain at a convent of the Little Sisters of the Assumption in Paris. Duties would be light, he was told, only morning Mass and Benediction. One of the Sisters could speak a little English and would introduce him to a Mlle Pierre Edmond-Roger who would teach him French "provided he could find her place". He thought two months in France would be better than "basking in the sun in Co Down" so he accepted the offer. He arrived in Paris in August and remained until October 7.

The war not long over, Spartan conditions still prevailed in France. He hadn't been overfed in Cambridge, but food was even scarcer in Paris. The convent was located in a poor area in the suburbs and suffered from many privations. The summer turned out exceptionally hot. Ironically, Owen developed a cold which he couldn't shake off. Nevertheless, he enjoyed his Parisian experience; everyone he came in contact with was "kindness itself".

Back in Cambridge, he made plans to do more French during the following Christmas holidays. This time he wrote to the novitiate in Belgium. Its Superior was welcoming, but told him to get a letter from his Provincial. When requesting this, he added a few choice words about the university, "Cambridge is as self-opinionated and self-assertive as ever and consequently as boring". He liked to make such remarks, mainly intending to be humorous and, though they often contained a grain of truth, they didn't tell the whole story.

He wasn't bored in Cambridge; on the contrary he was busy and looking forward to Part II of his tripos. He had gained a "II, 2" in his

June '46 exams. Now he was looking forward to some new courses: the 'History of the USA', the 'Expansion of Europe' and 'Early Franciscan history'. The latter course especially attracted him, largely, because it was to be given by a renowned medieval scholar, Dom Cyril Knowles osb who had recently left Downside Abbey and been 'defrocked'. But, "He's still considered doctrinally sound", said Owen. Taking his cue from the course on the 'History of the USA', Owen dropped another 'choice remark', "For lack of ideals, and for having a cultural background that worships the great god Mammon, America is hard to beat".

Regarding the 'Expansion of Europe', he was already planning an essay, 'Colonisation in Africa, treating of the benefits, or the opposite, that missionary enterprise brings to the native people'. As this would be covering a relatively new field, few of the lecturers were equipped to deal with it. Owen thought he was fortunate in having as supervisor Dr Parry, a recognized authority on Spanish colonization. He concluded his letter to Harrington, "I fear that both James (Jim McCarthy) and I have been bitten by the jolly old University bug". Unfortunately, his ebullient mood was in for a dreadful shock.

He had not shaken off his 'Paris cold' in fact it was getting worse and he was coughing a lot. Hoping for a quick cure, he visited the college infirmary. Asked about his medical history, he mentioned his brush with TB as a boy. The doctor, not over concerned, treated him for bronchial catarrh. After a fortnight, during which Owen had a high temperature, the doctor thought he should be x-rayed as soon as he was well enough to go out. Confined to his room and not allowed out even to say Mass, it wasn't until the middle of November that he was fit to go for an x-ray. While waiting for the results, Fr Corboy informed the Provincial, no longer Stephen Harrington but Doctor PM Kelly[2], about Owen's worrying state of health. Owen himself was more concerned about missing lectures.

Though he didn't know much about it, tuberculosis was rampant in Britain and Ireland at the time and was very contagious. People wishing to reassure him, said that his boyhood encounter with TB would make him immune. English friends told him that it was the poor food in France that weakened him. Owen defended the French, saying if anything helped to run him down, it was the slender rations and strenuous work of the summer in England.

A few days after being x-rayed, he received the bad news. Tuberculosis. Fr Corboy informed the Provincial that he would have to be sent home immediately. Corboy urged that Owen be treated as soon as possible, adding, "As you no doubt well know already, one has to be very firm with him for he tends to ponder every step suggested on his behalf". Dr Paton Philip, tuberculosis officer for the County of Cambridge, on 28 November informed Owen's tutor, Mr Whalley-Tooker, that Owen was suffering from pulmonary tuberculosis of the left lung in a marked and active stage and was urgently in need of treatment in a sanatorium. Furthermore, all his fellow residents at St Edmund's should be examined for contagion.

The Cambridge professors, some of whom Owen had thought 'standoffish', now turned out to be most considerate and helpful. Unfortunately, there was little they could add to his academic record for that Michaelmas term. Dr Parry said, "He has been sick for several weeks and I have only seen him twice – he has done no written work for me yet". Mr White, said, "I saw him but little owing to his illness. A competent man: a sound 2nd, I thought, from my short knowledge of him". Mr Whalley-Tooker, did all he could to make his departure as easy as possible, getting an 'Allowance' of the term for him from the University senate. The staff of St Edmunds and of Downing College, genuinely concerned and sympathetic, wished him a full recovery to health and a speedy return to Cambridge.

Contracting a serious illness at this time of his life was a hard blow – he had barely celebrated his twenty-sixth birthday. He wrote to Fr Harrington, now Vice Provincial, telling him very briefly that he had tuberculosis. Later, he wrote him a long, eight-page letter which, however, contained more about the university than about himself. In it he admitted, "My x-ray revealed more than I expected. It came as a terrific shock. Unlike St Ignatius[3], I have not recovered perfect serenity of mind within five minutes, nor in five days either". Putting it in a spiritual context, he attributed the setback to God's will, "What He ordains is for the best". With wry humour he added, "God alone knows what harm I might have done on the missions next year". He ended the letter sadly, "I can't help feeling that I am a millstone tied around the Society's neck. I must have at least six month's rest and begin treatment at once".

1. Fr Henry Van Straelen svd, 1903-2004, spent over thirty years in Japan, and was professor of philosophy at Nanzan University in Nagoya. After Japan entered the war with the bombing of Pearl Harbour, 7 December 1941, he was interned. On being released, he left Japan in July '42 and went to Cambridge. An advisor at Vatican II, he was the author of over sixty books.

2. Dr Kelly, elected Provincial in July 1946, was the first member of the Irish Province to gain a doctorate in theology and so was called 'Doctor', or more often 'Doc', by his confreres.

3. St Ignatius of Loyola, author of the 'Spiritual Exercises', 'The Thirty Days Retreat'.

Chapter 5

TUBERCULOSIS 1946-1950

On the 3ʳᵈ of December, Owen flew to Belfast. He was met at the airport and brought to Dromantine where he spent the night. Fr John Cadogan, the superior, had already tried to find a place for him in a sanatorium in Northern Ireland, but all were booked up five months in advance. Cadogan recalled that when Owen was a student in Dromantine, he had been inclined to get run down and, as a precautionary measure, had been sent for a chest x-ray; the results then indicated that he was free of any traces or symptoms of tubercular trouble. From Dromantine he was sent to *The Cedars,* a home run by Mercy Sisters in Dun Laoghaire, Co Dublin, where the Provincial had made arrangements for him.

After a few days, he was moved to the Mater Private Home in Dublin where he came under the care of Dr Kevin Malley.[1] On the 16ᵗʰ of December, the doctor commenced what he termed "an artificial pneumathorax", a collapse of Owen's left lung. Following it, a few weeks would be required before the doctor could say whether the procedure was proving effective or not.

Two days after the commencement of the procedure, Owen wrote a letter of gratitude to his tutor, Whalley-Tooker, saying he felt in "excellent form" and, wishing his tutor seasonal greetings, said he was looking forward to returning to Cambridge the following year.

Sending Christmas greetings to Stephen Harrington, he thanked him for all his help and repeated that the x-ray result had come as a great shock, "the last thing I expected". Trying to make sense of it, he said,

"I hope it is God's way of making me atone for past sins and indiscretions. If I consecrate my inactivity to Him, I may succeed in meriting something even yet".

Early in the New Year of 1947, Dr Malley, pleased with Owen's progress, had him moved back to *The Cedars,* or '*The Lourdes Hospital*' as the sanatorium in Dun Laoghaire was now called. He was given a bed in a single room with a pleasant view; he could even see the lordly Sugar Loaf mountain in the distance. In February he wrote again to Whalley-Tooker saying, "The situation is ideal. Even now in the depths of winter the surrounding countryside looks lovely. Attention too, is first class". He was responding well to treatment, but didn't know whether he would be permitted to resume studies in October or not. He would send the Doctor's report and medical certificate as soon as he received them.

To closer friends, he was less cheerful, admitting that, feeling weak and confined to bed, he wasn't in much form for scenery and felt very lonesome. Dr Malley, a rather silent man, one of the rare ones Owen failed to draw into conversation, came daily to further deflate his lung. Owen noticed that a sombre hush followed Dr Malley on his rounds. Staff members appeared to be in awe, or even afraid, of him. After some time, the daily deflation of the lung became less frequent and, finally, was reduced to once a week.

In February, Owen got a pleasant surprise, the receipt in the mail of one of Henry Van Straelen's recently published books, *A Missionary in the War-net.* On the fly-leaf, Henry had written, "As a small memory of many pleasant talks in Cambridge and with best wishes for a complete recovery, H. Van Straelen svd, Cambridge, 7 February 1947". The book was about Henry's imprisonment in Japan after Pearl Harbour.

That month, February 1947, arctic conditions set in all over Europe. In Ireland the great freeze continued until Patrick's Day, following which the thaw gave rise to the worst flooding in living memory. Despite the awful conditions outside, Owen, in his heated room, began to hope that he was getting better. In April, feeling good, though confined to bed, he told Stephen Harrington that he was "in the best of form". However, on the 17th, Dr Malley certified that he was not fit for studies and that, in his opinion, he would not be able to return to Cambridge even in October. Owen was disappointed, but admitted that he did not really feel up to serious study.

Jim McCarthy visited. He was not in his usual good form as he was facing final exams in June. Though envious of Jim, who would soon be heading for the missions, Owen was very happy to see him. In August, Whalley-Tooker, after twenty years as tutor to Downing College history students, retired. Mr Clive Parry replaced him as Owen's tutor.

In the single room in the sanatorium, days lengthened into weeks and months; summer gave way to autumn and then winter. A year of hospitalisation passed. Owen remained confined to bed, weak and disinclined for activity. He missed very much the company of friends and longed to hear some Society news. In a letter to the Provincial at the end of November '47 he said, "The last confrere I saw was Fr Deeley from Ballinafad". Bill Deeley was bursar in the Society's College, in Ballinafad, Co Mayo. He regaled Owen with mission news and stories of Nigeria and of Egypt. He had been appointed to Egypt after being invalided home from West Africa. Owen commiserated with him for him being sent to Egypt, there were few Irish confreres there, he thought. However, Bill said he didn't remain long there, he fell ill again and was sent home.

Dr Malley, satisfied with Owen's progress, told him he could begin saying Mass once a week in December and, if he continued to make good progress, he might be able to discharge him in the spring of 1948. Owen told the Provincial the good news and asked him to send a *celebret*, a certificate of entitlement to say Mass, as the hospital chaplain had asked him for it a few times. A few nurses and patients gathered for his 'first Mass'. He felt quite good but, when he bent over for the *Confiteor*, he nearly collapsed. Hardly able to breathe, it was quite a while before he could continue and only with difficulty did he get through the whole Mass.

In Cambridge, despite the pressure of work, the freedom and the distractions, he had persevered in a regime of prayer and spiritual exercises; in the hospital he let everything go. Mass was relayed to all the rooms over the radio but he didn't follow it. At other times, he did listen to the radio, being about all he could do, it was his main pastime.

As well as Society life and confreres, he missed home and neighbours. Two of his cousins had died from tuberculosis, so he appreciated how worried Annie and Mark must be, yet they never came to visit. However, realizing that Mark was nearly seventy and that Annie wouldn't leave home without him, he forgave them. Tom came.

He made friends with some of the nurses and, as he regained strength, began to leave his room and visit other patients: an eighteen-year-old from Co Cork who talked a lot about horses, a girl from Glasgow who talked about mountains and the Lough Ness monster, a Christian Brother who introduced him to crossword puzzles and chess, a priest from Kilkenny who talked about hurling. A young Tipperary girl who, everyone knew, had little chance of recovering, looked forward very much to his visits. After she died, others told him how much his visits had meant to her.

Though he didn't pray, he was impressed at how much the lay patients and staff did, and how deep their faith was. Chaplains visited frequently, young men bent on cheering up the patients. He wished they would drop the jocularity for a while and engage in a serious conversation but that, it seemed, was *verboten*.

A foolish notion, current at the time, was that TB patients were more sexually indulgent than others. Whatever about that, a sanatorium, Owen found, was a place where human needs and weaknesses surfaced. Numerous patients and staff, women in particular, confided in him; he was quite shocked at some of the things he heard. Naturally, he felt attracted to some of the women, but the commitment he had made at holy orders and the respect with which they held him, helped him to keep his relationships wholesome.

Orphan girls from various institutions worked in the hospital. They were particularly vulnerable to predatory males. He discovered that his name was used as a deterrent, "If you do that, I'll tell Father Maginn". It gave him a kind of rueful satisfaction that his priesthood was of use to someone.

Dr Noel Browne, the Minister for Health, who riled in particular the Archbishop of Dublin, John Charles McQuaid, was one whom Owen greatly appreciated because of what he did for TB patients, raising funds to combat the disease, building sanatoria and, in 1948, introducing the new drug 'streptomycin'. First tried on a man in *The Lourdes Hospital,* where Owen was, it worked and the patient departed cured.

Dr Malley, who intended keeping Owen's lung collapsed for two years, wondered what kind of work the Provincial might have in mind for him, should he be discharged; anything strenuous was out of the question. Believing that the Doctor would not sanction a return to Cambridge, Owen thought of requesting an *aegrotat* – a degree awarded to a candidate who was unable to sit exams because of illness, provided, in the judgement of the faculty, he would have passed if he had not been ill. On his behalf, Ned Harrington, his former philosophy professor, now Provincial Secretary wrote to Fr Corboy. Corboy replied that Downing College was keeping a place open for Owen, but would hardly grant an *aegrotat* as he had missed nearly three academic terms. However, saying it was worth a try, he told Ned to send him a doctor's certificate with a brief account of Owen's illness. Owen's tutor would then take up the matter with the University Board.

When the Provincial heard that the University was holding a place for Owen, he thought it best that he should return to Cambridge in October '49 if he was fit. Malley was hopeful that he would be. But, when October came round, the doctor reported that not only was Owen not fit, he had developed "a non-obstructive duodenal ulcer", probably caused by the medication he was using. To remedy it, he was put on a strict diet which he would have to maintain for a long time.

Months dragged into years. The greatest relief in his monotonous existence was the visits of confreres especially classmates on their first home leave after five years in Africa; among them Johnny Browne, John Moorhead, Tommy Lennon, and Gerry Scanlon. Others came too; all of them had stimulating missionary stories. After they left, Owen felt a twinge of jealousy that they were so active while he was confined to a hospital bed. Bishop Tom Hughes of Ondo, whose niece was a patient, usually called on him too when visiting her. Stephen Harrington came and, one whose visits he greatly appreciated, Ned Harrington.

By the end of 1949, he definitely seemed to have turned a corner and, in the New Year, Dr Malley transferred him to Beaumont Nursing Home in Drumcondra. Gaining strength day by day and free to move around, he found a large number of priest patients there who proved to be great company. In April, Malley informed Fr Corboy that he proposed to re-expand Owen's lung soon and that he should be fit to resume studies the following October, he was clear of tubercular bacilli and was no danger to others. Though fit for studies, he should be allowed a few hours rest every day.

After an absence of four years, Owen returned to Cambridge in October 1950. In the relatively large correspondence pertaining to Owen's illness and absence from Cambridge, it is noticeable that the most positive of the correspondents, the one most given to gratitude and awareness of other-worldly dimensions, was the patient himself! Nowhere is there a word of complaint or self-pity. On the contrary, his letters bore witness to a deep faith, quiet courage, and much hope.

On his return to the University, he found some new confreres, John Creaven, Sean McCarthy, Benno Wolff, Paddy Carroll and Larry Skelly. With less naiveté, but also with less energy than when he first arrived, he took up studies again and, after an intense year, sat for his final exams in May 1951. His new tutor, Clive Parry, had already arranged that, in view of work completed in Part I of his *tripos*, his long illness and absence from classes, he would not have to sit for all Part II examinations, only for papers 1, 2, 3, 8 and 11. Grateful for that, Owen sat the required exams and acquitted himself very well.

In June, when all was over, he wrote to the Provincial, "Now that exams are a thing of the past, I am beginning to wonder about the future. I believe that I should get a degree on what I have done, even if I don't cover myself in glory". He was awarded a 'Bachelor of Arts' which, according to Cambridge custom after one year, became a 'MA Cantab'. Characteristically, though he hadn't yet departed from Cambridge, he asked the Provincial what his next appointment would be so that he "could be preparing for it from now on".

1. Dr Kevin Malley, was one of a distinguished Mayo family. His brother, Earnan (who included an 'O' in his surname), was author of *On Another Man's Wound,* a novel about Ireland's War of Independence and Civil War, in both of which he fought. Severely wounded in the Civil War, he was captured and sentenced to death, but not executed as, due to his injuries (twenty-one bullet wounds) doctors said he would never walk again. He did and led a very active life up to his, non-violent, death in 1957.

Chapter 6

EGYPT 1951

At home in Co Down, before the end of June, Owen received a letter from the Provincial Secretary, informing him that he had been appointed to Egypt. The Secretary, Ned Harrington, told him to get inoculated against smallpox and typhoid, see that his passport was endorsed for as many countries as possible, and buy his tropical outfit before the bursar went on holidays on the 1st of August.

The SMA had been working in Egypt since 1877. The successor of the Founder, Augustin Planque had first sought Egypt and other places in Africa "to give our missionaries a chance to live". The West Coast of Africa was costing the Society dearly in premature deaths. The average length of survival of young missionaries on the Coast was less than two years. Planque, seeking missions in places with a less severe climate than West Africa, succeeded in getting co-operative missions in Algiers, Oran, Egypt and South Africa. Of these, only the Egyptian mission continued. It was staffed mainly by French confreres. In 1936, the Irish Province agreed to take over their English-speaking schools. During World War Two, over twenty Irish Fathers taught in Alexandria, Port Said, Suez, Shubra, and Heliopolis. After the war the schools were gradually closed down until only St George's, Heliopolis, remained.

Before the Moslem conquest in the 7th century, Egypt had been the centre of a flourishing Christianity with its ruling patriarch residing in the great city of Alexandria at the mouth of the Nile. A considerable number of Christians survived the Moslem invasion and continued practising their faith. In the nineteenth century one of the Coptic churches reconciled with the Latin west to become 'Catholic Copts'. Though united to Rome, the Catholic Copts continued to have their own Patriarch in Heliopolis and another one in Alexandria. The patriarchate of Heliopolis had about 2,000 members and that of Alexandria over 11,000. It was to these especially that Rome sent the SMA. There were, and still are, in Egypt, 'Orthodox' Copts and other ancient Christian Churches who are not in union with Rome.

Initially, Owen was disappointed on being assigned to Egypt. Only seven Irish confreres worked there in what was basically a French mission served by about forty French confreres. Mgr André van den Bronk sma[1], a lone Dutch man among the French, was Vicar Apostolic of Heliopolis. He visited Ireland in 1951 and, after returning to Egypt, wrote to the Irish Provincial repeating his request for more Irish Fathers. In his letter, significantly written on the feast of St George, 23 April, he requested only one Father by name, Owen Maginn, whom he wanted for St George's College.

In Owen's time, Egypt was regarded by Society humorists as a '*refugium peccatorum*', a 'refuge of sinners'; officially, it was still a place where men who did not enjoy robust health could be sent. Owen was asked to go to St Georges's before the beginning of the school year in the first week of October.

*

Before his departure for Egypt, a significant event took place in the parish of Drumaroad and Clanvaraghan. On the 9th of September 1951, on the summit of the hill of Drumnaquoile, an imposing cross, erected by Fr Cahill and parishioners, was blessed by Bishop Daniel Mageean. The twenty-five foot granite cross commemorated the Franciscans of Downpatrick who had taken refuge in the area after their expulsion by Elizabethan soldiers and the killing of three friars in

1570. The friars remained working in the Drumnaquoile area until the end of the eighteenth century. Theirs was the last Franciscan presence in the county.

Owen, who hailed from Drumanaghan, very near Drumnaquoile, was master of ceremonies at the formal blessing when Bishop Mageean accompanied by a great throng of people climbed the hill. In his few words on the occasion, Owen said, "The Franciscan friary was erected in dark and

The Cross of Drumnaquoile;
Owen is on left in surplice.

evil days. It served a people who were oppressed by unjust laws. The cross that pays tribute to their patience and steadfastness is a worthy monument". His father, Mark, wrote a commemorative poem, "The Cross of Drumnaquoile":

> *They raised a cross on the hill-top high / The hill in Drumnaquoile*
> *Where the sons of good St Francis / In ages past did toil*
>
> *They toiled for their heavenly Master / In a sorely stricken land,*
> *Where the priest was a hunted outlaw / And their holy faith was banned.*
>
> *Where the lives of the suffering people / Through the cruel penal years*
> *Were filled with dread and anguish / With sorrow grief and tears...*

The last three verses of the fifteen-verse poem are:

And thousands climbed that steep hill-side / Their memory proud to honour
That September day when the cross was blest /
By Daniel of Down and Connor.

And the cross, it stands as a symbol / Of the Church that cannot fail;
For the Saviour has promised, against it / Hell's gates shall not prevail.

And you who climb to that sacred spot / As you stand by the cross that's there,
For the souls of the Friars long dead and gone / Please kindly breathe a prayer.[2]

It was draughty on that hill-top high and even before the day of the blessing, Owen was suffering from 'flu. That evening he thought it best to inform the Provincial Secretary in Cork of his condition and ask that his departure for Egypt be delayed. He felt miserable physically and mentally, one of the few times in his life, he said, when he felt really down in the dumps. Dr Moore in Castlewellan detected "a rasping sound in his right side" and, considering Owen's recent medical history, advised that he should not travel for some time.

Eight days later, Owen's passport arrived; the very next day, he wrote to Ned Harrington saying he felt much better and was ready to go! The Provincial, aware that Owen's Egyptian visa was valid up to the 8th of November, suggested that he remain at home until nearer that date. Owen acquiesced and used the extra time to read up on Egypt. He wrote to Fr Harry Baker, one of the Egyptian veterans, currently on leave in Ireland, requesting information about the mission. But, apart from telling Owen not to burden himself with too much luggage, especially if he was travelling by plane, Harry didn't say much and, "some of his information was inaccurate" said Owen!

In October, he flew to Egypt in the company of fellow Co Down man, Johnny Murtagh, who was, not only an experienced Egyptian missionary and staff member of St George's but, an accomplished Egyptologist. The pair travelled by Air India and arrived at Cairo Airport at 4am in the morning. After negotiating customs and immigration, they emerged from the airport as the sun was beginning to rise. Outside, Owen was astonished to see

The mosque of Mohammed Ali, Cairo

hundreds of men in white robes on their knees, facing east. "They're Moslems praying to Allah", Murtagh explained as he hailed a taxi.

It didn't take them long to reach St George's, at 15 Sharia Quait Bai, in Heliopolis, 8 kilometres from the centre of Cairo but quite near the Airport. The ancient city of Heliopolis, meaning 'city of the sun' built in honour of the sun God 'Ra', lay in ruins a few kilometres from the new city of the same name. New Heliopolis had been designed by a Belgian architect for Europeans engaged in the construction of the Suez Canal. Once a splendid place, over the years it had become run down.

St George's, founded by a Coptic Bishop in the 1940s, ran into financial difficulties. In 1950, it was amalgamated with St Austin's, 'British Boys' School', the last of the SMA English-speaking schools in Cairo. The two schools then continued as one under the title 'St George'. The patron saint, who may have been a Roman soldier, was martyred in Lydda, Palestine, in 303; not much more is known about him. Stories of dragon-slaying arose in medieval times. It wasn't until the fourteenth century that the English made him their patron saint. The Society of African Missions was regarded as the 'owner' of the school but, by an agreement of 1953, it was paying rent for it to the Coptic Patriarch.

The Fathers had spent nearly £2,000 on building and repairs, but much still needed to be done. Located in a crowded quarter of Heliopolis, the college offered elementary, primary and secondary education. A major problem was the lack of space. Classrooms were overcrowded, and there was no sports field or recreation ground. The Fathers lived 'upstairs' in an apartment built on the flat roof of the school. When Owen arrived, the school had about 250 pupils. They hailed from an astonishing variety of backgrounds: Catholic Copts, Orthodox Copts, Maronites, Melkites, Maltese, Greek Cypriots, Armenians, Chaldeans, and Lebanese. Less than half of them were in the secondary part. The number of pupils was about seventy less than the previous year as the Government had opened schools offering free education. Without fees, the SMA would not have been able to continue. The British Government gave a grant for British subjects, mainly Maltese and Greek Cypriots. As St George's was intended for the education of Christians, the Fathers endeavoured to restrict the numbers of Moslems to below 20%, but the Government had recently demanded that at least 25% be Moslem.

The teaching staff comprised of Fathers Davy Hughes the headmaster, Johnny Murtagh, Joe Barrett, Harry Baker, Pat Crystal, Pat McCarthy, and fourteen lay teachers. Shortly before Owen's arrival, there had been a 'shake-up' of the teaching Fathers. Bishop Van den Bronk's request for six or seven men "of average health and behaviour" had been something of an understatement. Recently departed were, Louis Kinnane, Patrick McHugh, and the O'Shea brothers, Jack and Kevin. Despite the shake-up, Owen noticed that the present staff still had more than a normal share of a high age profile, poor health, personal problems, or a combination of all three.

When school started, the new man was asked to teach nearly every subject on the curriculum. He took on English, Religion, History, and Science. To his surprise, there was a well-equipped geography room, which he wasn't using, but the Science laboratory, which he was using, was poorly equipped. While a variety of languages was spoken by the pupils, English, French and Arabic dominated; English was the language of tuition. Finding his French very useful, Owen determined to get lessons in Arabic as soon as possible.

For a start, he found many pupils in the senior classes quite unruly, and he set about instilling some discipline. One big youth openly mocked his efforts. Owen stood next to him and laid a hand on his shoulder. The youth sprang to his feet and, with a wicked-looking knife in his hand, threatened, "See this knife, it belonged to one of the men who assassinated '————' (Owen didn't catch the name) in the mosque in Jerusalem. Touch me again and I'll stick it in you". Owen didn't touch him again! And, as often happened in his rapport with 'foes', he succeeded in turning them into friends.

It took him some time to realize that foreigners were, at best, only tolerated in Cairo. Ironically, Irish men were taken to be English, who were regarded as oppressors and enemies. Owen liked to walk around the fascinating city and take photographs. The desert, never far away from anywhere in Egypt, intrigued him. One day leaving Heliopolis he began walking towards it. On the way, he stopped to admire and photograph a monument. No sooner had he done so than a crowd gathered around him murmuring sullenly. Before long there were scores. The mood was not friendly and, gesticulating angrily at the "Englesi", they were becoming more incensed by the minute. Fortunately, a group of Christian visitors led by an Egyptian Air Force officer arrived on the scene. The officer, taking in the situation quickly, told one of his companions to fetch the police and, standing next to Owen, calmed the crowd. He whispered urgently to Owen, "When the police come, go with them immediately, if you don't these people will kill you". A police jeep quickly drove up. Before it came to a halt, Owen jumped in. Whisked away to the station, the police questioned him. Hughes and Murtagh were called and, with their explanations about the new man who didn't understand how things were in Egypt, he was released.

Back at St George's, the Superior warned him about wandering in places where strangers shouldn't go and, for his own good, confiscated his camera! Fortunately, he had already taken a few rolls of film and, when writing home, usually inserted a photo or two. One to whom he wrote regularly was Mr Fitzpatrick, the primary school headmaster. A number of the Maginn-Fitzpatrick photo collection survived. They included one of two Arabs and a priest. On the back Owen wrote, "Our cooks, Ahmed and Hassan with Fr Murtagh.

'Daisy', priests and pyramid

Staunch opponents of the law of monogamy". Another photo showed a Reverend Father on a disdainful camel with a pyramid in the background. Owen's caption was, "Can you blame 'Daisy' for holding her head a little high?" On a visit to the French SMA house at Tanta, he photographed the ageing community of long-bearded confreres and, on the back of the photo wrote, "Abraham and the Prophets are dead??"

Another 'perilous incident' occurred when Owen and Joe Barrett went to see "*Joan of Arc*" in the local cinema. During a scene when the English were being slaughtered by the French, the empathetic patrons wanted to join in but, as they couldn't get at the English on screen, they began to vent their rage on the furniture. Joe and Owen, the only two in the hall who looked like Englishmen, fearing the lights might come on, put their jackets over their heads and beat a hasty retreat.

To Owen's disappointment, he found that the Fathers were but little involved in pastoral work. They helped out when asked and when able among the Catholic Copts and did some chaplaincy work for a few expatriate religious communities. The only permanent commitment they had was to St Clare's, a school for girls run by Irish Franciscan Sisters from Bloomfield, Mullingar. Apart from this, he said Mass in a Coptic church near St George's, occasionally went to say Mass for a De la Salle community in Cairo and took turns in saying Mass for various groups of Sisters.

A place Owen liked was the Chaldean church of Fatima. It had been built by a Mgr Rasam and was still administered by him. Two humorous incidents occurred while Owen was saying Mass there. The first occurred on the 2nd of March 1952, Pope Pius XII's birthday. Mgr Rasam, a great admirer of the Holy Father, at the end of Owen's Mass, asked the people to remain. Then hurrying off to the sacristy, he re-appeared pushing a mountainous birthday cake on a trolley. Standing next to it, and waving a bread knife like a conductor, he led the non-English-speaking congregation in "For he's a jolly good fellow". As the Monsignor wasn't a great singer and the congregation weren't well acquainted with either the words or the tune, the result was hilarious.

In the same church, on another occasion Owen noticed that no small hosts had been left out for consecration, nor were there any in the tabernacle. He informed Mgr Rasam who sent his sacristan, a likeable villain called 'Johnny', to the *Basilique,* the basilica of Nôtre-Dame, to get some hosts. Père Gaignoux, a very conscientious French confrere, who didn't suffer fools gladly, was the administrator of the basilica.

When Johnny burst in with his braces undone and trousers unbuttoned, Père Gaignoux, in the middle of Mass, exploded, as Johnny explained afterwards *"Comme le bombe atomique"*.

At first, Owen was disturbed by the muezzin's early morning call to prayer but before long hardly noticed it. Again and again he was impressed to see Moslems praying publicly even in busy city streets. He was fortunate in having Johnny Murtagh to explain things to him and show him around the old quarters of the city. Murtagh, very knowledgeable about Egyptian history, archaeology, and the ancient Christian churches, was one of the few expatriate priests who had permission to celebrate Mass in the old Coptic rite and language.

Murtagh also told Owen about contemporary Egypt. It was only three years since the state of Israel had been created. The Arabs were bitterly opposed to it and the hope of crushing the Jewish State was never far from their minds. King Farouk still reigned but was not popular. High ranking military men coveted his position and regarded his playboy lifestyle with distaste. Virulent among Farouk's opponents was the militant 'Moslem Brotherhood'. They were not only hostile to Farouk but also to everything western and Christian. Owen began to see for himself the effects of the Brotherhood's activity when, in January '52, they burned down British and other foreign owned buildings in Cairo. A contingent of them, marching on Heliopolis, intending to torch Christian houses and property, were stopped by the army.

Owen saw the beginning of radical change in Egypt when, on 23 July, army officers, under General Mohammed Neguib, forced King Farouk to abdicate. Known as the 'July Revolution', Neguib was installed as President. Colonel Gamal Abdul Nasser became his deputy.

*

Meanwhile, in January '52 in Ireland, members of the Society of African Missions were buzzing with news of a different kind of 'revolution'. The Provincial Superior, Doctor Kelly, and his Council, had been asked to resign by an Apostolic Visitator! Dr PM Kelly's preoccupation with avant-garde development schemes in Nigeria and failure to address disciplinary problems in Ireland led to Rome's action. The Visitator appointed a new Provincial in February, thirty-four-year-old John A. Creaven, then pursuing doctoral studies in Cambridge. One of the first things he did, as Provincial, was to tour the missions in Africa. He visited Egypt in April 1953.

At St George's, Creaven found a relatively good spirit among the Fathers, despite frustration stemming mainly from lack of pastoral opportunities and a feeling of being unappreciated. The previous year for instance, in an effort to rationalize and economise, Fr Hughes closed the school's 'Egyptian section' which was difficult to staff and a drain on the school's finances. Cardinal Tisserant in Rome, Secretary of the Congregation for Oriental Churches, reacted strongly and instructed Mgr Alberto Levame[3] of the Internunciature in Cairo to have it re-opened immediately. In general, the Cardinal appeared to be critical of the Society's efforts in Egypt.

*

Certainly, Egypt had a less humid climate than West Africa, but it was nevertheless very hot. In summer, temperatures rose to over 100 degrees Fahrenheit. Adding to the discomfort, the temperature could drop to near freezing point in winter. Houses were not equipped with heating and the sudden change in temperature caused colds and 'flu. Owen, who never liked cold weather, suffered from it in winter and from the heat and dust in summer. While he found his first two years in Egypt exciting he also found them tiring. However, it was not the heat or the cold that was affecting him at this time, but his stomach.

Thinking the problem was not really serious, he put off doing anything about it until he went on home leave. Because of their special circumstances, the confreres in Egypt were allowed home leave more often than those in West Africa.

At the end of May 1953, writing to Ned Harrington, Owen said that the political situation in the country was tense but, "If the Egyptians wait 'till I go on holidays they can amuse themselves as much as they like then in ridding the world of 'Englishmen'. Fortunately at present the faithful have not sufficient energy to spit. They are exactly half-way through their Lent, and are worn out with heat and fasting". Continuing in his humorous vein, he said there was great activity in St George's, drawing up programmes to make it "a second Eton". "We have barely time to scratch ourselves". Intending to leave Egypt by June 19th, he commented, "It can't come too soon".

The last stage of his journey home was by train. When he got off the train at Goroughwood, near Dromantine, he had to go through customs. An inspector, flicking through his passport said, "So you've been to Egypt. How are the

Owen and Hassan the cook

wogs getting on?" Owen didn't like the derogatory word or the man's attitude. Sympathising with the Egyptians, he didn't blame them for being anti-colonial. Some of his fellow missionaries acted as if they were superior to the ordinary people. Confreres in St George's, were given to calling Hassan, the cook, "Boy", even though he was over sixty.

In Dublin, Owen went to see Dr Malley who, after examination, told him that he was suffering from a severe duodenal ulcer and must undergo major surgery. Dr John Corcoran operated on him on the 25th of August in the Mater Hospital. After the operation, Malley reported that the surgeon had removed two-thirds of Owen's stomach. His post-operative response was satisfactory, but full recovery, the doctor said, would take time, "he would not be fit to return to Egypt before the beginning of 1954".

Three weeks after the operation, Owen, was sent to Beaumont Nursing Home for convalescence. Though still weak, he was concerned about his return to Egypt and, conscious that his visa would expire in October, asked the administration in Cork to have it renewed. Fr John Reddington, acting for the Provincial, who had departed for Nigeria, advised him not to worry, the provincial secretary would see to the visa and he should not think of returning until fully fit. In December, Malley and Corcoran agreed that Owen would be ready to return to Egypt in the New Year. On the 5th of February, he sailed from Southampton on board the *Carthage*.

Not long after his return, politics in Egypt took another significant turn. In April, Gamal Abdul Nasser accused Prime Minister Neguib of absolutist ambitions. In October, following an assassination attempt on Nasser by a member of the Moslem Brotherhood, the movement was suppressed. In November, Nasser ousted Neguib and, taking over the premiership and presidential powers, began to transform Egypt into a socialist state.

Of lesser moment in the affairs of Egypt, Owen was appointed Dean of Studies in St George's. At the end of the school year, June '55, Davy Hughes reported that Owen was doing a good job but, "was still not very robust". In that, Owen was not much different from most of the Fathers in St George's. The SMA community then consisted of:

Fr Harry Baker, 67: his curriculum vitae included being invalided home from Liberia; then appointment to Egypt in '37 where, over the years, he had served as teacher, headmaster and superior. Now he was scarcely able for school work due to age, deafness, and inability to control a class.

Pat Joe Christal, 57, was twenty-one years in Egypt. A former headmaster of three schools, he had suffered from tuberculosis and was often ill. Run down and suffering from the heat, he too was unable to control a class.

Patsy McCarthy, 58, after fifteen years in Liberia was appointed to Egypt in '37. He was not well and his qualifications restricted him to teaching in the junior school.

Johnny Murtagh, 42, apart from a full teaching programme in the senior school, was supervising the teachers in the junior. Since his arrival in '39, among other roles, he had been headmaster of two schools. Though revelling in Egyptian antiquities, he was not enjoying life in contemporary St George's. In '42, he had tried to join the Jesuits in Syria and, in '51, had spent some months in parish work in England. Despite being relatively young, his health was not good.

George Chester, the youngest, arrived in Egypt in October '54, a few months after his ordination in June of that year. Possessed of youth and a BA, it was hoped that he would be a great asset to the school but, though he had only thirteen periods a week, it seemed to be taking a lot out of him. He was losing weight and was attending the doctor.

Davy Huges, 38, as well as being headmaster, was taking senior Maths. All told, the SMA community in St George's in '55 was not exactly bursting with energy or facing the future with absolute confidence.

As well as the seven Fathers, there were eighteen lay people on the staff. Of these, twelve were male and five female. Three of the men had University degrees and five were attending University. The lady teachers did not have university qualifications and, rating high in the marriage stakes, frequently had to be replaced. The school population continued to rise, mainly in the junior part, and now had 370 pupils but, as the number of Christians had decreased and that of Moslems increased, Fr Hughes feared that the school would soon lose its Christian character. The Ministry of Education had recently issued another spate of instructions about teaching Arabic and the Koran, requiring all pupils, including non-Egyptians, to sit for Arabic examinations annually. Financially, Hughes thought they had enough funds to get by for the present but, if teachers' salaries were increased or, if the Patriarch insisted on a large increase in the rent, then they would be in difficulties.

On a brighter note, the head reported that gymnastics and games had improved with the hiring of a sports ground in Shubra. Though ten miles from the school, it was the best they could get. The school basketball team had done very well, winning the 'Part time Cup' and the Cairo Senior Championship. They were now favourites for the All-Egypt championship to be held in Alexandria.

Owen with Frank and
Fayez Nafekh

At the end of May '55, Owen wrote to the administration in Cork saying, that the closing weeks of the school year were, as always, extra busy. As dean he was involved in examinations and marks, but also with concerts and the production of the first school magazine of which he was editor-in-chief. The teachers were supposed to write the articles but getting them was like extracting teeth.

The school was due to close for holidays on 23 June, then Murtagh, Baker, and McCarthy would go on home leave. The confreres "are in good form", Owen wrote, "at least we can all walk and none have died yet". On the political front things were quiet. The only excitement was a few robberies in religious institutions and a shooting in a nearby church in which the sacristan was hit by four bullets. He recovered after two weeks – much to the disappointment of parishioners who were hoping for a martyr!

Owen got used to using the dusty, noisy, crowded city trams, sometimes on Legion of Mary work and sometimes to attend the American University, where he was doing a course in Arabic. After classes he liked to spend time discussing religion and the problems of the world with students. He enjoyed these sessions and, overall, seemed to be settling in rather well.

He visited the families of pupils especially if he heard of a special need. He got to know very well the Hazbouns, a family who had been forced to flee from Palestine when the United Nations partitioned the country in 1948 to create the state of Israel. Louis Hazboun was a pupil in St George's. Three of his sisters, Madeleine, Etty, and

Miranda attending St Clare's, were members of the Legion of Mary praesidium of which Owen was spiritual director. The group met with him every Thursday after school.
Miranda, a very bright girl, at age

Etty Hazboun on Owen's right, Madeline on his left.

twelve was stricken with bone cancer in her left leg which had to be amputated. Owen visited her daily, bringing Communion and spending hours chatting and praying with her. Occasionally, he said Mass in her room. She breathed her last on the 11th of November 1955, smiling and repeating "Jesus Mercy! Mary Help!" The family never forgot Owen's solicitude, "He was always there with a kind smile on his face", said Ray, Miranda's older brother.

When Madeleine, Miranda's older sister, realized how seriously ill she was, she wrote to Padre Pio in Italy. He replied that Miranda was not for this life. On the day of her funeral, traffic was diverted from the main street while her remains were carried to the basilica of Nôtre-Dame. The SMA Fathers, Franciscan Sisters, pupils of St Clare's, friends and neighbours attended. The young girl already had a reputation for sanctity. After her death, people prayed to her and a number said their prayers were answered. A Dutch priest of the parish, Fr Waterreus wf, asked Ray if he wished to introduce the process for her beatification. Ray, then beset with many difficulties supporting the family and making ends meet, had to decline.

Miranda Hazboun

On the 40th day after Miranda's death a memorial Mass was said in the basilica. An Italian priest, Fr Tarcisius, came from San Giovanni Rotondo, where Padre Pio resided. During the Mass, Tarcisius was seen gazing intently above the altar. Afterwards, he explained that Padre Pio had been there throughout the Mass. No one else saw the renowned holy man though some said they felt his presence. Padre Pio was canonised by Pope John Paul II in 2002; among other phenomena, he was credited with the power of 'bilocation'.

Ray, the eldest son of the family, had been top of his class in high school in Jaffa, but the terrible events of 1948, just before he matriculated, spoiled his promising career. Forced to flee, in Egypt aged only seventeen, he was the sole wage-earner of the family. After Miranda died, Owen thrust £50 into his hand to help buy a coffin. Ray never forgot the kind deed.[4]

*

In March 1956, Davy Hughes reported that Owen had put on some weight, seemed fit, and was absorbed in the task of producing the second edition of the school magazine. Owen, having sent the Provincial a copy of the first magazine, asked him to write an article for the second one. In his letter, he indicated that things in general were going alright, "Not much strange here. All the Fathers are well, and the weather is delightful". He was looking forward to going on home leave once school closed in June.

The apparent peacefulness in Egypt was soon to be disrupted. In June, the sole presidential candidate, Gamal Abdul Nasser, was elected President. The following month, he upset World powers by nationalizing the Suez Canal! Because of its importance in international trade, tension between the great powers escalated and fears grew that the canal affair might trigger off a nuclear war.

By this time Owen was on board ship in the Mediterranean on the first leg of an adventurous homeward journey. After a pleasant voyage, he disembarked at Bari on Italy's Adriatic coast and continued by bus towards Rome where he hoped to pick up some money held for him at the SMA Generalate. Meanwhile, he would have to survive on his wits for, after paying his bus fare, he had hardly any money left. The bus was scheduled to stop at interesting places like Naples, Vesuvius, and Monte Cassino.

His fellow passengers included a cheerful group of tourists. Owen fell into conversation with one of them who became very excited when he heard that Owen was a missionary in Egypt. Telling Owen that the group were hoping to go there, he asked him to tell them about Egypt. Owen stood at the front of the bus and gave a mighty exposé on Pharaohs and sphinxes, pyramids and tombs, Tutankhamen and mummification, scarab beetles and camels. He concluded with a blessing in Coptic and then in Arabic. The tourists were delighted; Owen's 'friend' passed round his straw hat; Owen received more than he needed for the rest of the journey, including a taxi fare to the Generalate.

After a good holiday, much of it spent in Drumaroad reading John Creaven's Cambridge doctoral thesis in philosophy, he booked a passage on the *Corinthia* and sailed from Marseilles on the 20th of September. From the time of his Cambridge doctorate, the Provincial was usually addressed as 'Doctor' Creaven.

Tension over the Suez Canal was higher than ever. In October '56, Israeli forces invaded the Sinai Peninsula and raced towards the Canal. Britain and France demanded that all troops be withdrawn ten miles from the canal and requested Egypt to allow their troops to occupy key points in the Canal Zone. Nasser refused and, after the Anglo-French ultimatum passed, aircraft from Cyprus began to bomb Cairo and troops invaded the north end of the canal. The Suez War had begun.

A state of emergency was declared, schools, including St George's, were closed, and a 'black-out' was imposed at night. On the first night of the war, Owen and some of the other Fathers were relaxing on the roof terrace of St George's. In the darkness – all lights were off – they heard a plane approach. It dropped two flares which lighted up the whole area. Then, bombers came – French and British, "using NATO planes" said Owen disapprovingly, and began the attack which Nasser termed the 'Tripartite Aggression' of Britain, France, and Israel. Near St George's, Egyptian anti-aircraft guns opened up. Between flares, rockets, bombs, multi-coloured tracer bullets and anti-aircraft fire it was, Owen thought, the most marvellous display of fireworks he'd ever seen. Some fifteen minutes into the firework display, the Fathers became aware of pieces of metal dropping on the roof – shrapnel! They hurried inside and after that rarely went out. The planes continued to attack every twenty minutes or so, seeking, especially, hidden oil storage tanks.

Though safe enough within the house, it was very monotonous. After some days of enclosure, Owen went out on the roof to read his breviary. No sooner had he taken a few steps on the roof and blessed himself than a plane flew overhead. He rushed back but, just as he was re-entering the house, a shot rang out and a bullet, fired from the street below, shattered the door frame near his head. An angry mob stormed into the building, searching for "the English spy on the roof". They raced upstairs, pulling out telephones and wires as they went. Laying hands on Owen, they accused him of giving signals to enemy planes. Owen's explanation that he was only blessing himself fell on deaf ears; they marched him to the nearest Police Station.

There, he found other Europeans being interrogated. He was glad he had an Irish passport; when the police saw it they became less hostile; they were not at all well-disposed to those with British or French passports. On seeing a big Egyptian sitting on a bench weeping inconsolably, the horrors of war and violence struck Owen more intensely than they had during the World War. Two of the weeping man's young brothers had just been killed in the air raid.

People overseas who had family members in Egypt were worried about their safety. On the 2nd of November the *Irish Independent's* front page headline read, "Anglo-French warships approach Suez Canal". Its lead article reported that, after desert battles, Israel claimed to have captured the Sinai Peninsula; ships were sunk in the canal blocking passage; oil pipelines were threatened; Egypt had broken off diplomatic relations with England. The paper said there were about fifty Irish citizens, mainly missionary priests and sisters, in Cairo and neighbourhood. The principal house was that of the Society of African Missions, St George's, and adjacent to it, St Clare's where there were about twenty Sisters.

On 5 November, the Provincial wrote to Owen's mother, saying he had been informed by the honorary Irish consul in Egypt, Mr Herne, a personal friend of the Fathers, that all Irish citizens in Egypt were safe and that there was no need to worry about them. (He was unaware of Owen's narrow escape on the roof!)

The fighting ended on the 7th of November after the United Nations, under pressure from America, ordered a cease-fire. Britain, France, and Israel withdrew their forces and UN troops occupied the territory. On the 10th of November, Dr Creaven, having received more news from the Department of Foreign Affairs, wrote again to Drumaroad, stating that all the Fathers in Heliopolis were well and their property had not been damaged.

The Suez War increased Nasser's prestige in the Arab world and facilitated his aim to establish an Arab empire across North Africa and the Middle East – an empire he attempted to found in February 1958 with the creation of the 'United Arab Republic' with himself as first President.

After the Suez War, schools remained closed until 24 December, the date, no doubt, a snub to Christians. After re-opening, 'foreign' schools, like St George's, found that they had lost much of their prewar autonomy.   British subjects were expelled from Egypt and other westerners, unable to find employment or retain ownership of businesses, left. Christian Copts, never regarded as 'first class' citizens under Moslem rule, experienced an increase in antipathy towards them. The Government's promotion of Arabic was raising the level of frustration in the 'English' colleges. "The Koran is the main interest of the inspectors and the main annoyance of the headmaster", complained Davy Hughes. Owen, though sympathetic with Nasser's policy of 'Egyptianisation', also felt the discomfort of those who were not Moslem. His work load as Dean increased as he had to re-organize school curricula and timetables to satisfy increasing Government demands.

Ministry inspectors, suspecting that foreign schools were externalising money, began scrutinising finances and demanding detailed accounts of each *piaster* in their books. St George's was not transferring money but Owen, later, recalled one parent who asked the Fathers to transfer £7,000 to England for him. Ironically, the same man, on enrolling his three sons, claimed he was desperately poor and, as a result, had been dispensed from paying fees!

After the war, the cost of living rose dramatically.   School fees remained the same but grants decreased. With growth in Arab militancy, compulsory military training was introduced for youth. Anti-western propaganda increased. Communist influence gained ground and Russia paid for Nasser's pet project, the Aswan Dam!

1. Van den Bronk, working as a missionary in Ghana, in 1946 had, surprisingly, been appointed Coadjutor to Mgr Girard, Vicar Apostolic of the 'Nile Delta'. On the death of Girard in 1950, he became the Administrator of the Vicariate renamed 'Heliopolis'. In his nomination in 1946, it seems Rome had hoped he would give a new impetus to the apostolate among the

Copts. In 1954, he was re-appointed to Ghana as Bishop of Kumasi, while a French confrere, Mgr Noel Boucheix, was nominated Vicar Apostolic of Heliopolis.

2. The whole poem was included by Fr Gerald Park, parish priest of Drumaroad and Clanvaraghan 1977-1987, in his book about the parish in 1985.

3. Not long after this, Mgr Levame was appointed Apostolic Nuncio to Ireland and, as such, attended the SMA centenary celebrations in Cork in 1956.

4. Thirty-five years later, Ray Hazboun, resident in California, sent a generous cheque to the African Missions for Owen.

The Hazbouns have a fascinating, as well as a tragic, family history. Descended from a well-to-do Catholic family of Bethlehem, their forefathers first arrived in Palestine with Christian crusaders who remained Catholics of the Latin rite. Ray's father went to Central America where he established a large department store. In 1920, he returned to Palestine and married. Investing in an orange grove near Jaffa, he developed a highly successful export business. "Best Jaffa Oranges; Hazboun Brand" became famous in Europe, including Ireland.

In April 1948, the town of Jaffa suffered a massive seven-day bombardment. Ray's older sister, Julie, was seriously wounded by mortar shrapnel in the neck. Forced to flee, the Hazbouns, after a difficult odyssey, settled in Egypt. In 1960, Ray, Madeleine and some other family members began a new life in America.

Chapter 7

DROMANTINE 1957

In June 1957, Davy Hughes in Heliopolis received a letter from the Provincial informing him that Owen Maginn was being re-called to Ireland. The idea of a home appointment was not a new one, it had been considered when Owen graduated from Cambridge, but had been shelved to allow him some mission experience first. Now he was being appointed to the staff of Dromantine Seminary. Eugene Melody, whose health had not been too good in Liberia, would replace him in Egypt. Dr Creaven requested Davy to send Owen on his way as soon as possible to allow him a holiday before Dromantine re-opened on 3 September.

Owen, seemingly in no great rush to leave, sailed from Port Said on the *P&O Corfu* in July. On the 31ˢᵗ somewhere in the Mediterranean, he wrote to the Provincial, explaining that it had been impossible to travel earlier owing to the difficulty of getting a berth. The *Corfu* was expected to reach London on 6 August, but he did not know how long it would take him to get to Ireland after that as he had "no tickets and plenty of luggage". He continued, "I believe I am to teach Church History in Dromantine. Further than that I have heard nothing … I should like to know what my obligations are". As always, he was obedient but, saying he had "heard nothing" was one of his ways of indicating displeasure.

Despite the isolation, frustrations, and dangers of the Egyptian mission, Owen said his six years there had been "a very happy time" and, no sooner had he left, than he missed its "excitement". The prospect of being a member of staff in a home-seminary for the rest of his life did not appeal to him and he may well have instigated a little conspiracy to get himself back to the missions. In April 1958, a letter from Dr Malley, arrived on the desk of the Provincial in Cork. The doctor stated that Fr Maginn, who had formerly been under his care for pulmonary tuberculosis, had recently been troubled with recurring attacks of moderately severe rheumatic pains which were difficult to relieve, particularly in this wet and damp Irish climate. The doctor recommended that he be sent immediately to a mission in a warm dry climate!

Unfortunately for the conspiracy, if such it was, the Provincial was in West Africa. His secretary, no longer Ned Harrington but Jim Lee (a Drumaroad man), acknowledged the letter, and there the matter remained – as Owen also did, in Dromantine!

He was resident in Dromantine a few months before his duties were clarified. By this time, the no-longer 'brand new' Provincial, Dr Creaven, had judged that change and improvements of one kind or another were called for in all the houses of formation. Fr John Joe Conlon had already succeeded Larry Carr as Superior in Dromantine and other changes, ranging from major building work to modifications of the chicken run, were under way. In July '58, Owen, receiving more duties than originally intimated, was appointed "*Magister Spiritus* as well as Professor of Ecclesiastical History". *Magister Spiritus* was a new title for the Father in charge of student discipline. Most of the staff preferred the older title 'Dean', but the students, who referred to themselves as 'monks', liked the sound of *'Magister'* and used it.

On a visit to Cork, Owen was enlightened on his new role by Dr Creaven who, among other things, exhorted him to study Pius XII's 1956 Apostolic Constitution on religious formation. Following this with a letter, the Provincial recommended that Owen aim at, "A living interpretation of his duties rather than a literal application of directives, keeping in mind the missionary vocation and the requirements of the future missionaries ... Study the particular needs of the various categories of students, interview them frequently – the Philosophers more than the Theologians – and be guided by a student's general showing, his response to his vocation and the questions <u>he</u> asks rather than what he says about his own progress".

In August 1958, Dr Creaven returned to Fr Conlon the new Dromantine Rule and timetable with his comments. He instructed that each professor draw up a syllabus for the subjects he taught. Following previous investigations, he had found that students were subjected to a bewildering variety of courses from which they derived little benefit. He thought a good course on pastoral theology should replace subjects like patrology, catechetics, 'Catholic Action', and sociology.

The academic staff in 1958 was composed of: Alfie Glynn, dogmatic theology and missiology; Gerry McGahon, moral theology and plain chant; Bob Molloy, scripture and canon law; Michael Mahony (transferred from Clough) pastoral theology and Latin; Martin Walsh, philosophy and English; Owen Maginn, Church History and Religious Instruction, the latter being a new course for Philosophers.

On assuming office in 1952, one of the aims of Dr Creaven had been to increase accommodation in all the houses of formation. Student numbers were steadily increasing and Dromantine was already overcrowded. While Owen was settling in, a new three-storey dormitory wing, capable of housing 62 students in single rooms and a new assembly hall capable of seating 400, were nearing completion. Under Fr Conlon, the college's surroundings were being improved, a new lawn in front of the house and new grass tennis courts were already completed. A new sports field was being levelled, and a path around the lake was being made.

One of the few advantages, for Owen, of being at home was that he could see family and friends more frequently. His brother Tom occasionally called out to Dromantine to see him. Tom and he were close, but one thing Tom hadn't discussed with him was his forthcoming marriage; it was somewhat by chance that Owen discovered he was to be married in Drumbo Church, Belfast, on the 27th of November 1958. Tom had wanted a quiet wedding but Owen got wind of the event and officiated at it. The bride was Sarah, 'Sadie', Magee from Kilclief. An athletic and talented young woman, she was captain of the very successful Co Down senior camogie team which reached the All-Ireland final in 1948. John Maginn, a brother of Mark, was the best man and Carmel Magorrian, a cousin of Sadie, was bridesmaid. Mark, as broad-shouldered as ever but a bit stooped, was there. Annie remained at home as also did Sadie's mother.

Tom and Sadie's wedding

Owen gave Sadie, who liked to sing, a gift of a gramophone and some long-playing records, saying "They'll be company for you in the house when you're alone". Bride and groom went to Cork for their honeymoon and toured a bit of the west coast. Sadie recalled that it was her first time in a pub! Four years later, Owen gave her another 'wedding gift' – a wristwatch which she still wears and "In all that time", she says, "it has never gone wrong or needed repair".

Sadie enjoyed the gramophone but, in fact she wasn't alone that much. Apart from Tom, there was Mark, with whom she got on very well, and Annie. Neither was she in want of something to do, daughter of a farming family, she was ever active in fields and byres in Drumanaghan. The following year in November, her first baby was born who, according to Maginn tradition, was called after his grandfather, Mark.

Being at home also gave Owen the opportunity to attend funerals. On the 21st of March '59, he attended the funeral of his neighbour John Doran, whose son, Sexton, was a student in Dromantine. John, a prominent Republican, well-known to Eamon de Valera and other leaders in the struggle for independence, was a highly respected member of the south Down community. He had died suddenly at home on the 20th.

As *Magister,* it was Owen's duty to grant or withhold the radio from the students on special occasions – usually major sporting events. Generally he was lenient, especially if a game was on a Sunday afternoon. Sometimes, if there was a power failure or reception was bad on the 'wireless', he would give his own battery operated radio. From his largesse, the students enjoyed the broadcast of the international rugby match between Ireland and England on Saturday, 7 February 1959 which Ireland lost; and the Leinster-Connacht Railway Cup match on the 15th which Leinster won.

Owen, wishing to interest the students in a broad spectrum of activities, encouraged them to write articles for the *African Missionary*, and to speak in the Literary and Debating Society. Also, keen on the Young Christian Worker movement, he invited Canon Arbuthnott, the National Chaplain in England, and Mr Bernard Wilkinson to speak about it in Dromantine.

The building of the new residential block 'St Colman's', and the new assembly hall was completed in March '59. Though expensive, £60,000, the two units were a great asset to the college. They were blessed and opened by Eugene O'Doherty, the bishop of Dromore, on 31 March. At the Pontifical High Mass sixty clergy assisted and afterwards were treated to a lunch prepared by the Sisters of Our Lady of Apostles who were in charge of domestic affairs in the college.

In the afternoon, the College Dramatic Society staged a serious two-act play *The Strong are Lonely*. The play was ideal for an all male cast as most of the dramatis personae were staff members of a Jesuit college in Buenos Aires in 1767. Produced by Willie Foley, it boasted of some remarkable actors including, Don Burke, Jim O'Kane, and Sexton Doran. Outstanding in their own fields were Oscar Welsh, stage manager, and Terry Gunn, the special effects artist. O'Kane from Omagh, and Doran from Loughinisland gave inimitable performances as two Inca guards, 'Candia' and 'Acatu'. When Owen saw his tall neighbour from Loughinisland in a short Inca skirt, he took a fit of laughing which convulsed him for days. Sexton vowed he'd never act again and obliterated the play from memory.

The VIP guests, Bishop O'Doherty and Dr Creaven, were so pleased with the performance that the play was staged again on the 2nd of April (not the 1st). This time, the Dromantine Céili Band and the 'Drom Dreamers' lightened the evening with some music and song. Among the audience were Tom, Mark, and Mark's good friend, Johnny

McGrady. They always came whenever there was a play or concert and enjoyed a cup of tea with Owen afterwards.

After the summer holidays, the drama committee consulted the *Magister* about a play for November. Owen suggested the *Pot of Broth*, a one-act farce by WB Yeats, but the committee rejected it, choosing instead two one-act plays, *Home Guard*, and *Safe at Last*. For a subsequent evening, the Dean agreed with the committee's choice of a documentary film about 'automation' in the Ford motor works in Detroit. Seeing the hub of the American motor industry on screen, brought back memories to Owen. The following February, he rejected the committee's choice of *Dry Rot* for Easter as being "Too frivolous" and, encouraged by the Provincial to aim high, recommended *Richard II*. The committee agreed but, disappointingly, when staged, the Shakespearean play was poorly attended. For its second performance, Owen dragooned reluctant students into attending. Fortunately, it went down well the second time.

Early in 1960, work on the new football field was completed and the first game was played on Sunday the 28th of January. Though rain-sodden, the field was praised by players and spectators as "tops". Owen used to join in the students' games in those days and, not wishing to catch a cold, always wore a black beret which, in fact, rarely left his head on field or off it. He played left cornerback and was noted especially for having a fine pair of boots. Following a visit by Dr Creaven, staff participation in games became strictly forbidden. An enterprising student, after comparing the size of Owen's feet with his own during history class, asked Owen to sell him his boots. Owen said he might as well as he'd have to hang them up anyway. A few days later, another student made the same request and, forgetting that he had already promised them, agreed. Before supper, he came on two students preparing to fight over his boots.

There was much student dissatisfaction with the 45-minute spiritual lectures given twice weekly by the Superior and once a week by the Spiritual Father. "Too long and too frequent" was the general student opinion and they requested that, at least the final fifteen minutes be given them to make their own summaries. Fr Conlon, aware that the lectures were not going down well and, wishing to dispense himself of the chore, suggested to the Provincial that they might, with more benefit, be given by the Spiritual Father and the Dean. The rapport between 'John Joe', as the students called the superior, and 'John A', as they called the Provincial, was very good. In quick time, the lectures were reduced to one per week for philosophers and one for theologians and <u>both</u> were to be given by the <u>Dean</u>. Owen couldn't help feeling that he was left holding the baby that other people had delivered. He took on the task and made a good beginning by calling a representative twelve-man group of students to discuss with him suitable themes for the talks.

In 1960, the 'gods' (the Fathers) thought that a general stiffening of the Rule was called for. In compliance, Owen introduced a few 'extraordinary' items. Two outstanding ones were: banning electric "shavers" and forbidding "Smoking in bed when sick". An in-depth investigation found that forty-nine students used electric razors. When all of them were in operation at the same time, the noise was possibly construed as breaking the nocturnal *Grande Silence* which was supposed to continue 'till breakfast or, that the modern mechanised contraptions were contravening Papal teaching on 'Modernism'. More likely the real reason had to do with fire risks and insurance policies. Surprisingly, smoking (even when not in bed) was very common among staff and students. Practically all the 'gods' smoked even the Dean despite his lung problems.

Jubilation was experienced in the 'northern camp' in September 1960 when, for the first time ever the Sam Maguire cup crossed the border after Down beat Kerry 2-10 to 8 points in the All-Ireland senior football final in Croke Park. Owen, rejoicing with everyone else, except the Kerry men, admitted that he didn't think he'd be asked to play for the county any more.

'Nineteen-sixty' was something of a special year in Dromantine, not because it was exactly 300 years since the house had been acquired by Sir Hans Hamilton who leased it to Colonel William Lucas the man commissioned to hunt down and capture the archbishop of Armagh, Oliver Plunkett,[1] but because the college had the biggest number of students for ordination since it had opened as a seminary in 1926. On 21 December, twenty-two students were ordained; previously the biggest number was twenty, in 1936. The ordaining prelate, Mgr Francis Carroll sma, a Newry man, had only been consecrated Vicar Apostolic of Monrovia, Liberia, the previous May. A very big congregation attended and no less than forty-seven priests laid their hands on the heads of the *ordinandi* during the impressive ceremony.

'Nineteen-sixty-one', the 'Patrician Year', was another significant year, the 1,500[th] anniversary of the death of St Patrick. Ceremonies were held on the hill of Saul where a towering granite statue of the Saint had been erected. Saul, near where Patrick landed in Strangford Lough on his return to Ireland, was the spot where he founded his first church and where, it is thought, he wrote his *Confessions* shortly before his death in 461. A week-long Missionary Exhibition was held in Downpatrick. At it, the SMA displayed the work of its six hundred Irish missionaries over the past half century in West Africa.

The climax of the Year for the Society was the ordination of sixteen of its members on Sunday 10 December, not as usual in the cathedral of Newry but in St Peter's, Lurgan, in St Patrick's see of Armagh. For the first time ever, an ordination ceremony was televised live by the BBC. Bishop Eugene O'Doherty of Dromore presided, supported by many priests and a choir of fifty Dromantine students under the expert baton of Fr Gerry McGahon. Fr Agnellus Andrew was in charge of TV production. The *Armagh Observer,* of December 14, gave the event a full centre page with many photographs. The *African Missionary* of February 1962 on its back cover published a very fine photograph of the sixteen new priests with Bishop O'Doherty, Fr JJ Conlon, President of Dromantine College, and Fr Owen Maginn, Vice President. The *Irish News,* Belfast, and other papers also gave the ordination and the seminary excellent coverage. In those times there was very positive media support for missionary work, in particular that of the Irish Province of the SMA and its seven dioceses in Nigeria and one in Liberia. Owen couldn't help grumbling that the Society's work in Egypt was hardly ever mentioned.

As Dean, Owen needed to know what was going on among the students. One way to find out was to interview them regularly on a one-to-one basis. Another was to take an odd look at their notice board. All sorts of things appeared on it and an innocent-looking note might lead to the exposure of a nefarious underground movement. One day, Gerry Holland, a new student late in arriving, was studying the notice board to see which room he had been allocated. Owen, dressed in an ordinary soutane like the students,

A student's impression of Owen

sidled up beside him. Gerry, who hadn't yet met the Dean but had seen his photograph, mistook him for a student. Owen gave him a welcoming smile and shook his hand. Surprise registered on Gerry's face, "My God, you know you're the spitting image of Maginn!" and he went on to ask, "What's he like? I heard all sorts of things". "Oh, what did you hear?" asked Owen cutely. Unfortunately, the bell for history class went and Owen had to run.

For class, he prepared well but, he knew too much, wanted to say it all, and credited his class with knowing more than they did. Many students found him boring. He read his notes and didn't interact much, except on one famous occasion when, dealing with the scandalous lifestyle of the Renaissance popes, a student 'innocently' asked, "What's a 'mistress' Father?" Owen, controlling his 'risibility', paused sagely before answering, "A mistress is a lady who's invited for supper and stays for breakfast!"

On Friday 13th of April 1962, he attended the funeral of Canon Dinny Cahill, his former parish priest. Fr Dinny had been made a canon of the Diocesan Chapter some four years before being transferred from

Fr Cahill presenting a chalice from the people of Drumaroad and Clanvaraghan to Pius XII, Holy Year 1950

Drumaroad. In 1957, he had been appointed to the parish of Upper Mourne near Kilkeel and died there on 11April. It was Owen who dictated the Latin inscription on the plaque that marks his grave at Massforth, Upper Mourne. Canon Cahill was survived by many relatives including two nephews in the SMA, Sexton Doran and Sexton Cahill; another nephew, Sean Cahill, became a priest of the diocese.

The work load of a willing horse tends to increase. In 1962, as well as being Dean, teaching Church History and giving spiritual talks, Owen was lecturing in liturgy and catechetics. The last two were not really his subjects but, the era of Vatican II had dawned and 'change' had become everybody's business. Already, Fr Johannes Hoffinger sj, a leading light in methods of imparting religious doctrine had begun a new way of teaching catechism. His 'kerygmatic' approach based on 'salvation history' was a welcome change from the old 'penny catechism' method. Owen was fascinated by it, "The *Magister* went wild on Hoffinger!" said the students.

Hearing that Hoffinger was giving a seminar in Dublin, Owen booked places for himself and one of the newly-ordained deacons. The seminar was excellent. Owen was inspired not only by the content, but by the 'Dialogue Mass' and new-style liturgies led by Fr Hoffinger. Back in Dromantine, he began to put into practice what he had heard and seen. With the help of the deacon, a good singer, he introduced the beautiful Gelineau Psalms at Mass, and at morning and evening prayer. However, in so doing he was encroaching on Fr Gerry McGahon's chant territory. One day at lunch, Gerry, known as 'Gentleman Gerry' for his gentle manner, uncharacteristically turned on Owen, "Who put you in charge of music?" Owen readily admitted that "he hadn't a note", but he continued with his up-dating.

In class, taking a cue from Hoffinger's 'Dialogue Mass', he tried to interact more with the students but, he didn't get it right. He had a habit of calling them by their surnames. Some resented this, "Does he think he's a Cambridge professor?" Others didn't like his habit of omitting the Gaelic 'O' from their names as if he, or they, were Protestants. Others said he had favourites – those who laughed at his jokes or were fellow Northerners. His neighbour, Sexton Doran, was about the only one he always addressed as 'Sexton'. Furthermore, as Dean, as well as lecturer, he could fly off the handle, even for a minor offence like finding dust in a corner or catching someone whispering in a corridor and, not everyone like to be admonished, "Wash your neck", "Comb your hair", or "Clip your nails".

One of his tasks was to teach the newly-ordained deacons how to administer the sacraments and perform correctly at the altar. For weekly Sunday evening Benediction, he used to appoint two deacons to prepare the altar and expose the Blessed Sacrament. On one unforgetable Sunday, two keyed-up beginners were about to put the sacred host in the monstrance, when Fr Gerry McGahon, the organist, accidentally hit a wrong note and the organ squealed. The deacons, unable to contain themselves, began to laugh. The student body, ever-ready for diversion, followed suit and bedlam ensued. The Dean, livid, gave the two deacons a severe tongue-lashing ending with, "I can't trust ye, I will have to do it myself next Sunday!"

When the following week's Benediction came round, the grim-faced Dean did everything with tight-faced seriousness. As he was about to expose the Blessed Sacrament the incredible happened, Fr McGahon hit a wrong note again. The student body went rigid, each individual fearing he'd be the first to laugh. Owen, at the tabernacle with his back to the congregation, remained immobile. The students, watching him nervously, noticed his back and shoulders begin to shake and a kind of seismic shudder overtake him. Realization dawned – the old devil of risibility had struck; the *Magister* was overcome by laughter! Unable to compose himself, Owen beat a hasty retreat to the sacristy. No more was heard about the deacons' lapse.

In the days before Eucharistic concelebrations, the seminary Fathers said their individual Masses on the numerous side altars of the main chapel. Owen always chose the altar dedicated to St Therese of

Lisieux. Though a cloistered Carmelite, Therese was patroness of the missions. It was not for this that Owen was drawn to her as much as for her "Little Way" in spirituality and for the fact that she had died of tuberculosis aged only twenty-four. At her altar, he often prayed to have some of her strength, resilience and humour and, that if he was not re-appointed to Africa, at least he might become reconciled to working at home.

Though his time as Dean in Dromantine was not his finest hour, he maintained his integrity and sense of humour. A respite came in December 1962 when an emergency arose in the novitiate in Cloughballymore and he was sent to man the breach.

1. Executed in Tyburn in 1681, St Oliver Plunkett, Archbishop of Armagh, was canonized a martyr in 1975.

Chapter 8

CLOUGHBALLYMORE 1963

The African Missions novitiate at Cloughballymore received a large group of forty-five young men in September 1962. It was no longer a place of two years philosophy as it had been in Owen's time but a house of one year's probation comprising of some general studies and spirituality. Called a 'spiritual year', it began in the middle of September and continued until the end of the following June. Two weeks after beginning, the 'aspirants', of average age eighteen and fresh out of secondary school, began the famous 'Thirty Day Retreat'. The director, no longer Fr Counihan, was the superior of the house, Fr Jim Byrne, a mild-mannered missionary, noted for the promotion of the Legion of Mary in Nigeria. He now faced the daunting task of leading forty-five new yahoos in the spiritual exercises of St Ignatius for a whole month on his own.

His spiritual talks were serene and pious. The aspirants gamely took notes and biblical references. In the chapel, round the walks, and in the woods they practised *lectio divina, meditatio,* and *contemplatio.* Some reached 'great heights' (in the trees mainly), and some were bored. Thirty days in silence (even without Fr Counihan) was no joke. Though some things had changed, silence and isolation from 'the world' had not. The students had no access to radio or newspapers, were not allowed letters, and contact with outsiders was strictly forbidden.

During the long retreat, unknown to them, the world had become an increasingly dangerous place. The cold war between Russia and the United States had warmed to near boiling point. In October, Soviet warships carrying nuclear warheads were sailing towards Cuba where

Fidel Castro had established bases from which missiles could be fired at America. One morning Fr Byrne opened his conference in the chapel with, "The world is on the brink of the Third World War" then, rolling his eyes towards the 14th Station of the Cross, he continued with his conference as if he'd said nothing unusual. Fortunately, Nikita Khruschev called home his destroyers and … the Thirty Day Retreat was able to continue. However, during it and afterwards, Fr Byrne became very run down and, in December, had to leave for health reasons.

By January 1963, the Provincial realized that Fr Byrne's illness was more serious than at first thought and he would have to remain away from Clough for some time. In February, Owen was sent to replace him. Another man, Frank Doyle, was sent to replace Owen in Dromantine.

Owen's first view of the novices nearly gave him a heart attack. As he drove in the long avenue from the main gate, he noticed a number of them perched like birds on the castle roof. Visions of fatal accidents and himself trying to explain what happened to bereaved parents swam before his mind. Jumping out of the car, he waved his arms and shouted to attract the roof-top students'

Checking for loose slates on the castle roof

attention. This wasn't difficult as they were already all eyes to see what the new man was like. Trying not to be profane, he asked them what they were doing on the roof? Craning over the rusty guttering, they shouted down that the *'socius'* (assistant to the superior) had told them to check for loose slates. Owen commanded them to come down at once "carefully". He became aware of another racket going on behind the castle. On top of very high trees, he spied other students, pillaging crows' nests and tossing out young birds who, as yet unable to fly, tumbled down to earth where, before they landed, a student armed with a blood-stained hurley 'doubled' on them. The hurler told him that the *socius* wanted to get rid of the crows.

Once over the shock, Owen settled in quickly. Away from the peer pressure of the bigger seminary and the awkward job of Magister, he began to relax. He liked the students, less numerous and more 'innocent' than the 'monks' in Dromantine, and he didn't have to deal directly with matters of discipline, his assistant, Fr John Clancy, did that. Class work was looked after by two veterans, John Keaveney and, a man who had been there when Owen was a novice, Jerry Sheehan, now nicknamed 'Rip van Winkle" by the students. Michael Moorhead was farm manager and bursar; OLA Sisters looked after domestic affairs. The students quickly took to the new Acting Superior and thought he was like 'a breath of fresh air'; in Dromantine, the students thought the same of their new man.

Among the forty-five novices were three men preparing to be brothers in the Society. In Ireland and in Africa they would collaborate with the priest members especially in building and other practical work. Their training was supposed to be different from that of the priest aspirants, but not much thought had been put into organizing it. The Provincial gave Owen the extra task of seeing how it could be improved.

Owen, understandably, was acutely aware of the danger of tuberculosis spreading among a large group living in close proximity. In Dromantine most students had single rooms but in Clough they slept in dormitories. Dr Creaven, the Provincial, desired that all have chest x-rays, but the hospital in Galway, with inadequate facilities and too many patients, would only accept six Clough students. Owen picked out six of "the more doubtful and delicate-looking ones" and, after persuading them that they had nothing to worry about, sent them off with Michael Moorhead to Galway. After the x-rays, while waiting for Fr Moorhead to take them home, one of the 'delicate' ones chanced on going into the famous Lydon's café on Shop Street for tea and buns. On taking a seat, to his consternation he saw Fr Moorhead sitting at a nearby table. In those days, a student entering such a 'den of iniquity' could merit expulsion. Either the bursar didn't recognise him or chose to 'forget' to report him as the bun man is still a member of the Society. Others, who made illegal excursions to céilís and such in nearby Ballindereen, were not so lucky. After snow fell one night, telltale footprints to a ground floor window were still visible on the front lawn next morning.

Thanks to Owen, the crisis of not having a superior in the novitiate had been averted. He wrote comforting letters to the authorities in Cork, "All going well here ... The house is still standing ... All the Fathers are peaceable". In general he was pleased with the aspirants and commended them for their "enthusiasm", "They have just staged a play, a noteworthy effort".

Occasionally he found himself attempting to suppress mirth beneath a serious mask of authority. After the Easter vigil Mass, the students continued revelling noisily in their recreation hall. With appropriate stern face, Owen appeared and began to berate them but, on pausing for breath, a smile broke through and he departed laughing. Once more 'risibility' got the better of him.

Clough being a place of probation, the Superior had to get to know the students pretty well. This began with basic health and fitness. A doctor came to examine them. As it happened Dr Chater was Indian, the first dark-skinned person most of the would-be African missionaries ever encountered. Some of them became very apprehensive, fearing he might practice juju on them! Once the medical and other types of requirements were satisfied, Owen still had the delicate task of dividing the class in two. After the year of probation, half of them would go to University College Cork while the other half would go to Dromantine. Unfamiliar with the educational system and university entrance requirements in the 'Republic', he corresponded with his counterpart in the Society's house of studies in Cork before making the division.

While in Clough, he maintained contact with friends in Co Down. In April, the Downpatrick De la Salle Union asked him to be their spiritual director on a pilgrimage to Lourdes in August. He agreed, but the pilgrimage plans met with setbacks and had to be cancelled. Instead, Owen arranged to go to England to do parish work. During the year, he collaborated with Fr Patrick McEnroe in producing a radio tribute to Canon Dennis Cahill. Previously, Fr Dinny himself had broadcast Sunday Masses from Drumaroad and Clanvaraghan which were relayed on the BBC Overseas Service. These were very well received; among appreciative listeners, was Fr Paddy Jennings of Castlewellan who heard the broadcasts in his mission in Nigeria.

Owen and Jim Byrne

The 'spiritual year' quickly came to an end. In the middle of June, Fr Dick Tobin, a missionary from Ilorin, Nigeria, came to give the students a short retreat to help them make up their minds about continuing on the road to missionary priesthood. After the retreat, on the 25th of June, the day the Founder died in 1859, forty-one students took the first temporary oath of membership of the Society. The same month, health restored, Jim Byrne returned.

Perhaps it was not all due to Owen's influence but, the Provincial Council at this time decided that permission would no longer be given to aspirants to embark on corporal ascetical practices such as had been encouraged by Fr Counihan and, secondly, that retreats for the aspirants should henceforward be directed by members of the African Missions. The Provincial was very pleased with the manner Owen had acquitted himself as acting superior. Writing to Fr Byrne he said, "Fr Maginn did a very fine job under difficult conditions. It was really remarkable how he was able to get down to such a large class – all strangers to him – and get such a shrewd knowledge of them in a very short time ... You will find it useful to have long talks with him on every aspect of the Clough regime".

In September, Owen returned to Dromantine but, as Spiritual Director, not as Magister. The change of role suited him and he began to enjoy his work more than previously. However, his tenure this time was very short. In June '64, to his great surprise, he was re-appointed to Egypt. Maybe the Provincial hadn't ignored that 1958 letter of Dr Malley after all!

Chapter 9

EGYPT 1964

In August 1964, Owen went to Dublin for a final check-up with Dr Malley and to arrange his departure for Egypt. After the medical visit, he got a tourist visa from the Egyptian embassy, bought a light soutane in Clery's and, in Heffernan's travel agency, booked a flight from Dublin to Cairo via Lourdes and Rome, departing on 10 September.

He was welcomed back by Johnny Murtagh, Harry Baker, Pat Christal, Patsy McCarthy and Eugene Melody. The current Vicar Apostolic of Heliopolis, Amand Hubert, welcomed him too. Hubert, a long serving French confrere, regarded Owen as "an old friend, well known and appreciated for his kind character and his smile". Davy Hughes was gone; in '58 he had been transferred to Nigeria and Murtagh had taken over as Superior. Some lay teachers, whom Owen had known, were also gone and, of course, all his former pupils were gone. Once he moved around a bit, he sensed a depressed spirit among the people. Gone were the high hopes in Nasser's earlier promises. The great union of the Arab world had not materialized, economically the people were worse off than before, and the country was burdened with a costly war in Yemen.

George Chester was gone. In 1957, before Owen's departure, a new teacher, Linda Eskinazi, a Jewess, whose mother was Italian, had requested baptism. At first Owen instructed her in the faith but, after a while, handed over the task to George. She was baptised at Easter. The following year, George and Linda 'disappeared'. After various peregrinations, including teaching in Turkey for a year and a half, the couple went to Milan where they started an English language school.

George's departure from the priesthood, well before the post-Vatican II exodus, caused quite a sensation.

The school population had risen greatly since Owen had left; it was now over 900. With the departure of British and other expatriates during the Suez crisis, 'English' schools were taken over by the government but, without the well-qualified expatriate staff, standards had gone down. St George's now was the only 'English school' in Cairo run by English speakers. That these were Irish Catholic priests added to the school's prestige. Government ministers and high-ranking army officers all wanted their children enrolled. Among the pupils were President Nasser's grandchildren and Vice President Anwar Saddat's children. To deal with the great increase in numbers, Johnny Murtagh had recently acquired another school premises, the 'Armenian school', just a ten minute walk from St George's. More spacious than St George's, it would facilitate the primary and preparatory parts of the college.

Despite the school's growing reputation, nineteen-sixty-three had not been a good year for the administrators. The Head of the local Zone had obstructed progress at every opportunity. One of the teachers, acting as 'a spy', reported to him any 'anti-Egyptian' acts on the part of the Irish Fathers. One ridiculous report was that Murtagh had torn up a picture of Nasser and trampled it underfoot. Among other things, the Zone Head had refused the Fathers permission to use the Armenian school; had accused them of misappropriating £5,000 from the hire of school buses; and had complained about the salaries they were getting. The tables turned in December when Murtagh went directly to the Minister of Education. The Minister, having already received several complaints about this Zone Head, acted immediately. Permission was granted to use the Armenian school, all accusations against the Fathers were dropped, and their salaries were approved. The Minister also endorsed their nominee for a new lay headmaster.

Meanwhile in Rome, Society superiors were seriously considering terminating the SMA mission in Egypt even though they knew that this would run counter to the wishes of the Congregation for Oriental Churches, the views of the Pro Nuncio in Cairo and the Coptic Patriarchs. These leading ecclesiastical authorities all held that the SMA apostolate was a great support for Egyptian Catholics, the Coptic Church, and other minorities.

At this time, politics and policies began to have an increasing influence on the Society's future in Egypt. In 1964, the Government brought out a decree that all schools must fall under Egyptian ownership by 1 October 1965. Murtagh, with Mgr Hubert's approval, initiated discussions with the Coptic Patriarch, Cardinal Stephanos I Sidarous, about handing the school over to him.

Privately, Johnny told Owen that he had had enough of St George's and teaching and had already asked the Provincial for a transfer. He described his twenty-five years in Egypt as "a life of continual frustration"; if the Provincial agreed he would be leaving in June 1965. He was attracted to other pursuits; recently he had written five Catholic Truth Society pamphlets about the Eastern Churches, preached five retreats in Pakistan during the summer holidays and, when Owen arrived, had been giving a retreat to the Sisters of St Clare's.

Along with this disquieting news, Owen received the sad news that his father had passed away. Mark, eighty-four, had finally succumbed to cancer and Alzheimer's disease on the 18th of October 1964 – Owen's birthday. Feeling sad and empty at the loss, Owen was particularly sorry that he could not have been at the funeral. However, Mark had suffered a lot and Owen appreciated that his demise was a happy release. Subsequently, he could rarely speak of Mark without a catch in his voice or tears coming to his eyes.

Along with his request to be transferred, Johnny Murtagh had asked the Provincial to send to Egypt someone who might be able to replace him as Superior. On hearing this, Owen began to suspect that this was the reason for his own sudden transfer from Dromantine. No doubt the Provincial thought he would be able for the post. Murtagh thought so too at first but, in May '65, wrote in a worried manner to Dr Creaven, "Despite a good beginning ... the [new lay] headmaster nearly ruined the school ... he has lost the respect of teachers and pupils ... Fr Maginn has had a very trying year, I fear he is much too nervous to put up with the very difficult situations which life in Egypt is sure to produce".

Nevertheless, when Murtagh departed in June '65, Owen was appointed Superior of the community and deputy headmaster of the school. His double role was not an easy one; there was tension in the community and plenty of problems in the school, "I feel anything but happy at the appointment", he said. He wrote to Dr Creaven outlining the problems: difficulties in the transference of school ownership, low finances, shortage of teachers, poor discipline, and difficulties with the headmaster. Murtagh's panacea of a quick transfer of ownership had not materialized, mainly because the Patriarch feared the school might prove to be a serious financial liability. Owen couldn't help thinking that 'His Beatitude' did have a point. The school deficit for the past year was over £5,000. Their accountant estimated that the next year's expenditure would exceed income by £3,500 and the shortfall would continue to grow unless fees were increased. Murtagh had requested permission to raise the fees but, although Government inspectors appeared to be sympathetic and had examined the school's accounts, nothing came of it.

The Fathers owed two years arrears of rent to the Patriarch and, ironically in view of their wish to transfer ownership to him, His Excellency was vociferously demanding payment and even threatening 'seizure'! Owen feared a court case. The college also owed rent to the

Armenian Patriarch for the use of his school. Adding to his worries about rent, was the question of Government taxes which, though officially charged to the Patriarch, by the 1953 agreement were to be paid by the missionaries. Unpaid taxes had accumulated into the considerable sum of £1,200. The school's lawyer advised Owen not to pay. Murtagh always said that tax was not their business but the Cardinal's. Cardinal Tisserant, in Rome, was the 'legal' owner and he had persistently argued against paying. Murtagh hadn't worried about taxes in his time, but times had changed. For payment of the rent, Patriarch Sidarous had given a deadline, December '65. Owen, very worried, knew that they couldn't pay unless they borrowed money which he was loath to do.

These anxieties drained Owen's energy and left him with little time for internal school affairs. The lay headmaster, since his appointment, had taken on an authoritarian, over-bearing manner and, in a short time, had alienated the rest of the staff. In a knock-on effect, relations between teachers and pupils had also deteriorated. Absenteeism of teachers was rampant, standards were falling, and parents were complaining. Owen was exasperated especially by the headmaster's simplistic plan to 'Egyptianise' everything immediately, a plan he had submitted to the Zone authorities. As the head had managed to establish good relations with the Zone, Owen thought it best not to try to have him replaced for the moment.

School transport was another headache. More than half of the pupils, about 550, used the six school buses. As alternative means like public transport were inadequate, the buses could not be dispensed with. The cost of running them, including salaries for driver and supervisor on each bus, was high. Breakdowns were frequent and repairs expensive – in the past year alone £5,600 was spent on repairs. The small bus fee charged by the school barely covered ordinary expenses and the Zone would not permit it to be increased. It was hoped that a new

Mercedes bus, on its way from Germany, would ameliorate the transport problem.

The college, now located in three places, secondary in Qait Bai, preparatory in Iman Aly, and primary in Aly Ibrahim, had about 1000 pupils and the number was growing all the time. The largest increase was in the primary and preparatory sections. This would soon create problems in the secondary school where classroom space was inadequate even for the present single stream of about thirty-five pupils per class. Multiple streams couldn't be accommodated unless expensive building work was undertaken. St George's, with only fifty-three teachers, was understaffed but, with debts looming, the school couldn't afford to employ more.

The Provincial, who had been in Argentina negotiating the opening of a new mission, replied to Owen on his return to Cork in November '65. He commiserated with him for the series of difficulties he had encountered so soon in his stewardship. To help, he wrote two formal letters, one to the Minister for Public Instruction and another to the Coptic Patriarch. To both he stated clearly that unless certain conditions were fulfilled, the SMA collaboration in St George's would be terminated and the Fathers withdrawn. To the Patriarch he reiterated the missionaries' wish that he take over proprietorship of the school. He said that the Fathers would remain on as teachers provided they were given adequate living quarters and salaries. Referring to transfer of ownership, he gave a deadline – before the end of January 1967. Owen was mandated to report on progress.

School and community problems inevitably took their toll on Owen. However it was only because of an alarming report sent to the Superior General that he felt obliged, in September '65, to inform his superiors in Cork about his state of health. He said he had been very ill in July and had been treated at the Italian Hospital in Cairo. The cause of the illness had not been immediately diagnosed but, whatever it was, it had left him very weak. On the 31ˢᵗ of July, he had been detained in the hospital for two weeks and, eventually, paratyphoid fever, an infectious bacterial disease like typhoid but less serious, was diagnosed. The doctors treated him for that but remained concerned that his tubercular trouble might recur. A chest x-ray gave no reason for alarm, but Fr Gaignoux of the basilica of Nôtre-Dame, informed the Superior General that a cavity had opened in Owen's left lung. Owen, who had seen the x-ray himself, said it showed no such thing. He felt quite well and was confident that he was on the way to full recovery, "The doctors think the same", he added. Clearly, Owen did not want a fuss, or a rest, and did not want to leave Egypt.

The Government's deadline for the handover of ownership of schools, October '65, came and went. Neither St George's, nor many other 'foreign' schools had succeeded in transferring ownership by then, nor was the Government ready to insist. Meanwhile, Owen had some other problems to deal with. Of the recently arrived Fathers, Eugene Melody was settling down nicely and taking on a heavy teaching load, but James Murphy, an excellent missionary, with teaching experience in Nigeria, Ireland, and Ghana, was not. He had not enjoyed good health in West Africa and so, after being invalided home, had been appointed to Egypt. But, he still hankered after West Africa and, despite the health risk, wished to return. He was transferred back to Nigeria in December and departed on the 2ⁿᵈ of January '66. Owen missed him; he had been a good teacher and a pleasant community man.

Recognising that there was tension in the community, Owen sympathised with his confreres; they had little opportunity for pastoral activity and recreational facilities were very limited. If they were proficient in French or Arabic more pastoral work would be available but, required for teaching as soon as they arrived, they had little time for learning new languages. A good knowledge of Arabic was becoming more and more important. Apart from the fact that the

Government wanted it to be the first language in schools, many meetings in St George's were already being conducted in Arabic alone and an increasing number of pupils' parents knew no English or French. Owen felt that unless the missionaries could find some way of relating more with the ordinary people, they would not settle down or would apply themselves to their work in a half-hearted fashion.

The SMA community was now very small – only Owen, Eugene Melody, and Patsy McCarthy. Patsy wasn't well and was neither teaching nor saying Mass. Owen was thankful that at least the weather in the New Year of 1966 was good. But, on the 25th of January, the day he was scheduled to meet the Coptic Patriarch about the transfer of ownership, the first sandstorm of the year occurred. He wondered whether it was a good or bad portent.

Despite Dr Creaven's ultimatum, Patriarch Stephanos was not to be rushed. At best he was indecisive, at worst stalling. At the meeting on the 25th, at which Owen was accompanied by Mgr Hubert and Eugene Melody, the Patriarch refused to be drawn into any decision, claiming he needed more time and wanted to consult the other Coptic bishops. On the 21st of February, after meeting the Bishops, he conveyed to Owen the news that he would be terminating the 1953 contract between Society and Patriarchate in September. Understanding this to mean that he intended taking over ownership of St George's, Owen began to look forward to the end of the tedious business.

On the 30th of April, His Excellency asked him to call. Hoping to finalize things, Owen brought Mr Rizkallah, the school's lawyer, with him. But, at the meeting, the Patriarch's whole attitude had changed. Claiming that the Coptic community was not satisfied with the financial state of the school and, professing to be highly offended that the SMA had not properly replied to a letter of his sent in February, he now said he would take only the Coptic part of the school (the smaller part) and not the Armenian part. On behalf of the SMA, Mr

Rizkallah immediately wrote a formal reply to the February letter. His Beatitude reacted to this strongly, saying it was insulting and that, in future, he would not meet with the Fathers if Mr Rizkallah was present! At subsequent meetings, he was represented by his lawyers and a Mgr Cabis.

In May, Owen, having studied the contract between the De la Salle Brothers and the Greek Catholic Patriarch, submitted to Patriarch Stephanos a draft 'Contract', basically that the Patriarch would assume ownership and that the Fathers would remain as teachers with a salary, accommodation and holidays. Valid for two years, the contract could be renewed if both parties were agreeable.

Towards the end of June, Owen felt that 'the cold war' between the Patriarch and themselves was thawing, but now the Patriarch began to argue that the SMA was asking too much in financial recompense. With debts of nearly £9,000, Owen had asked for remuneration for school furniture and buses. Owen agreed to accept £300 less, reducing the total amount requested to £7,300. The following day, the Patriarch met with his colleagues. In the afternoon, as Owen was finishing a letter to Dr Creaven, he was interrupted by a telephone call, which contained 'a rumour of good news'. Resuming his letter he said, "I have just heard that our latest offer has been received favourably, the Patriarch has instructed his lawyers to inform us that he has accepted. If the report is true, all that remains is to set things in order". Early in July the agreement was signed. It still had to be approved by the Government, but there was nothing Owen could do about that. In fact the transfer didn't receive final approval until the end of the year. Meanwhile, Owen took a week's holiday at the Red Sea. Feeling refreshed after it, he planned on taking another break before school opened in October.

Community life or the lack of it

As well as school problems in the academic year of '65-'66, all three Fathers had been sick. Nevertheless, the community spirit had survived quite well, "Probably because we were united against everyone else". In June '66, wishing he too could get away, he saw off Eugene Melody and Patsy McCarthy who were going on home leave. Eugene left first. "Desperate to get away, he'd work anywhere for the sake of a change", said Owen, "even in China"! Actually, he undertook temporary pastoral work much nearer home, in Birmingham. At the end of the month, Patsy was pacing the decks before a dawn departure. Owen remarked, "There's less trouble getting the Queen Mary off to sea than getting Patsy out of the house".

When they were gone, Owen joked that he could now settle down "to a life of peace and ease". More seriously, he admitted that he still suffered from the effects of the previous summer's illness but, as long as some matters of the school transfer were pending, he couldn't go away. In August, he began getting the school painted and repairs done on the ceiling of Patsy's room which had fallen in. Overall, it wasn't much fun sitting in the house on his own, inhaling paint fumes and swallowing dust but, "Apart from the heat, the flies, the food, the people and, in particular, some members of the hierarchy, there is little to complain about. We always have the consolation of rotten beer and worse brandy to fall back upon".

He had a number of friends among the Egyptians, especially teachers and parents. A Moslem couple, the wife a teacher in St George's and the husband a doctor in the army, impressed him very much. In the past, when one of the Fathers thought of leaving the priesthood, this couple talked him into persevering. As well as the Hazbouns, he was friendly with the families of many of his present and past pupils, among them Frank and Fayez Nafekh. The old college gatekeeper, Ibrahim, a Moslem, was another friend. Owen admired his deep faith in Allah and his prayerfulness, and said "He's one of the gentlest persons I've ever known".

Good as Owen's ability was to relate to local people, he missed news and gossip of home and Society. He was happy to have occasional visits from Irish priests, most of them confreres from Nigeria going on home leave. It didn't cost much more to fly to Ireland via Egypt. Among them that year were Tony O'Donnell, John O'Hea, and Donnie O'Connor, two Redemptorists from India, and a Fr Bennett from Athlone. Owen enjoyed their company, "We move in a narrow groove here and forget that there is a big bad world outside with its own problems".

Reflecting on the past year, he said, "The only things we preserved were our sanity and our vows". In an effort to solve the problem of lack of classroom space, some classes had been amalgamated and, to reduce expenditure, some teachers had been laid off. Unfortunately, the retrenched men threatened a lawsuit. While such was pending, their leader died suddenly of a heart attack. The others, seeing in it "the finger of God", dropped the law case, "and so far their health has remained good", observed Owen. He wondered if it would be expecting too much of Providence to solve another problem – that of the headmaster. The difficult man had actually been given a transfer to Upper Nile but, belonging to an influential Cairo family, he got himself reinstated. An unexpected death occurred on 16 January, that of Mr Emile Nashid, the school secretary. Owen, genuinely missing him, said "His death added chaos to the confusion".

At the end of 1966, two Coptic priests, Iskander Rozek and Maurice Boutros, came to St George's and, in the New Year, took over the running of the school. The missionary Fathers continued to teach English and to reside in their apartment on the school roof. On 8 January '67, when the school closed for holidays, Owen and Melody, enjoying their new freedom from administrative responsibility, took a break; Owen went to Luxor and Melody to Alexandria. Patsy stayed in St George's.

On the wider political scene, relations between Egypt and Israel steadily deteriorated. Palestinian guerrilla groups based in Syria, Jordan, and Lebanon increased attacks and Israel retaliated with increasing violence. One Israeli raid on Jordan in November '66 left eighteen people dead. On 5 June '67, after Nasser closed the Gulf of Aqaba, Israel made a pre-emptive attack. Thus began the **Six Day War**, which resulted in a resounding victory for the Israelis and a humiliating defeat for the Egyptians. The Egyptian Air Force was destroyed before its planes got off the ground and the army was put to flight in Sinai with the loss of some 10,000 soldiers. Israel occupied Sinai and the Suez Canal became the new 'border' with Egypt. The short war brought an end to the Nasser era. When Nasser died in September 1970, Vice President, Anwar Sadat, succeeded him.

After the Six Day War, Owen went on leave. In the Mater Hospital, Dublin, he had an operation for varicose veins and, in July, spent another ten days in hospital. In August, he attended a five day renewal course in Dublin which afforded him a welcome opportunity of meeting other missionaries. Many of them were interested in the situation in the Middle East. "Thoughts of the coming year in Egypt give me a butterfly feeling in the stomach", Owen told them, "Last year was rather unpleasant". Egyptian resentment against Israel was very strong and a renewal of war or even of civil war, were distinct possibilities. Thinking that it was unlikely that any hostilities would commence before October, he intended returning in September.

While at home, he wrote to the Provincial, "If fighting resumes, I presume you will leave it to us whether to stay or leave. I favour remaining on unless the conflict becomes widespread. All Africa is in turmoil. It could be that we are in the safest place of all!" Under normal circumstances he would wish to have more teaching Fathers, but now he said, "If fighting starts again, the fewer of us there are the better".

Early in '67, he had entertained hopes that Fr Paddy Burgess, a missionary with experience in Liberia, including two years as secretary to Archbishop Francis Carroll, would join the community in St George's. But, when Burgess heard that there was little chance of getting the post he sought in the Nunciature in Cairo, he lost interest. Patriarch and pupils' parents pestered Owen to get more men from Ireland, but none were available. Far from receiving more, Owen feared he might lose one; Eugene Melody appeared to be increasingly disenchanted with St George's. On the other hand, shortly before leaving Ireland, Owen heard a surprising bit of good news, a newly ordained man, unable to get a visa for Nigeria, had been appointed to Egypt!

A day or two before his departure, Owen made his usual round of friends and neighbours in Co Down to say goodbye. Mrs Doran[1], the mother of Sexton, now a missionary in Nigeria, sensing Owen's feelings, wrote to her son saying, "Fr Owen is returning to his lonely mission in Egypt".

The man of the surprising appointment to Egypt, Michael Moloney, arrived in Cairo in October. To get a young man on his first mission was a great boost for the ailing community. Owen met the twenty-seven-year-old at the Airport and escorted him on a tram back to St George's. Michael was amazed at the vigour of his former seminary professor who, heedless of heat, dust, and the crush in the tram, imparted a fund of interesting information about every remarkable place they passed. After a light meal and a brief rest, Owen took him out and, setting a fast pace, brought him to some shops where he could equip himself with clothing suitable for the climate.

Though a science graduate, Michael was given English and geography as subjects to teach. The science subjects had already been allocated to other teachers before he arrived. In school, as in the streets, Michael found that the main topic of conversation was still the Six Day War. With the Copts, Lebanese, and ordinary people you could joke about the war. President Nasser had for long favoured the military, especially the officers, so much so that now the ordinary people had little sympathy for them. Typical jokes were that Egyptian tanks had only one forward gear but four for reverse and that their commanders drove into battle reading the 'How to operate a tank' manual. Though Owen enjoyed the humour, his sympathies lay with the Egyptians.

He took Michael on a pastoral visit to the crews of two ships immobilised in the Bitter Lakes in the demilitarized zone of the Suez Canal. The canal was blocked by sunken ships. Crews remained on board trapped vessels to see to their maintenance and guard cargo. Owen also took him to see the pyramids of Giza where they enjoyed a *sonne et lumiere* performance. Mission in Egypt, Michael thought, was proving to be better than he had expected. Owen encouraged him to see as much as he could, and often joined him in excursions around Cairo.

Moloney's teaching schedule for English and geography was not heavy and allowed him time for language study. Owen arranged French lessons for him with a Madam Lelia and, in the New Year, a course in Arabic at the American University in Cairo. Owen joined him for the Arabic course. There was no shortage of opportunities to practise French or Arabic in school or in the street. Before long, the new man was saying the daily Mass in French in the convent school of the *Dames du Déliverance*.

Dr Creaven, visited Egypt again in October '67. He found the four missionaries in reasonably good form but, seeing that they were very confined, authorised Owen to buy a car. Owen investigated, but found the cost so prohibitive that the community agreed to stick to trams and taxis for the time being.

Having often dined at the 'Evêche', the bishop's house, Owen invited Mgr Hubert for dinner at St George's on Patrick's Day 1968. Michael was the special chef for the day and, with a little help from Owen, prepared an elaborate four-course meal. On being introduced to Moloney, Hubert joked that the name in French, *'mal o nez'*, meant 'a bad smell'! He acknowledged that the food smelt good and, hardy Breton that he was, he had a hearty appetite, but he 'shocked' his hosts when he piled all four of their carefully prepared courses onto his soup plate and ate the lot with a spoon!

Owen liked to be with young people and readily joined Michael and the pupils in a major excursion to Luxor. It entailed a journey of some eighteen hours by train south from Cairo along the valley of the Nile. After four days in Luxor, visiting the ancient temples in the Valley of the Kings and Valley of the Queens, they visited the nearly completed Aswan Dam.

Michael was settling in but, unknown to him and Owen, his days in Egypt were numbered. Bishop PJ Kelly of Benin City, Nigeria, where Moloney had been originally appointed, wanted him there and threatened all sorts of penalties on the Provincial if he didn't deliver him. The bishop wasn't the only one who wanted him, the staff of the minor seminary in Oke Are, Ibadan, which desperately needed a science teacher, were outraged when they heard that Moloney wasn't even teaching science in Egypt!

There was a little excitement in Cairo over Government elections in April '68, but much more enthusiasm about apparitions of the Virgin Mary above the Coptic church at Zeitoun. Since the first report of her appearance on 2 April, thousands of people claimed to have seen her. Every evening an expectant crowd, including Moslems, gathered to watch, pray, sing, and hold processions by candle light. The Patriarch and some Moslem leaders seemed convinced that the apparitions were authentic. The Catholic parish priest of Zeitoun, Joseph Porcherot sma, declined to comment but observed that the apparitions were certainly bringing Christians and Moslems together in peaceful prayer. Owen, curious, dragging Moloney with him, kept vigil for three nights, but saw nothing. In June the apparitions ceased.

The same month, Moloney departed for holidays. Owen looked forward to his return in August when he would take a break himself. But, far from returning, Michael received word during the summer that he was to take up studies in Galway University in September. Owen, annoyed, complained that the Province should either supply men for Egypt or close down the mission, "All we are doing here is accelerating backwards".

Eugene Melody also went on holidays and, before the middle of June, Owen was on his own again, "monarch of all I survey". With temperatures over a hundred degrees, "It's no place for a teetotaller", he said.

Earlier in the summer of 1968, at Society headquarters in Rome, the SMA held its first General Assembly since the close of the momentous Second Vatican Council. The Council's spirit and documents were having a profound effect on the church everywhere. Moved by its spirit of renewal, the General Assembly Fathers re-investigated the aim of the Society and concluded that it was 'primary evangelization'.

At the Irish Provincial Assembly, Larry Carr, whom Owen knew since novitiate days, was elected Superior. The new Provincial Council, in the light of the re-stated aim of the Society, took a hard look at the apostolate in Egypt and, for a start, decided that Michael Moloney would not be re-appointed there. A man invalided home from Nigeria, Pat Murphy would replace him.

As the hot summer wore on, Owen, alone in St George's, was getting more anxious to have a break. He had had quite a bit of fever in the past year and very much wanted to have a serious talk with the new Provincial about the future of the mission in Egypt.

1. Susan Doran, nee Cahill, was the sister of Fr Sexton Cahill who died in Nigeria in 1942.

Chapter 10

LEAVING EGYPT

The new Provincial Superior, Fr Larry Carr, missionary, seminary rector, and canon lawyer with a reputation for achieving his aims, visited Egypt in October 1968. Bringing Owen with him, he made a formal call on Patriarch Stephanos and told him that the work of the African Missions in Cairo was not really within the Society's proper aim. In November, he informed the Patriarch that Fr Maginn, would enter into discussions with him about withdrawing from St George's. Carr, desiring that the withdrawal would be fair to both parties, said the Society would be willing to underwrite the expenses of training Coptic priests to take over from the missionaries.

The Patriarch protested that the Irish Fathers were indispensable and that their work <u>was</u> missionary, in fact it was the only kind of mission possible in the circumstances. Fr Carr spoke to others. The Egyptian headmaster, adamant that the Fathers should not leave, said they increased the school's prestige and could be relied on to teach English well. Fr Iskander Rozek, now in charge of school administration, supporting the arguments of Patriarch and headmaster, spoke glowingly of the Christian witness that the Fathers were giving and said that Coptic priests would not be able to run the school on their own for at least fifteen years. Owen and his confreres, agreeing that their presence lent some prestige to the college, argued that they were not fulfilling any worthwhile pastoral or missionary role and that their withdrawal would not be detrimental to the Coptic community as a whole.

Meanwhile, the school's population had risen to some 1,600 pupils, only 15% of whom were Catholic. In fact there were only four

Catholic Copts in the secondary section. More than 50% of the students were Moslem. While the Patriarch saw these figures as a motive for the Fathers remaining, Fr Carr saw them as a reason for leaving.

Unfortunately for the community, after only one academic year in St George's, the very acceptable Pat Murphy was re-appointed to Nigeria. Having taught in West Africa and in Ireland, he was not enamoured of teaching in Egypt and described the pupils of St George's as "The toughest, roughest, and rudest he had ever seen". Owen defended them, "They have good qualities but it takes some time to discover them".

The Superior of the SMA Province of Lyon, Paul Falcon, visited Egypt in October 1969. Of the more than twenty French confreres still in Egypt, practically all were of advanced years. And, as the younger Fathers of the Province did not want to go to Egypt, Falcon saw little future for his Province there. Owen felt sorry for Mgr Hubert, "He must have great faith for he sees little to give him courage, in another five years about half his priests will probably be dead and buried".

The few Irish Fathers remaining weren't all that vigorous either. Patsy McCarthy in particular had been poorly since his return from leave in '68. Owen sent him to the Italian Hospital where he was detained until the New Year. But after being discharged he felt no better. Owen then booked him into a convalescent home but, fearing there might be something seriously wrong with him, advised the Provincial that he should be re-called to Ireland. Patsy departed in May '69; only Owen and Eugene Melody then remained.

Not desirous of a sudden, complete withdrawal from St George's, Fr Carr appealed to other Provinces of the Society for help and looked for lay volunteer teachers as well. He had some success with the British Province. A Fr Liam Wilcock who had a licentiate in theology and was continuing studies, specialising in Islamic and Arabic subjects, agreed to go. Michael Walsh, the British Provincial Superior, hoped Liam would study in the Islamic University in Cairo. Owen remembered Liam as a student in Dromantine, and recalled with a smile his performance as a French jockey in a rehearsal of *Dry Rot* which Owen had cancelled in favour of *Richard II*. Apart from equestrian high jinks, Liam was a quiet, gentle sort and Owen wondered whether he would be able for the rough and tumble of St George's.

Even on his way to Cairo in December '69, Wilcock was dogged by misfortune. Due to a strike, his luggage was lost at Marseilles, "As a consequence", said Owen, "we had to clothe the naked!" Enthusiastic about his Arabic studies in the Islamic University, Liam was not keen on teaching in St George's. Beset by personal problems, he did not settle and left in June. Subsequently, he took up parish work in England and was content but, tragically, one Christmas Eve riding his motor cycle to say Mass in another church, he was killed in a collision with a car.

Another member of the British Province, John Desmond, arrived shortly after Wilcock. After ordination, he had been appointed to the Gold Coast (Ghana). On the voyage out in 1941, his ship had been torpedoed near Freetown. He survived and, in the Gold Coast, did pastoral work, taught in Amisano seminary, and was secretary to the bishop of Tamale. Owen hoped he'd be a success in Egypt but, like Wilcock, he too was unenthusiastic about teaching and, also beset with personal problems, departed within a few days of his colleague.

For the half-year or so that the two were present, the community's relations became severely strained. Owen referred to the period as "stormy weather". Having enough problems with priests, Owen was not at all put out that Fr Carr had failed to find lay teachers. To the Provincial he described the year as "a most trying one"; to a friend, "a bloody awful one".

Hoping to stimulate his little community – only Melody and himself – he asked the Provincial to send out one or two of the new well-qualified professors of Dromantine to give them a course and mentioned John Quinlan and Peter O'Connell. However, Fr Carr, with a lot on his plate, especially difficulties following the Nigerian civil war, replied that the men were not available.

In July 1970, Fr Rozek, thanked Fr Carr for two new buses funded by the Irish and British provinces. The Patriarch also expressed his gratitude and again asked the Provincial to re-reconsider the decision to withdraw; he needed at least five years to organise his own priests. To Owen, the Patriarch itemised a few more reasons why the Irish should remain: the school was much admired by the Moslems – even the Governor of Cairo's son was enrolled there now, and the Fathers would be sadly missed by the English-speaking community, especially by the Sisters and pupils of St Clare's. He pointed out that there were thirty-three female congregations of the Latin rite in Cairo with over 1,200 members, and almost all of them depended on missionary priests, like the SMA, for sacramental and other spiritual support. Finally, he said he would ask the Congregation for Oriental Churches to forbid withdrawal.

The case of the opposition to withdrawal was strengthened by the furore caused by the selling of the French SMA College of St Louis in Tanta. After negotiations lasting a number of years, the Patriarch there finally refused to take over ownership and the school was sold to the Government. The loss of the school was a bitter blow to the Coptic community.

Frustrated at his inability to get really involved in Arabic-speaking pastoral work, Owen registered for another course in the language during the summer of 1970. In July, a young confrere from Strasbourg, Jean-Marie Guillaume, visited him. Jean-Marie had just completed post-ordination Biblical studies and was touring the

Middle East. Spending over a month at St George's, he was impressed that Owen was, not only studying Arabic but, delving into its literature as well. In the evenings on the terrace roof, Owen and Jean-Marie discussed the problems of the world, the Society, and the Church. One topic that exercised Owen at the time was how the Church could impose Sunday Mass on Catholics and then declare it a mortal sin not to attend! He felt this was an abuse of power.

Owen assisted the French Fathers in the basilica on Sundays. That summer, 1970, the French confreres were particularly short-handed. Only Mgr Hubert, who was not well, and Père Colson were there. Hubert had suffered a suspected thrombosis the previous year and a recurrence was feared. Owen, however, did not remain all summer. Wishing to discuss the Egyptian mission with the Irish Provincial, he departed on the 13th of August on a month-long return ticket.

At the Generalate in Rome, the Society's leaders were discussing the closure of the SMA mission in Egypt. The new Superior General, Joseph Hardy, a French man, and his Vicar General, Jackie Power, Irish, visited Egypt in February 1971. They saw the Patriarch and, despite his protests, it seemed inevitable that the SMA would proceed with its plans to withdraw. Owen accepted the inevitability of, at least, his own departure and, expressing his feelings to Fr Carr said, "I shall naturally be sorry at leaving a place in which I have spent so many years and a people whom I like. I have been reasonably happy here despite everything and, if someone had to stay on for a while longer, I would not be averse to doing so ... I would much prefer to stay on to being posted at home". Regarding an alternative mission appointment, he said he'd be willing to go to the new mission in Argentina.

At a General Council meeting in Rome in April '71, it was decided to end the commitment to St George's in July. Owen and Eugene Melody could remain on a voluntary basis, if they wanted to.

Owen with Coptic priest and school staff

A religious community of two is a difficult one. Owen's and Eugene's relationship had been strained by the recent tensions in the community. Eugene possibly exaggerated Owen's clout as superior, "When Owen Maginn tells me to jump, I jump and, on the way up, I ask how high?" Whatever was between them, Owen decided that he would prefer to depart if Eugene decided to stay. As it transpired, Eugene decided to leave. Some time after his departure – he was transferred to Nigeria – Owen said, "It is only now that I am beginning to appreciate some of the work he did, and he did a lot". As well as teaching, Eugene had been the chief supervisor of teachers and, apart from school work, was organizing lay apostolic groups, including English-speaking groups of undergraduates.[1]

Fr Carr made a quick visit in October 1971. "He didn't seem well" said Owen, "and wasn't at all impressed by what he found; he wasn't even interested in the play that the school wanted to put on for him". Somewhat in a hurry (he was on his way to visit another new mission in Australia), he made it clear that no new young men would be appointed to Egypt. Owen had no argument with that, there wasn't sufficient work to keep himself occupied not to mind more men, especially young men. He would depart too only that Frs Rozek and Boutros, both French speakers with little enough English and no experience in school administration, had implored him to stay on to help run the school. "Anyway, where would I go? I am fit for little else now", he said.

In 1971, tension rose again in Cairo and there was more talk of war with Israel. Owen, writing to a friend, said that the possibility of war was not remote but, "So far our lives are not in danger". What bothered him more was that mail was censored and hardly anything from Ireland was reaching him, not even the Provincial Newsletter! The little news he got of home was from the BBC and most of that, unfortunately, was about violence in the North. As the months wore on towards Christmas, he observed that there were no festive decorations evident in Cairo, "Just as well. Generally, I find it a sad time of the year".

Now the only Irish man in St George's, he was able to report that at least he was getting on well with the Coptic Fathers, Iskander Rozek, "a good man and very zealous", and Maurice Boutros. Three more were teaching religion in the school. Owen spoke of all of them as, "Hard workers and easy to get on with". Glad to be free of administration, he described the new Fathers' task as "an almost impossible one": the school's resources were dwindling, pupil numbers were soaring, Islamisation was intensifying. Among 'minor' problems, Iskander was having great difficulties with the importation of school buses. Following exhausting procedures with officialdom, he finally gained possession of one new bus from overseas. No sooner was it on the road than an unregistered lorry driven by an unlicensed driver smashed into it!

Owen helped provide Iskander with Mass intentions. The stipends would go towards school expenses. As administrator of an 'English' school, Iskander felt the need to improve his English. Owen helped him get a short course overseas. Previously, the British Province had organized a course for Maurice Boutros in Manchester from which he had benefited greatly.

Sadly, Fr Alexandre Gaignoux sma, the administrator of the basilica of Heliopolis, died of cancer of the lungs on the 30th of March '72. Despite poor health he had served most effectively in Egypt since his ordination in 1929. His work had ranged from being parish priest to Vicar General and regional superior. Committed to the cause of equality, he had spent a spell in prison for protesting against anti-Christian laws. In 1970, His Beatitude Maximos V Hakim honoured him with the title 'Archimandrite' for his services to the Melkite church.

Gaignoux was succeeded as administrator of the basilica by an Egyptian member of the SMA, forty-eight-year-old, Gabriel Haddad. Owen sympathised with Haddad, thinking he would have a difficult time – an Egyptian in charge of French missionaries all senior to him in age. But, before long, Owen observed that he was doing remarkably well and said, "I like him he is a pious sincere man". In April, Owen got some sad family news. His eighty-three-year-old mother had died on the 13th. Suffering from cancer, Annie had spent three months in a nursing home, was moved to hospital in Belfast and, finally, returned home where she passed away.

Owen went home in August 1972, spent time at his parents' grave and assisted the parish priest in Drumaroad and Clanvaraghan. He returned to Egypt in September and, reflecting on the year that had nearly passed, felt that it had been "a very unsatisfactory year from the point of view of teaching". Things did not improve as the year drew on, even the weather turned unfavourable. Torrential rain fell in November, the heaviest he had ever experienced in Egypt, "Part of our ceiling fell in", he said. But, despite the rain, a church in the neighbourhood was burned down maliciously, apparently by members of a Moslem sect. Nationwide, eleven similar arson attacks took place. The Government, more concerned about war against Israel than outrages against Christians, played down the incidents.

Helping to compensate for lack of news from overseas, Fionnbarra O'Cuilleanain came on a visit from Nigeria. The news from West Africa was disconcerting, quite a number of young men had left the mission and the priesthood. However, it had happened also among the 'Egyptian confreres'. George Chester was only the first. While studying in Galway University, Michael Moloney became friendly with another student, Marjorie whom, eventually, he married. Both teachers, the couple went to Zambia on a teaching contract in 1970.[2] Owen kept up correspondence with George and Michael.

Nineteen-seventy-three proved to be a better year in St George's. Teaching and school affairs went quite well, at least, from January to June. As the number of pupils continued to increase by leaps and bounds, Owen commented that "sometimes we don't know where two or three hundred are, but what is that among so many?" Despite overcrowding in the classrooms, he enjoyed the work.

The following year, a few more Irish-Nigerian missionaries visited him, among them Vincent Bartley and Donie O'Connor. Vincent, who hadn't got himself inoculated against smallpox before arrival, was confined in quarantine, "I could only speak to him through iron bars", said Owen, "his only request was for food".

Apart from student demonstrations in Cairo in February 1973, the country seemed quiet but, with increasing threats about crushing Israel, Owen thought there was little chance for peace. He noticed a mushrooming of prayer groups, though he wasn't sure whether it sprung from genuine spirituality or merely a lack of something to do. He himself joined a group that met twice a month. Composed of Catholic and Protestant missionaries, religious and a few lay people, it was a kind of ecumenical Pentecostal group. He found it "really good".

He planned on doing an advanced French language course in July. Even though his French was good, he felt it was not up to the standard of addressing an educated audience in public. Near the end of the school year, however, he decided to give himself a break instead and, in response to an invitation from George Chester and Linda in Milan, decided to visit them and go on home leave. After an enjoyable visit, he commented to a priest friend, "We were born out of time".[3]

Owen's presentiment of war materialised on the 6th of October 1973. This time, it was the Israelis who were taken by surprise. On the Jewish feast of **Yom Kippur**, the Day of Atonement – the holiest day in the Jewish calendar – when most Israelis were either praying or relaxing, the Egyptian army crossed the Suez Canal and, breaking through the fortified Bar-Lev line, advanced into the Sinai desert. Called the 'Yom Kippur War', the Egyptian army redeemed its honour, raised the country's morale, and enabled President Sadat to negotiate peace terms.

Irish UN officers

Since the Six Day War of '67, the United Nations had maintained an international group of army officers in Cairo as observers. From 1971, Owen had got to know a number of the Irish officers and their families. "A fine lot" he said, who were "not only very supportive and friendly but gave outstanding example of Christian living".

One of them, Captain Barry Studdart, was second in command of the UN force. From Cork, he had grown up near the African Missions College in Wilton, where he had served Mass as a boy and got to know many of the African missionaries.

In Heliopolis, on Sundays and feast days, the Irish attended Owen's Mass in St Clare's. Barry often read at the Mass and, if ever there was a scriptural allusion to the Egyptians smiting the Israelites, he'd notice a quiet grin spread on Owen's face. Owen had some difficulty coping with the 'anti-Egyptian' themes of the Easter readings such as the drowning of Pharaoh's army in the Red Sea. Though the Egyptians often gave Owen a tough time, Barry realized that beneath the surface he had a great *'grá'* (love) for them. Barry and his wife Frances's two children received their First Communion from Owen in Heliopolis. When they first arrived, Owen took Frances and other army wives to visit the markets and showed them where to shop and how to bargain. They were impressed with his friendliness with the people and his knowledge of Arabic.

The Studdarts visited Owen at St George's and in turn he often visited them. Some of Owen's relatives were well known to the Irish officers, all of whom had trained in the Curragh camp in Co Kildare as cadets. In 1922, Pat Maginn, Owen's uncle, had left Co Down and settled in the Curragh where he started a shop. Pat, his son Owen, and grandson who continued to run the family business, were well known to the officers. As cadets they regularly bought loose biscuits by the ½ lb from Pat who used to break one into small pieces to get the weight exactly right. Owen enjoyed the detail about his Uncle's thriftiness. As a seminarian, Owen, on a number of occasions, accompanied by Mick Toner, had cycled to Kildare to spend time with Pat and family.

On Owen's first visit to the Studdert home in Cairo, he was wearing his usual white soutane. Barry's young son opened the door and, leaving Owen standing there, told his father there was an 'Egyptian in a *gallabaya'* outside who wanted to see him. Owen's white soutane was not at all unlike a *gallabaya,* the every-day dress of the Egyptians.

Another officer Owen got to know was Captain Joe Fallon and his wife Marguerite. Arriving a few months before the Yom Kippur War, they found him very helpful as they tried to settle into what was for them a very strange and, at times, hostile environment. Owen shared with them his understanding of the tense situation. They regarded him as one of 'nature's gentlemen'. Owen liked to visit the Fallon's place which was little more than a mile from St George's. In the relaxed atmosphere of their home, he could give vent to his witty comments on national affairs without fear of being reported.

He became friends with Captain Pat McMahon, his wife Ann, and children, Joan, Jim, Dara, and Orla. In Cairo, Ann gave birth to Aisling – giving Owen a rare pastoral opportunity of performing a baptism; he gave Dara[4], her first communion. Owen praised Pat, saying he had foreseen what would happen when Israel and Egypt agreed on a truce at the end of the Yom Kippur War, thereby facilitating UN preparations; however others got the credit for it.

Baptism of Aisling McMahon

The aftermath of the Yom Kippur War was, for Owen, a time of pondering on his own future in Egypt. The lack of Irish SMA contact was especially troubling him. As normal mail was not functioning, members of the many religious Sisters' congregations in Cairo with mother houses in Europe were willing to take letters when travelling there or back. Mail became 'fe-mail'. A Sister Josephine brought Owen a Christmas card from Larry Carr. Owen replied with a New Year letter carried by a Mother de Lourdes. In it he reflected on his life in the two and a half years since he had volunteered to remain in Egypt.

The first thing he mentioned was isolation. Though he was in contact with the French SMA Fathers, their work, interests and ages, were different from his. Also, they had their own problems, not least the recent tragic death of Père Gabriel Jouanne at the railway station of Mahallah. Caught in a press of people struggling to get on a train which was already moving, he had fallen onto the track and died, apparently, of shock.[5] Secondly, Owen said that his work was no longer personally life-giving; it consisted in teaching English and little else. Going over and over the same piece of grammar with very large classes was exhausting. Thirdly, his priestly ministry was stagnating, in the past ten years he had performed only one marriage and two baptisms.

Realizing that he might not find a satisfactory alternative, he said the Egyptian mission was not "altogether unrewarding" but, he hoped the Provincial would consider his case and enlighten him about other possibilities. The Vice Provincial, Joe Donnelly, acting for Larry Carr, responded that it might not be difficult to find something more fulfilling. He pointed out that Owen was in Egypt on a voluntary basis and it was entirely up to him either to stay or to leave. The decision was not an easy one for Owen, especially as the Province had not yet indicated alternatives. In March, Fr Donnelly told him that if he came to Cork in the summer they could discuss the matter.

Sure-footed when advising others, Owen was not so sure in his own case. For the next few months he was undecided whether to stay in

Egypt or not. Options he entertained were: leaving the decision until he met the SMA Vicar General, Jackie Power, who was to visit in April '74; waiting 'till he heard what alternatives might be proposed by the administration in Cork; hanging on for another year before deciding or, even remaining indefinitely. If he opted for the last, he would insist on being given an opportunity to study Arabic properly so that he could engage in pastoral work. In May he decided that he would go to Cork and commit himself one way or another.

The Vicar General, accompanied by the new Provincial of Lyon, Jean Bonfils, arrived in Cairo on the 19th of April and began to make a thorough study of the Society's Vicariate Apostolic of Heliopolis. At the time, nine of the twenty French Fathers were over seventy years of age and six were over fifty. The one Irish man, Owen, was fifty-three.

Having studied the situation from all points of view, Power and Bonfils presented their report to the Superior General on the 2nd of June and sent a copy to the Secretary of the Congregation for the Oriental Churches. In brief, they said that for nearly a hundred years the Society had served the Church in Egypt, but now a decision was being forced upon it, either to revitalise the Egyptian mission with a younger group or to close it in favour of primary evangelization in West Africa. The apostolate in Egypt was a "discreet presence" in which "the invisible and secret values of the Kingdom" were promoted. The bottom line of the report was that they would not advocate a continuation of the mission in Egypt unless the Congregation for Oriental Churches insisted. Furthermore, the report stated that the Society made no claims over the position of Vicar Apostolic. Mgr Hubert would be seventy-five in July and it was not likely that a suitable successor would be found among the confreres in Egypt.

Despite their well-reasoned case, Paul Cardinal Philippe, Prefect of the Congregation, requested the Society to continue, concluding his brief letter with the hope that "on the eve of the centenary of the Society's arrival in Egypt, it would commit itself to strengthen and rejuvenate its presence in the region". A long time before, not too far away from Egypt, St Augustine of Hippo had said, "When Rome has spoken, the case is closed"; the Society remained in Egypt, though in a reduced and modified form and, it is still there.

In July, Owen met Fr Donnelly in Cork and discussed with him other mission possibilities: West Africa, Argentina, U.S.A, Britain, Ireland, and a new mission in Zambia. Only the new mission in East Africa appealed to him. Both Fr Power, when on a visit to Zambia, and Sexton Doran, the superior in Zambia, had written to him and, during Owen's leave in Ireland in the summer he had spoken with Mick Igoe, one of the Zambian missionaries. All had sown seeds. Owen's main worry was, whether at his age he would be able to adapt to a new mission in tropical Africa. After a long discussion with Fr Donnelly, he decided on taking a year off from Egypt and doing "a sort of sabbatical" in Zambia. During this sojourn he would start learning the local language. After it, he would be in a better position to make a final decision about Egypt. In Zambia, Sexton Doran applied for a work permit for him.

By September, the work permit had not yet arrived in Ireland, so Owen returned to Egypt to wait for it there. While waiting, he made preparations for departure, telling a worried Fr Rozek that he would be away "for a short time only" but, deep down, he hoped that it would not be short. He very much wanted to settle down and enjoy a sense of belonging in a worthwhile but, not solitary, mission. Near the end of September, Rozek, who had just returned from France where he had been visiting his brother, a pharmaceutical student residing at the SMA foyer in Strasbourg, gave Owen a nicely wrapped package. On opening it, he found a box of *Mercator Cigarillos*, a gift from Jean-Marie Guillaume, who had visited him four years previously; Jean-Marie was now a member of staff at the Strasbourg house.[6] The gift cheered Owen "tremendously". He wrote in thanks, "I really do appreciate it. I had given up smoking but, when I saw the *Cigarillos*, I started again".

By 30 September, Owen's work permit still had not arrived and he was "marking time" impatiently. That evening he postponed his enjoyment of a 'cigarillo' until after a charismatic prayer meeting in the convent school of *Sacré Coeur* to which Mgr Hubert – much better after a holiday in France – was also going. The charismatic movement was really taking off in Cairo. There was a well-established French-speaking group in Heliopolis, an English one in the parish of Sakkakini and two more French ones in Shubra. "It is the most powerful thing that has come into my life in years", said Owen.

Fretting at the delay over the work permit, he wrote to the Provincial Secretary on the 13th of October asking for news. This was to be his last letter from St George's.[7] In it he mentioned that Sexton Doran, had written saying that a language course would begin in November and it would be good if he could attend it.

When the work permit arrived, he lost no time in making his final arrangements and, early on the morning of 13 November 1974, Captain Joe Fallon drove him to the airport. Joe had an airport pass which might prove useful if there were any difficulties. In the reception area, customs officials roughly emptied the contents of Owen's suitcase onto the floor and rummaged through them. When they were done, Owen quietly gathered his bits and pieces. Joe, fuming at the treatment, admired Owen's calmness. He helped him re-pack the suitcase and bade him a heart-felt *adieu*.

1. At least one of these groups still survives and calls itself "The Melody Club"! A prominent member is Dr Magdi Wissa, a former pupil of St George's (Mattie McNeeley, see note 7). After suffering from malaria in Nigeria in 1974, Fr Melody returned to Ireland and was incardinated in Clonfert diocese in 1976. He died in 2001.

2. From 1970 to 1973, Michael and Marjorie taught in a Government school in Kalabo, Zambia, before settling in Ireland where they raised their four children. Sadly, Marjorie died in 2005. Subsequently, Michael desirous of taking up priestly ministry again, after due process, was received into the diocese of Kildare and Leighlin in a ceremony in his parish church in Naas on December 11, 2008. He was then assigned by Bishop Moriarty to work in the parishes of Daingean and Killeigh in Co Offaly.

3. Years later, after separating from Linda, George went to Canada where he spearheaded work for homeless people in an organization called, 'Out of the Cold'. He died in 2006.

4. Dara became the first female President of the prestigious, male-dominated, Malahide Golf Club, Dublin, in 2008.

5. Père Jouanne from Reims, the parish priest of Mahallah, died on the 3rd of December 1973 aged sixty-nine; he had been in Egypt since 1931.

6. Jean-Marie Guillaume is the present Vicar General of the Society; formerly he was the Provincial Superior of the Est Province which is based at Strasbourg.

7. In Ireland in 2006, Owen met Mattie McNeeley sma, a lone Irish man who works in Egypt, but not in St George's. He told Owen that the school was still in the hands of the Coptic Patriarchate. Owen was cheered by the news and commented, "If that is so, then we really did make a lasting contribution". (In interview with E. Hogan sma.)

Chapter 11

THOUGHTS OF HOME, DRUMAROAD

Flying from Cairo to Zambia, Owen dozed and dreamed of home. By now, Tom and Sadie had six children, Mark, Owen, Patrick, Colette, Dermot, and Yvonne; another child, Martin, had not survived infancy. The children regarded Owen as a

The old home refurbished

second father and felt the family was only complete when he was home.

In his will, Mark Maginn had specified that Owen should have two rooms in the family home, an upstairs bedroom and a downstairs sitting room. The two rooms, known as 'Fr Owen's' were comfortable, of good size, and both had fireplaces, and windows affording pleasant views. In these, Owen always felt at home. It was the house he had been born in and, apart from his sojourn in America, the place where he had grown up. When on leave, though he spent a lot of time visiting, he hardly ever missed a meal in Drumanaghan.

A ritual had been established over the years before his homecoming. His rooms were swept and painted, new bed linen and towels bought. The rest of the house got a touch of paint too, Sadie doing most of the work herself. Once she put so much paint on the cooker that she couldn't open the oven door afterwards. Floors had to be scrubbed and the yard tidied. Tom, after removing buckets, ropes, and bits of farm machinery from the car, and washing it inside and out, warned the children to be on their best behaviour, there was to be no squabbling or fighting during Fr Owen's holiday.

'Major', the dog in the yard, was always the first to greet him. A bond existed between the two which was deeper than the canine's appreciation of the extra titbits he got when Owen was home – he knew that Sadie cooked only the best for Owen.

On entering the house, Owen took everything in, especially any changes Sadie had made since his last holiday, "Why did you do that?" he'd ask as soon as he spotted something different. On such occasions she wished she had her camogie stick handy to belt him. She worked hard in the house and on the farm and, apart from rearing her own large family, had looked after Mark and Annie in their advanced years, and also Annie's brothers Hugh and Tom. Owen would apologise if he thought he'd gone too far.

Accustomed to early morning rising in Africa, he rose with the lark and trumpeted the fact to all by a series of loud nose-blows. The family had no need of alarm clocks when Owen was around. Early as he was, Sadie had to be up before him to light the fire in his sitting room for he was always cold even in summer. When the fire was crackling he'd descend to begin his morning prayers. Meanwhile, Sadie was busy in the kitchen preparing his breakfast of porridge, a hard boiled egg, toast, and piping hot fresh tea. The family's best China ware and cutlery were laid out for him. Breakfast was carried in on a large tray when his matins and lauds were finished. Eating meditatively at the table near the window, he could gaze over the fields towards Drumaroad village and see Slieve Croob and Dunmore Hill in the distance. Once finished, he praised Colette or Yvonne who came to clear away his breakfast things. Normally, Tom joined him for meals; Sadie and the children ate in the kitchen.

Before 9 am, he'd walk the mile or so to the church saying the rosary as he went. Tom followed later in the car with the family, especially the boys who would serve the Mass. They were quite good at it, occasionally even singing a hymn which greatly pleased Owen. He celebrated the Eucharist with great reverence and devotion but, on the occasions when his acolytes' singing was off key, he found it hard to keep a straight face. Neighbours attended the Mass and even small children like the headmaster's children sensed something special was going on. After Mass he'd take a lift home with Tom in the car and partake of a cup of coffee with him in his sitting room or, if he walked, he'd visit neighbours on the way.

A man used to routine, he expected his lunch at 1 pm precisely. He loved Sadie's thick 'homemade soup' and reminded her frequently to write down the recipe for him. She never did, not wishing to reveal her secret – two packets of shop-bought soup powder! Owen could be finicky about food. Sometimes she went through six eggs making an omelette for him that didn't have bits of shell in it. After lunch and siesta, he was ready for more tea with cream crackers and cheese. Despite the abundance, he liked to have a standby and would send one of the children to buy four packets of cheese and onion flavoured Tayto crisps for him. After opening one bag, he'd tell the child to put away the other three carefully for him in the kitchen! Woe betide the kids if a packet disappeared.

Before supper, he'd mix himself a drink – a cocktail of brandy, Martini, and two limes. His nieces watched, fascinated, as he shook the concoction which, he explained, was for his digestion. His supper of salad, potato and a piece of red salmon, eaten late was followed by rosary for all including visitors. Then he showed slides or photographs from the missions. He would be really pleased if the children showed interest. At one session, young Patrick used a colourful swear word. Tom was mortified, but Owen could scarcely contain his mirth.

For the duration of his holiday, the television was transferred to his sitting room, but he encouraged the kids to watch it with him. He loved cartoons. 'Tom and Jerry' and 'Mickey Mouse' made him laugh even more than the children. Show jumping with Eddie Macken and Harvey Smith, and the quiz game 'Call my bluff' were other favourites. Interested in everything the children did, he tried to engage each of them in a serious conversation about their lives and aspirations at least once during the holiday. While his 'interviewing phase' was on, Tom found his sons unusually anxious to help him on the farm.

In the evenings, if he wasn't showing slides or entertaining visitors he would call for the Ludo or Snakes and Ladders' boards and play in a fiercely competitive manner. If he didn't win he'd accuse the children of cheating. Games would go on all night if Sadie didn't whisper, "Let him win or we'll never get to bed". He wouldn't retire himself until he had his nightcap, a hot whisky with sugar and a slice of lemon, "I'll not go to bed 'till I've had my wee nibble".

His first port of call on homecoming was to his cousin, Mary Joe Laverty, on Carnreagh Road. Depending on his form, he walked or took Tom's car, which was always at his disposal. Mary Joe and Owen had an amiable argumentative relationship. Born a Mallon, she was determined, outspoken, and never stuck for a word – rather like Owen himself. On principal, she disagreed with everything he said, and he responded in like manner. Conversations went on for hours and included subjects like, "Why Bishops wear tall hats" and "Who, or what, is God?" Mary Joe's children, Eddie, Marie, and Margaret, barely caught the drift of the weighty discussions. By contrast, young Eddie's favourite memory of the Maginns was when Mark Maginn, his godfather, gave him a whole ten-shilling note for himself on his confirmation day.

On leaving the house, if he was walking, the children accompanied him to the gate. Margaret often escorted him the whole way home. On leaving school, she joined the Assumption Sisters in Ballinahinch. After her novitiate in South Africa, she was appointed to study medicine in UCD. His own niece, Colette, joined the Nazareth Sisters. After 'Cemetery Sunday' ceremonies, which Owen never missed when he was home, he always repaired to Laverty's for refreshments especially after Eddie married Roisin McNamara and built his own house in a beautiful secluded spot with a fine view of the Mournes.

Owen liked excursions. A favourite one was to Saul Mountain where he'd bring Sadie and the kids to say the rosary. "Mary has a special role to play in our lives", he'd explain as he sat into the car and begin the joyful mysteries. He was always saying the rosary in the car, even when Tom was rushing to fetch the vet for a cow in trouble. Every holiday, Owen planned a pilgrimage to Knock with Tom. Tom always fell in with his plans but, after a day or two at Knock, would murmur that they'd better go home or Sadie would be wondering what they were up to. If Owen wished to make the long journey to the African Missions headquarters in Cork, Tom would drive him but take Sadie too. Owen praised highly the flask of tea and egg sandwiches she made for the journey. She'd have preferred a few hotel stops on the way, but Owen would allow only one, saying, "Why go into a hotel when we have Sadie's wonderful sandwiches?" Not only did she suffer in the same way on the homeward journeys but, on reaching Drumanaghan, Owen would invariably announce that he wouldn't mind having something to eat!

He liked to visit everyone in Drumaroad and Clanvaraghan, being careful not to omit the sick and elderly in whose homes he occasionally said Mass. He spent a lot of time in the church in quiet prayer. Across the road from Drumaroad church lived Dan Fitzpatrick's family. Dan, for forty years headmaster of the primary school, had died of a heart attack in January 1970. Owen missed him but continued to visit Annie and the nine children most of whom became teachers like their father. Often, before he returned to mission, the parishioners would organize a fund-raising concert. Dan had been to the fore in these, not only for Owen but for Canon Cahill too, staging plays in McIlroy's loft like *Professor Tim*, *Quinn's Secret* and *Grogan and the Ferret* which went down well and gave a great night out. Later, in McIlroy's lounge, Lily Cochrane organized a fund-raising night which raised a tidy sum for Owen's mission.

Among the many he visited were, Paddy Carlin, Mrs King, the Flanagans in Shanbally, Mickey and Rosaleen Laverty in Dunturk. Mickey liked to tease him about his long Masses and sermons on Sundays, especially when the Down footballers were playing and the congregation wanted to get away quickly. He visited Des and Malachy Magorrian and was very pleased when he got from Malachy the true story behind his father's poem, "Six hard Slaps". Somewhat embarrassed, Malachy explained that playtime in Drumaroad primary school was segregated. Girls were allowed to play on the lawn, the boys were not. Malachy was caught on the grass one day by a new teacher, Miss Sharkey, who reported him to Master Fitzpatrick. Malachy got six hard slaps. When Mark heard the story he was inspired to write:

> *There's a rule in our school and they made it a law*
> *That if you kiss a girl she will tell her Maw*
> *Her Maw tells the master the boy to chastise*
> *I think it is wicked and not very wise,*
> *For the boy will remember till his heart beating stops*
> *That for kissing a girl he got six hard slaps.*
>
> *I know all about it, I've been through it once;*
> *I loved a wee lassie and kissed her on chance,*

I was reported, it was very cruel;
I made no excuses just took my gruel
When the master he called me I thought I'd collapse;
And for just one wee birdie I got six hard slaps.

The Irish race, it is dying some writers now say;
The young will not marry, so we'll just fade away;
Now a fellow won't marry if once on a time
He kissed a wee lass and they made it a crime;
And when he was punished, they were no gentle taps
For every kiss he gave her he got six hard slaps.

In preparing for marriage, great ideas are expressed,
But a wee bit of courting I think still the best;
If a fellow is courting and for her has a grá
Oh boy he will linger round her under-jaw.
And if she says 'Yes' when the question he pops
He'll forget her cross Mammy and all the hard slaps.

Now all you young maidens just listen to this
Don't tell on a boy if he gives you a kiss;
Don't run to your mother and start to complain,
If you do, it is sure he won't kiss you again;
While others for him will be tossing their caps,
You're sure to lose him if you get him six slaps.

Annie didn't approve of Mark's poetry, so he had to hide the manuscripts in a box in the barn. One day he showed the contents to Malachy and recited a few of the poems. Malachy and his brothers loved Mark and worked for him every year helping to harvest his thirty or forty acres of the finest potatoes. During lunch break the workers, some forty at a time, were well fed by Annie and Sadie and, when the ladies weren't listening, Mark told stories or recited poems.

As well as feeding so many, Sadie took her turn picking and was one of the fastest in the field. The children also helped. On one occasion, Colette's cardigan sleeve caught in the cogs of the sorting machine and pulled her arm into it. The eight-year-old nearly lost her arm but, what she remembered most was the sweet the nurse gave her in Downpatrick hospital when her arm was being stitched.

Owen visited Nina Smith in Clanvaraghan to thank her for the many socks she had knitted for him. Every time he called, she gave him more. He visited Raymond McBride and family, who farmed near the Maginns and, among others, the Walshes, McBrides, Kellys, Murphys, Cochranes and Steeles. When Joe and Mary Steele heard he was coming by car, they opened both halves of their gate. Joe's mother, Kitty, was the Maginn children's nanny and always remained very close to them. Owen called on the Dorans in Loughinisland and the Valentines. He drove to Kilcoo to visit his Uncle John and Aunt, Rosie O'Hare – the last of the Maginns to live in Fofanyreagh.

Owen and Canon Dinny Cahill became close friends. Owen helped the sometimes over-serious Canon to relax. When they walked the parish together, they delighted in observing the rural scene, commenting on the strengths and foibles of the folk they knew so well. Dinny's nephew, Fr Sean Cahill became a good friend too. Since seminary days, Owen had kept up his friendship with the diocesan students, now priests of Dromore and Down and Connor dioceses; he always called on them when on leave.

Travelling a bit farther, he visited his classmate of 1934, Des Egan who lived in Newcastle. When Owen first visited him after recovery from tuberculosis and mission in Egypt, Des was shocked to see how thin he had become. The tall, burly lad with the chubby face he'd known in the Red High was scarcely recognisable. Des knew well the ravages of tuberculosis; his own brother, Teddy, had died of it in 1943 and he himself had been ill with it for a year. Owen met other classmates,

Gerry Nolan, Michael Sawey, Roddy Maguire, Derek King and Gerry Milligan. Whenever he was on the way to Cork, he'd call to see Pat and Owen Maginn and their families at the Curragh in Kildare. They were especially interested to hear about their UN army friends in Egypt.

Finally, the day of return to mission came. The chore of suitcase-packing had begun at least a week in advance with Colette and Yvonne taking charge of it. He didn't have many things to pack, nevertheless re-packing had to be done many times and the case weighed on the bathroom scales after each change to make sure it was not overweight.

The house was sad the morning of his departure. The family lined up in the yard to say Goodbye. Major followed him round and got a farewell pat. At Belfast Airport, he walked to the departure gate without looking back.

Chapter 12

ZAMBIA 1974

Owen woke from his reverie as the plane's captain announced their approach to Ndola. It was evening on the 13th of November. He felt tired but also excited. In comparison with Cairo Airport, Ndola's seemed very small. Customs and immigration officials were very polite, welcoming him and even calling him 'Father'. Sexton Doran, Mick Igoe, and one or two other confreres were there to meet him. "Secky", as the superior was called, taking his suitcase, led him to a yellow station wagon in the un-crowded car park. They drove off to the SMA headquarters, 'Francisdale', thirteen miles from the city centre. As they drove, Owen was pleasantly surprised at how clean and tidy everything appeared to be.

The tree-lined roads along the way were delightful. Purple jacarandas were beginning to give way to brilliant red flamboyant trees. Passing through a light industrial area, Owen saw well-maintained buildings, a

Francisdale

Dunlop factory, a tall grain silo, a high electricity pylon, a copper refinery, and an oil refinery. Secky, pointing and explaining, drove on a good tarred road for about six miles and then turned onto a reddish 'dirt' road, smooth and well-graded. Leaving signs of habitation behind, they reached Francisdale, a nice looking mission with a fine church and a well-kept garden.

Over a cup of 'Kawambwa' tea – grown in the country – Secky told him he needn't unpack as the language course had already begun, "Ilondola, where the school is, is 400 miles away but you can rest half way at the Irish Sisters' hospital at Chilonga". Secky was joking, "No, you can join the course up to two weeks after commencement; spend a few days here first and then go". Aware of Owen's health problems, Secky was conscious too that he was much older than the rest of the SMA team. With Owen they were eleven, "A few more and we'll be able to take on the Down footballers", he said. Though Owen, fifty-four, was old to be starting a new mission, he was young in his way of thinking.

In the two or three days before departing for Ilondola the other Ndola priests came to see him. Six were working in parishes and four were engaged in teaching. When he saw them, he couldn't help contrasting them with the men in Egypt. Most of these were young, some only just ordained, and all of them appeared to be in good health. The eldest, Mick Igoe, was only forty-two, while Secky, the next in

SMA 'pioneers' at Francisdale: Sitting: Gerry Hanna, Benno Wolff, Mick Igoe, Sexton Doran, Pat Byrne, PJ Gormley. Standing: Mick O'Shea, Liam Brady, Bernard Lynch, Sinesio Santamarta (Spanish), Jim Fegan

years, was forty. Already all seemed to have some "Chibemba". Secky, Mick, and Pat Byrne appeared to be quite good and even the teachers were able to say Mass in it at the week-ends.

The three senior parish men, Mick Igoe from Westmeath, Secky, from Loughinisland, and Pat Byrne, a thirty-eight-year-old Wexford man, all had worked in Nigeria. The teachers, Noel O'Regan, Cork, thirty-two and Páraic Kelly, Co Galway, thirty-three, were both in a teacher training college in a town called Mufulira. Two other men, both aged thirty, were teaching in secondary schools in Ndola, PJ Gormley, Co Tyrone and Mick O'Shea, Cork city. Secky resided in Francisdale where he ran a parish and outstations. His deputy, Mick Igoe, lived in Kabushi in the suburbs of Ndola where he was assisted by one of the newly-ordained men, Gerry Hanna, twenty-five, who hailed from Rathfriland, Co Down. Pat Byrne was a parish priest in Mufulira. Finbarr Kerr, twenty-five, from Cork city, was a parish priest in Kitwe and another Cork city man, Liam Brady, twenty-seven, was working with Spanish missionaries in Chingola.

Secky brought Owen to see the bishop, Nicholas Agnozzi, an Italian Franciscan Conventual. The Conventuals, having arrived in Ndola in 1931, were the first resident Catholic missionaries in the district. Nicholas, the second bishop of Ndola, had arrived in 1934.

At the door of the Bishop's house, Nicholas warmly greeted Owen and said he was glad that there was now an 'old man' to keep an eye on youngsters like Doran. With the bishop was his impressive-looking Vicar General, Mgr Dennis de Jong, a Zambian of mixed race. Offering tea, coffee and cigarettes, Nicholas asked Owen for his first impressions of Zambia. Owen had been

Bishop Nicholas Agnozzi

asked this already a few times. Clearing his throat, he said, "Well, in comparison to Egypt, this place strikes me as a semi-paradise. Though I haven't seen much of it, Ndola is a beautiful city and the economic situation seems to be very good. The country is peaceful and one is free to practise and spread Christianity". Nicholas offered Owen another cigarette and, rising from his chair, began glancing out the window as if he was expecting someone. Secky and Owen made to depart. On their way out, Nicholas whispered to Secky, "If you have any more 'old men' at home, send them out as fast as you can". He wasn't just being witty; three young confreres had already left the diocese.

On their way back to Francisdale, Owen told Secky that he was impressed by the SMA group and, counting on the fingers of his left hand, itemised, "Fair progress in Chibemba; new presbytery in Kabushi; two more houses under way in Mufulira and Kitwe; a number of new church buildings in the planning stage and, apart from the main stations, the men are looking after many outstations". Running out of fingers, he changed hands and continued, "The teachers seem to be doing alright too, at least they're happy and positive about their work. There isn't overcrowding in the schools as in Cairo and there's no anti-Christian bias. I get the impression that the Zambian Church is forward-looking, the Church in Egypt was very caught up with its historic past". Secky thought Owen was right even if he had presented a rather rosy picture. The departure of four confreres, three young and another one not so young, in the first year and a half of the mission was very worrying. Owen, realizing that he might have spoken as one less wise, added with a smile, "Anyway, there seems to be room for me, I just hope I'll be able to make a fist of Chibemba".

He set off for the language school at Ilondola in the Northern Province a few days later. Mick O'Shea, a teacher in Chifubu Secondary School, taking advantage of a long week-end and his 'new' second hand Fiat 124 was only too happy to drive him. Despite the distance, the journey passed quickly. Owen, interested in everything, was a great conversationalist and Mick was delighted to share his 'vast' experience of nearly two years in Africa!

Leaving Ndola, they went south to Kapiri Mposhi where the Copperbelt road met the Great North Road, the main artery of Zambia, stretching all the way from Livingstone in the south to Tunduma, over a thousand miles away in the north. A well-surfaced tarred road, there wasn't much traffic on it, one could travel for an hour or two without meeting another vehicle. Over half-way to Chilonga, Mick interrupted the conversation to point out the side road to Chitambo's village, the place where the missionary-explorer David Livingstone had died in 1873. They stopped under the shade of a big *museshi* tree for a flask of tea – with lemon juice for Owen rather than milk – and egg sandwiches moistened with tomatoes and fresh lettuce from Secky's kitchen garden.

About 300 miles from Ndola, they reached Chilonga Mission Hospital, a regular pit stop for the SMA confreres, two groups of whom had preceded Owen to the language school over the previous year. The hospital was run by Irish Sisters of the Sacred Hearts of Jesus and Mary. Among them was La Salette, a nurse about Owen's age who became a great friend of his later when she was transferred to Ndola. After a fine supper, a game of 'a hundred and ten', a restful night, and morning Mass followed by 'a full Irish breakfast', they continued on their way, confident of being in Ilondola for afternoon tea if not for lunch.

After Chinsali, 'the tar stopped' and they were on a gravel road corrugated in places, but it was only another twenty-five miles to Ilondola. After twenty-five and a few more miles, with the road narrowing to a rough track, they were forced to stop at a rickety wooden bridge. Mick finally admitted that he didn't know where they were. Owen, surveying the very empty plain stretching for miles said, "Maybe we should ask someone!" The bridge didn't look too good; planks were missing from the middle. Owen began hauling a heavy branch from the side of the road to cover the gap; Mick was impressed. Bridge patched up, they motored on and, after a lot of shunting and back-tracking, came on the language school as dusk was falling.

The school was run by 'White Fathers' – the 'Missionaries of Africa' – the pioneer Catholic missionaries who founded their first mission in Bembaland in 1895. After gaining a foothold, between the two World Wars they began to make great progress and, by the middle of the twentieth century, Catholicism was imbedded among the Bemba, the dominant people of the north. The large population of the hinterland of Ilondola, once the cathedral centre of the Vicariate of Bangweolo, had diminished until only a small number remained. The people had gone to the big towns, like Kasama, the capital of the north, or the copper mines of the south.

The Bemba, noted warriors and hunters, in the British era were compelled to seek salaried employment in order to pay the 'hut tax' imposed by the colonial government. Leaving womenfolk behind, the men went south to the booming mines where there was a huge demand for labour. The local people of Ndola district, the Lamba, were not keen on working in the mines, so the Bemba and their language came to dominate the growing labour camps. The camps developed into the modern towns of Kitwe, Mufulira, Luanshya, Chingola, and Chililabombwe. Ndola was the administrative centre. All the towns were Chibemba-speaking, hence new missionaries needed to learn it.

The language course lasted from November to the following March with a break at Christmas; about ten students participated in each course. The school's director, Louis Oger wf, had long experience in the country and a deep knowledge of the culture. Owen thoroughly enjoyed his classes and, in a hard-covered notebook, took copious notes about the sophisticated matrilineal Bemba tribe. In settled communities, the Bemba took to farming but not to rearing cattle. The chiefs were polygamous, the ordinary people were not. When the missionaries arrived, barter was the common mode of exchange and at their first station, Kayambi, they were the first to introduce the use of 'cash'.

Under red ink headings, Owen took notes on the people's attitude to life and religion. The people believed in one God, *Lesa,* the creator, Father of all. Popular proverbs reveal more about Him: "One does not ask God for meat but for life"; "O God, you who help the wasp from breaking in two, help me"; "God can snap the iron tree". Ancestors, *mipashi,* are held in high esteem and importance as intermediaries with God. Bemba males do not have initiation rites; females do and attain status after undergoing initiation. Men are given some importance after begetting children, but it is the mothers who have the more significant role in family relationships. Sin is considered to be a disturbing of the social order. Witchcraft is a grievous sin and is greatly feared. Sickness and death are not caused by 'something' but by 'someone'. "<u>Who</u> caused it?" not "<u>what</u> caused it?" is often the question asked in the case of death.

Owen also learned about the Lumpa Church founded by Alice Mulenga, 'Lenshina', of nearby Chinsali. She claimed that she had died and risen and had been given a mission by God to rid the world of witchcraft. Membership of her church quickly outstripped that of the Protestant and Catholic churches and her burnt brick cathedral at Kasoma was larger than the White Fathers' one at Ilondola. Rejecting politics and refusing to join the United National Independence Party, the first indigenous ruling party, she was opposed by its leader, Kenneth Kaunda. In the months before Independence, 24 October 1964, about seven hundred (according to official figures; 'thousands' according to others) were massacred by Government soldiers. It was a tragic beginning to Zambia's independence, one that was played down by both the colonial and the new government.

At the back of his notebook, Owen neatly wrote the Zambian National anthem, "*Stand and sing of Zambia proud and free*". After it, in pencil, someone tried to translate it into Chibemba but only completed the first verse.

Partial to Oger's lectures, Owen complained that the other teachers confused him! He despaired of ever getting the hang of the complicated language with its nine classes of nouns, uncountable tenses, strange pronunciations, and words like *mailo* which could mean 'tomorrow' or 'yesterday'!

In the middle of the bush, Ilondola was an ideal place to learn a language – there was nothing else to do. There was a small fresh-water swimming pool which one could dip in but, it was chillingly cold. Food was wholesome but unexciting; two Canadian Sisters on the course, good cooks, occasionally provided some variety. A small library contained books on Bemba history, language, and culture. In a letter to Secky, Owen said, he was enjoying the course "up to a point". As he had arrived late, he had only five weeks of class to get through before the Christmas break.

He went to Francisdale for Christmas, where he met all the other confreres who frequently called there. The SMA headquarters was a nice out-of-town place, the superior was welcoming, and the Dominican Sisters in the school 'next door' allowed the confreres to use their very fine swimming pool. Owen helped out with Christmas Masses; by then he could read Chibemba even if he couldn't preach in it.

While in Francisdale, he received a letter from Phil O'Shea, the Provincial bursar in Cork, informing him that Fr Rozek and the

Coptic Patriarch were wondering when he was returning to Egypt! Rozek had written to Cork first in October, protesting about Owen's departure and again in December. In the latter, he paid Owen a nice compliment, "Fr Maginn was one that was loved and respected by everyone. I hope he will not stay long in Zambia but return to Egypt".

Owen returned to Ilondola in January and persevered through more complicated grammar and vocabulary until the middle of March when the course ended. "I learned nothing", he complained when he got back to Ndola. Actually he had learned a lot, but he needed practice. Sexton appointed him to Holy Cross parish, Kabushi, where he would be in the midst of the people and learn from the parish priests Mick Igoe and Gerry Hanna.

The parish of 'Kabushi', meaning 'little goat', was founded by the Conventuals in 1956. Before Independence, colonial law required that white and black people live in separate areas. The Conventual religious rule required that its members live together in 'convents', hence the name 'Conventuals'. When they built their large centre, called the 'Franciscan Centre' in 1950, they went as near as they could to a densely populated black township called Chifubu in the suburbs of Ndola. After Independence, Bishop Nicholas desiring that missionaries reside among the people, requested the SMA to do so. The Spanish missionaries in Chingola and the Franciscans in Luanshya were already living in African areas. In Ndola, Mick Igoe and his first assistant, Bernard Lynch, a young man from Clare, were the first to live in an African township when they took up residence in Kabushi in May 1974.

Built, next to 'Holy Cross' church, the original Kabushi presbytery was very small – a two-bedroom house, measuring only 38 feet by 26. Later, it was extended to accommodate more priests. When Owen arrived, as well as Igoe and Hanna, PJ Gormley, teaching in nearby Masala Secondary School, was residing there. 'Holy Cross' church and presbytery were on, appropriately named, "Church Road" which, approved by the colonial town planners as a place for religious worship, had no less than six different denominations of Christian churches on it.

Mick Igoe, gave Owen a small catechism in Chibemba of the question and answer sort called *Mulanga Lesa* ('To show God') and told him to attend the children's instruction classes every day to hear and practice the proper pronunciation of the language. Owen, sat like Methuselah among his offspring and enjoyed it all or, at least, a lot of it! He also accompanied Mick on hospital visitation and picked-up some useful bedside conversation. The busy parish of Kabushi, with six Masses on a Sunday between main church and outstations, was a good place to start. By now Owen had little difficulty saying Mass in Chibemba and, for Sunday homilies, he enlisted the help of local *balumendo*, youths, to correct his written compositions, though he admitted, "My sermons must have been painful, half the time I didn't know what I was saying myself".

The presbytery was a lively place. Mick Igoe, the witty parish priest was a first class mimic and had a mine of humorous stories; aided and abetted by Hanna and Gormley, there was rarely a dull moment in the house. The pastors got their work done too, not only in Kabushi, but in their many other Mass centres, heavily populated areas like Lubuto, Ndeke, Mushili, and Kaloko. In these, Mick and Gerry were building new churches.

At the end of August '75, Owen went to Lusaka to give an eight-day retreat to a large group of Sisters at the Kalundu study centre. He found it a congenial break from Kabushi and it afforded him an opportunity of seeing the capital city. As well as reinvigorating the Sisters' spiritual lives, he replenished his own, knowing that his 'apprenticeship' in Kabushi was coming to an end for, when he got back to Ndola, he would be getting a proper work assignment.

Twapia

In 1975, Nicholas Agnozzi resigned as bishop of Ndola in favour of Dennis de Jong, whom he had been grooming for office. Dennis's episcopal ordination took place in Ndola on 28 September. The following month, he asked Sexton Doran to provide a temporary cathedral administrator until the Franciscans appointed one. As the Franciscans were by far the largest congregation in the diocese Dennis wished that one of them would be the administrator but it might be some time before they made the appointment. The Franciscans had about seventy priests and brothers in the diocese. The SMA, the next congregation in size, had eleven; the Bishop had only three local diocesan priests. Sexton asked Owen to take up the interim post. In addition, Bishop Dennis asked him to take charge of St Stephen's, Twapia, a small parish seven miles from Ndola.

Owen, sorry to be leaving the lively community and friendly people of Kabushi, packed his bags and moved to the Bishop's house, next to the cathedral. Among the residents there was the very pleasant, mild-mannered, Italian Franciscan, Tiziano Bragagnolo. He had been suddenly plucked from his rural mission St Theresa's, Ibenga, by Dennis to be his Vicar General. Tiziano welcomed Owen graciously and tried to make him feel at home. At their first supper, Owen abruptly asked him, "What's 'Religious Life'?" The Bishop was amused; understandably, he favoured the secular diocesan way of life and, at times, felt overwhelmed by the large number of Franciscans in the diocese. *"Mama mia",* Tiziano tried to answer, "That's a big question" and, praying for inspiration, continued, "Dear Father, I think it's trying to live like Christ". It was an answer Owen couldn't argue with. Henceforward the two got on very well and had many more theological debates.

Twapia lies off the main road to Kitwe. The parish, founded in 1962 by the Franciscans, was visited regularly by them from the Franciscan Centre. When Owen took it on, it was being visited by Stanislaus, a

Polish friar. With increasing numbers of Catholics in their big parishes and many other works, including running one of the biggest printing presses in the country, the Franciscans were glad of assistance. In the hand-over of Twapia, Owen discovered that Fr Stanislaus spoke good Chibemba, but was a beginner in English. Between Chibemba and English, Owen gathered that he was now the pastor of some 6,000 Catholics, that Stanislaus had had about 1,000 communicants at Easter and that he had performed six marriages in the past year.

Owen worked out that the Bemba word *twapia* meant 'We are burning'. Looking around the parish he thought the name appropriate, the place looked burnt out. A small congregation attended his first Mass, a few elderly women sitting on the floor on one side and even fewer elderly men on the other.

Power in the parish was concentrated in the hands of the parish council and a full-time catechist, Honore Kabwe. The council had been in office for four years, the catechist had been there for more than thirty! Already grey-haired, Mr Kabwe had come from one of the White Fathers' missions in the north where he had been trained as a catechist and then sent as a 'missionary' to the Copperbelt. Owen got on well with him, but many of the parishioners, regarding him as a 'blow-in', didn't.

With Owen's letter of appointment were instructions that he should visit the parish three times a week and see to the outlying areas which comprised of four 'outstations'. As time went on, the people warmed to him. In his first year, he generally acceded to most of their requests for baptism or marriage and he actually baptised over 600. Later, he realized that he had been too accommodating; some of the recipients were not fully instructed or had canonical impediments. Nevertheless, he wasn't all that soft as the following story indicates.

A particularly devout woman used to attend his Masses, but she always remained at the back of the church and never received communion. One day she surprised Owen by asking for baptism, he thought she had been baptised. "You must be instructed first", he said. "Why?" she asked. "Well, to know God", he said struggling to make it sound right in Chibemba. "I've known Him for years; why do you think I come here every time there is Mass". "Well, you need to learn how to pray". "I've been doing that all my life". Owen was

Preaching in Twapia

flummoxed; surely she already had faith and knowledge of God. He began to realize that it was he who could learn a lot about God from these people. As time went on, he got to like Twapia but found the struggle to speak Chibemba a terrible trial, "I almost came to believe I was deaf and dumb".

A result of his early 'liberal' attitude to accepting people for baptism was that the number of parishioners and church attendances increased. As his knowledge of the language and diocesan rules grew, he became stricter. Always one who cast a critical eye over things, he saw that the parish records, especially of baptism, were not in good order. He requested a young parishioner, Patrick Mpabulwani, to make a new register. When this tedious work was completed, Owen paid him – to his surprise – with a cheque.

Owen also realized that the figures he had accepted for the parish were on the high side. In his statistical report of June 1976, he recorded that while the total population of the area was about 6,000 (after which he put a question mark), only about 1,500 (again with a question mark) were Catholics. He stated that the parish had four outstations: Chichele, Dola Hill, Kwacha, and Zambia Compound. Dola Hill was a Government forestry work site and residential area. The parish and outstations had one paid catechist and five volunteers. Parish income over the preceding year had been K1,475 and the expenditure was K986. Before signing his name, he inserted the word *fairly*, "I certify that the above is *fairly* correct"!

The basic unit of Zambian currency is the 'Kwacha' (K). Established at the time of Independence, 1964, one Kwacha, which means 'dawn', was equal in value to £1 sterling. As time went on, it decreased in value and in the late Eighties was officially devalued. When Owen arrived in 1974, it was worth about ¾ of £1. Today, it is worth about 1/8000 of £1.

Once Owen got things moving in Twapia, he turned his attention to the outstations. In Kwacha and Dola Hill he began building new churches. By this time, the Franciscans had appointed Ambroz Knezic as permanent cathedral administrator. After moving in to the Bishop's house, he quickly made friends with Owen who continued to live there as there was no presbytery in Twapia.

Owen thought the hall in Twapia was too small, so he extended it. When it was being painted he noticed that the paint in large five-litre tins diminished overnight. Knowledgeable parishioners told him that it could be the heat! Owen took to bringing the tins home with him in the boot of the car. One evening, in a hurry to say Mass for the Sisters in town, he instructed his painter to put the tins in the boot of his car *"bwangu bwangu"* (quickly quickly). Next day on opening the boot, he found it had a nice thick coat of fresh green paint. The painter hadn't put the lids on the tins!

Another day rushing to Dola Hill – this time he was using a small pick-up van – he was flagged down by a man looking for a lift. Undecided about stopping, he slowed down. The man ran after the van and vaulted over the tail board just as Owen stepped hard on the brakes. The man shot forward, crashing his head through the cab window. Amazingly he wasn't seriously hurt. Owen, not knowing whether to laugh or cry, said to the head that had appeared next to him in the cab, "*Mulishani mukwai?* How are you Sir?

Far from Zambia, on 12 September 1976, Fr Larry Carr, the Irish Provincial Superior, died unexpectedly in Tenafly, USA, during a Society meeting. Fifty-six-year-old Larry had visited Zambia a few months previously and had seemed in good health. In Francisdale, a concelebrated requiem Mass was said for him at which Owen, who knew him since 1938, preached a fine tribute. Larry's brother, Fintan, a Christian Brother working in Mazabuka, Zambia, attended.

Basic Christian Communities
In 1976, the Conference of the bishops of East Africa, inspired by the thriving 'Basic Christian Communities' of Latin America, decided to introduce them in their own dioceses. The bishops, still greatly dependent on expatriate missionaries, hoped that through the 'BCCs' their dioceses would become more self-reliant. In 1977, Bishop de Jong, launching the plan in Ndola, invited experts to come to instruct the parish priests who, in turn, should see to the training of the lay leaders. The programme took off and, before long communities, popularly called 'sections', were forming in each parish. It was a community-based movement, very acceptable to Zambians who were well used to meeting in small groups to discuss affairs or to share a pot of beer.

Fr Joe Donnelly, acting Provincial Superior since Fr Carr's death, requested Sexton Doran to give him a report on the Basic Christian Communities. Sexton, in turn, asked Owen, Mick Igoe in Kabushi and Mick O'Shea in Chipulukusu to write accounts of the communities in their parishes.

Owen wrote his report in April 1978 and, though it was scarcely a year since the inception of the 'BCCs', he said progress had "far surpassed expectations". This time he gave 4,000 as the approximate number of Catholics in Twapia and outstations. The parish already had seven Basic Christian Communities with slightly over 400 members in each. Each had its own chairman, treasurer, secretary, and two voluntary catechists. They met weekly in their home areas, normally out of doors, sitting in a circle; office-holders – nearly always male – sitting on the only chairs. Catechism classes were held once a week in all sections. The parish's four outstations formed four communities of their own, making a total of eleven 'Basic Christian Communities'.

Following diocesan guidelines, catechesis for the reception of Baptism, Eucharist, and Confirmation was conducted over a two-year period for each sacrament. Always keen on catechetics, Owen was happy to give to each community a copy of *A way of life for the people of Africa* (in Chibemba), a book based on his 'old friend' Johannes Hoffinger's way of presenting the Christian message. Along with this, Bishop Dennis had picked up the series of catechetical handbooks called *Africa our Way of Life* by Michael McGrath sma and Sr Nicole Gregoire s.a., and had them translated into Chibemba for use in the diocese.

Owen met his catechists once a month for on-going instruction and visited each section every week accompanied by the parish vice chairman. The BCCs created more work for him but he found it worthwhile, at least five of the main parish sections were doing well. When the rains stopped, usually in April, he intended saying Mass once a week in each of the sections.

Apart from the Basic Communities there were also many traditional apostolic groups in the parish: the third order of St Francis called the

Tertiari; Young Christian Workers; women's and girls' groups called *Nazareti, Bana ba Maria,* and *Stella;* also choir groups, liturgical readers, Vincent de Paul, Legion of Mary, altar servers and youth groups. These did not compete with the BCCs but complemented them, the senior members of the groups were usually members of the 'sections' as well.

With the success of the Basic Communities, the Twapia parish council began to take over financial matters including support of the priest. The council decided to give Owen K100 per month and the Sunday collection. They also intended to raise all funds required for parish needs and contribute K300 per year to the diocese. Owen thought that this, from a parish that had many old and unemployed people, was very generous. Some priests in bigger parishes had problems with handing-over control; Owen argued, "If we talk about giving responsibility, we <u>should give it</u>".

He listed some of the effects the BCCs were already having in Twapia: an increase in numbers attending Sunday Mass and a slight increase in communions; an increase in numbers coming for instruction, in numbers involved in care of the needy, and in numbers of couples wanting to regularise their marriages. Sunday collections had doubled, "without once having to mention money from the altar" and, overall, the priest was left freer to concentrate on spiritual matters.

*

At the end of 1978, almost six years after the SMA's arrival in Zambia, Sexton Doran's mandate as superior came to an end. Under his leadership, the pioneering steps of the confreres had been successfully taken, the group had settled down, and a lot of progress had been made in different fields. A few men had left, but more had arrived, including two priests from the archdiocese of Tuam, Paddy Williams and Mick O'Malley. Called *fidei donum* priests, 'a gift of faith', they were volunteer diocesan priests who undertook a three-year renewable contract to work in Ndola diocese with the SMA. Two 'new' experienced confreres, thirty-nine-year-old Cork city man, Denis Collins, and thirty-eight-year-old Tony Gill from Dublin had also arrived. The four newcomers were destined for parish work.

The group, now numbering thirteen, elected Paraic Kelly as the new 'Society superior'. One of his early initiatives was to hold a spiritual-cum-mission-business meeting at Francisdale in February '79. Owen, having agreed to animate the spiritual part, prepared a paper on 'Personal Spiritual Renewal'. At the meeting, he commended the 1978 Provincial Assembly for highlighting the need for personal renewal, but was critical of its slight treatment of 'Poverty of Spirit', 'Obedience', and 'Devotion to Our Lady'. He spoke on themes familiar to missionaries: loneliness, disappointment, failure, and being misunderstood. Touching on celibacy, he described it as giving to Jesus "the exclusive love of one's heart" and, emphasising the importance of personal prayer said, "Listening to God is the essence of prayer" but, it should not be forgotten that "God often teaches us through His apparent absences". Regarding 'development work', he warned that excessive zeal for it can lead a priest away from his sacramental role, "We become what we do".

The confreres were pleased with his talk. Paraic Kelly sent a copy of it to Cork where it was published in the Irish Province's *Bulletin*. After the spiritual 'work' of the morning and siesta, the group met for 'business'. By popular acclaim, it was decided to have more of these 'Days of Recollection'. Six members wanted one every month and six wanted one every two months. Noted for his reconciliatory skills, Paraic decided to have one every six weeks.

In January 1980, Owen baptised many catechumens in Twapia and outstations. When Bishop de Jong arrived to confer Confirmation,

Owen had the large number of 110 ready for him. His 'concrete' projects were proceeding apace. He was especially keen that the builders of the new church at Dola Hill complete the work before 17 March, 'Patrick's Day', as it was to be called "St Patrick's". However they didn't manage; Owen had to wait until May for the opening and blessing. A man from Northern Ireland, Ed McCaul, director of the forestry works at Dola Hill, had been very helpful in building the church. Meanwhile, Owen was building two more churches, at 'Immaculate Conception' section and at 'Kwacha Compound'.

Zealous in pastoral work, Owen was irritated by some of his colleagues' excessive enthusiasm for 'development' of an agricultural type, "Conversation in the Bishop's House is all about hens and pigs and tractors and fruit trees. There wasn't half as much talk about farming in Drumaroad!" Bishop Dennis himself was promoting agricultural projects including a major one of training young farmers and settling them on plots of land procured by the diocese. Owen, though preferring church-related works was, nevertheless, involved in small projects to help the poor and, at the time, was raising funds for a 'Self-help project' in Zambia Compound.

According to the SMA-Ndola contract, the length of tour was three years, quite a bit longer than that of Egypt. By the end of his first three years, Owen, felt he was running out of steam and was looking forward to a break. He summed up, "All in all it wasn't a bad tour. Zambia isn't a bad old mission; all our grouses are very superficial". The thought of returning to Egypt hadn't surfaced, but a visit some time on his way home had.

Egypt re-visited, 1980
Owen re-visited Egypt at the end of his second tour in Zambia when he agreed to lead a group of missionary friends on a two-week visit to Egypt and the Holy Land. The group consisted of three German Dominican Sisters, Carla, Judith, and Siegfrieda, an Irish Sister of

Charity, Patricia, and Mick O' Malley, one of the Tuam diocesan priests.

In June 1980, the group flew from Ndola to Nairobi. There, while waiting for their connection to Cairo, Owen dozed. His friends wondered whether they had been wise in asking this frail-looking sixty-year-old to be their guide. Apart from Sr Siegfrieda, who was seventy, he was much older than the rest. But when he arrived in Cairo, he astonished them. It was as if he had stepped out of a time-warp. His back straightened, his step quickened, and his eyes lit up. He smiled broadly as he led his little flock through customs and immigration, switching from English to Arabic to French as occasion demanded.

Following his prior arrangements, the Irish Franciscan Sisters of St Clare's school in Heliopolis accommodated them. He had organized a mini-bus and driver and knew exactly where to go and what to do. His fellow pilgrims were amazed at his vitality. Despite the heat, he was running about like a ten-year-old.

First, he brought them on a tour of nearby sites: the old quarters, Jewish, Christian and Moslem; then to the famous Islamic University; Nasser's monument and the modern centre of Cairo. By noon the 'youngsters' were hoping he would ease up a bit and, using Sr Siegfrieda as an excuse, prompted him about the need for a rest room and some refreshments. Very attentive to the seventy-year-old Sr Siegfrieda – who looked after the altar linen and flower arrangements in Twapia – he immediately instructed their driver to take them to the Cairo Hilton! On parking outside it, the Sisters wondered, "Who'll pay for this?" "Follow me", said Owen, marching confidently into the foyer where he directed the ladies to a well-appointed bathroom, while he and Mick went to another. All set, he marched out again. Mick O'Malley grinned, "We didn't even spend a penny!" "I never do" said Owen with a wink. Then he took them to a beautiful, 'affordable', garden-cafe where they had a cool drink. After more sightseeing, he took them to a big park with a shaded open-air restaurant where the food was good and the prices reasonable.

Another day he shepherded them around the noisy dusty bazaars and helped them to buy souvenirs, real leather handbags, perfumes, and ornamental stone ware. The women were delighted. Owen's knowledge of Arabic and his jocular rapport with the stall keepers was a great help in making their purchases. They visited the pyramids of Giza and, on another day, went on an excursion to not-so-near Luxor and the Valley of the Kings and Queens. That day, Owen stayed in Cairo visiting friends.

He said Mass for the group in the basilica of Heliopolis. They were surprised at how many remembered him. He was delighted to meet old friends but, avoided answering their questions about when he was returning to Egypt! The week passed too quickly and the pilgrims flew on to Tel Aviv in Israel.

In the Holy Land they visited the usual sites, Jerusalem, Bethlehem, Nazareth, Jericho, Samaria and unusual ones like Zaccheus's sycamore tree. In the holy places Owen knelt or stood in reverent prayer with arms outstretched. At Jacob's well he drank of the water and told his followers to do the same. On the hilltop, where Jesus wept over Jerusalem, he said Mass – an emotional experience for him and the group. Again, the week passed very quickly; the 'not-so-old' guide was the first to leave. The others agreed that he had made the trip really worthwhile and, at least for Carla, his expertise in Egypt made the visit there even surpass that of the Holy Land.

While on leave in Ireland, he attended the funeral of Archbishop Francis Carroll sma, who died at his family home in Newry on 10 October, and was buried in St Mary's cemetery. A missionary in Liberia for forty-two years Mgr Carroll had been decorated four times by the Liberian government for outstanding work in education, health and social welfare.

Good though Owen's leave had been, after his return to Zambia, his health began to deteriorate. By Christmas he was feeling very poorly. In the New Year of 1981, the doctor, fearing that his tubercular problem was becoming active again, sent him for tests. The tests proved negative but he did not feel better and, by March, was experiencing chest pains. The doctor advised him to go to Salisbury in Southern Rhodesia for a thorough check-up. In July, he drove there with Ambroz who was also seeking medical attention. Spending four days in St Anne's Hospital, Avondale, they both underwent a battery of tests and x-rays which, thankfully, revealed nothing alarming.

Back in Twapia, having decided to extend the church, Owen engaged Ndola architect, Hamish Cameron Smith, to draw up plans. Owen wanted to extend the altar end of the church and raise the sanctuary floor level. A perfectionist when he wanted to be, he and Hamish had many arguments over designs. Eventually, they agreed to build a blunt arrowhead-shaped extension around the sanctuary enclosing two large transepts. Owen raised the necessary funds and construction work began.

A great event for the diocese of Ndola took place on 15 August 1982, the priestly ordination of five young men, Martin Bwalya, Joe Komakoma, Albert Chibuye, Bernard Chisanga, and Quintino Chisunka. Diocesan vocations were at last beginning to flourish. The ceremony was held in Roan Antelope mine football stadium in Luanshya. Along with most of the priests in the diocese Owen concelebrated. Ordinations in Africa are not noted for brevity and, when a concelebrant is seated in the middle of a football stadium, surrounded by a very large enthusiastic congregation, it is not easy to slip away quietly. Owen, sitting and standing under a hot sun for nearly six hours, began to feel weak. By the time he got home, he was running a high temperature and suffering severe chest pains. An Italian doctor, Maria Madalena, after examining him, sent him to Ndola Central Hospital. There, conditions were basic; the Dominican Sisters got him a fresh mattress and Ambroz brought him food daily. He wasn't able to rest much as all his parishioners came to visit him and stayed kneeling at his bedside praying for his recovery. Dr Maria advised him to go home.

After his departure, Sexton Doran, took charge of the parish of Twapia. He continued the building of the Church extension and completed it with some very fine Kasama stone and copper art work. Every time he drove into Twapia a cry was raised by kids and adults, "Ba Maginn! Ba Maginn!" "It was", said Sexton, "an exclamation of delight, appreciation, and love for Owen".

Another tribute to Owen's work in Twapia was encompassed in the statistics Fr Doran compiled for the parish in June 1984. The number of Catholics had more than doubled during Owen's tenure, from about 1,500 in 1976 to 3,032. A further 200 catechumens were preparing for baptism. There were fifteen Basic Christian Communities with twenty voluntary catechists including eight women. In the outstations there were about 700 Catholics and nearly 300 catechumens. As well as building three new churches, extending Twapia parish hall, and beginning the church extension, Owen had established a new outstation near the Dag Hammarskjold memorial site – the spot where the Secretary-General of the United Nations had been killed in a plane crash in 1961. All told, Owen's record as priest in charge of Twapia was an excellent one.

Sabbatical in Rome

After being hospitalized in Cork and treated against a recurrence of TB, Owen requested sabbatical leave, hoping that extra time would build him up for Africa. This was granted and, for his sabbatical, he arranged to study ecumenism and canon law in the academic year '83-

'84 at the Pontifical University of St Thomas Aquinas in Rome. In Rome, he would reside at the SMA Generalate in the western suburbs of the city.

Arriving at the Generalate on the Via della Nocetta in September, Owen was delighted with the vibrant community life that he found there. He loved the buzz of being "at the nerve centre of the Society" where Paddy Harrington[1], a former student of his in Dromantine, was beginning his mandate as Superior General. Owen cherished the social evenings in the 'bar' of the house where he enjoyed the lively conversations and witty story telling of Sean Kelly, Michael Evans, and Mattie McNeeley. Sean, like Owen, was on sabbatical and also attending the 'Angelicum' as the Dominican University was called, Michael was the Society's General bursar, and Mattie was the house bursar. 'Zambian' confrere, Mick O'Shea, was also there beginning doctoral studies at the Gregorian University. The three, Owen, Sean and Mick, attended a beginners' course in Italian in the city and an 'advanced' one in the house. Another confrere, Kieran O'Reilly[2], was studying Scripture in the Biblicum. These along with many other confreres of different nationalities comprised a very lively community at 'Nocetta'. Apart from the bar and the *craic*, Owen worked hard and, though complaining that the lecturers were not as good as those in Cambridge, he graduated with a *Magna cum Laude* in his diploma in pastoral theology.

As he was finishing his studies in May, the Provincial Superior, Con Murphy, offered him the job of editor of the Irish SMA Bulletin. Owen, not desirous of a home-based task, respectfully asked to be allowed to return to Africa; this was granted. He remained another month in Rome, "to see some of the sights I hadn't time to see all year".

Owen at St. Mark's, Venice

*With Provincial
Superior Con Murphy
in Rome*

1. Patrick (Paddy) Harrington, Superior General 1983-1995, is presently the Bishop of Lodwar in Kenya.

2. Kieran O'Reilly is the current Superior General.

Chapter 13

ZAMBIA 1984

Accompanying Owen back to Zambia on the flight from London in October 1984 was Fr Michael Joyce, the fourth priest from the archdiocese of Tuam to work with the SMA in Ndola diocese. Preceding him were Paddy Williams, Mick O'Malley, and Paddy Costello. For this his fourth Zambian tour, Owen received a new appointment, parish priest of St Mary's, Kamuchanga in the copper mining town of Mufulira forty miles from Ndola. Fr Joyce, after studying Chibemba in Ilondola, was also appointed to St Mary's. There, he and Owen became good friends and often worked in tandem.

Michael Joyce

St Mary's, a little over two miles from the centre of Mufulira, was first established as a parish by the White Fathers in 1968. The parish priests then resided with their community in the town centre. Pat Byrne sma took over St Mary's in 1974. At first he and Paraic Kelly, who was teaching in the town, lived in different places until the presbytery in Kamuchanga, about half a mile from the church, was completed. When the two took up residence there in May '75, they were the first priests to live in a black township in 'Muf' as the town was called. The population of Kamuchanga was over 40,000 of whom 11,000 were Catholic. After Pat and Paraic, Liam Brady, Pat O'Mahony[1], and other confreres worked there. All of them experienced St Mary's as a vibrant parish where, it was often said, more vocations to the priesthood and sisterhood were found than in any other parish of the diocese.

Owen joined Noel O'Regan, who had already been living in St Mary's for over a year as priest in charge of two smaller parishes in the area, Kawama West and Kansuswa. Kamuchanga, economically better off than Twapia and with a more developed parish, was not an area of "primary evangelization". Owen's work now consisted in running a busy urban parish.

Interested to see how Twapia and parishioners had fared in his absence, he made a return visit there with Sexton Doran. He was amazed and delighted to see how big and how fine the extension to the church was. Secky assured him that it was filled to capacity on Sundays and feast days. The people, very pleased to see their old pastor, were sorry to hear that he wasn't remaining.

Looking at his new abode in St Mary's, Owen felt the presbytery badly needed to be enlarged. With Michael Joyce they were now three priests and soon they would have to accommodate a number of long-term guests: Ndola diocesan seminarians and Irish SMA students appointed there to gain pastoral experience. Owen planned two extra bedrooms, a bathroom, and a lock-up garage – car thefts were common. After various appeals, he received funding from a Pontifical Mission Aid society in Austria. Construction work began and, despite difficulties in finding building materials, especially roofing sheets, progress was made. By the end of 1985 everything was completed including painting and furnishing. Characteristically, Owen gave meticulous accounts of money spent down to the cost of roofing nails and door locks, and an estimation of the shortfall of grants due to inflation then running at 20% in Zambia.

In Mufulira, as well as in the rest of the country, unemployment was a big problem especially in the poorer areas of the Copperbelt. Crime was on the increase; police had taken to shooting suspected thieves and smugglers on sight. Being near the Zairean border, smuggling was rife. Writing home Owen said, "Police shot eight smugglers fleeing to Zaire in the past week". Zambians believed that most *kabolala,* thieves, came from that side of the border.

The new man, Michael Joyce, thirty-six years of age from Mayo, before studying for the priesthood, worked with the Electricity Supply Board in Ireland. As priest he worked in Inishbofin and in Kilmaine and was a school chaplain. In Zambia, after the language course and a month in Francisdale with Paraic Kelly, he joined Owen and Noel in Kamuchanga. "It was an extraordinary exposure to a teeming population", he wrote, "People were everywhere and it seemed like a hundred experiences had to be assimilated every day, all clamouring in my brain for explanation and meaning. I was sometimes exhausted by 12 noon, such was the intensity involved in listening through conversations in Chibemba. I got great encouragement from my confreres and the people, and I developed a genuine love for the language, its musicality, tone, and subtlety".

If working in Kamuchanga was exhausting for the thirty-six-year-old, it must have been even more so for sixty-four-year-old Owen. He didn't complain but, after some time, handed over St Mary's to Michael while he took on an outstation, St Theresa's, Kawama East. This station had a population of some 6,000 people but, only about 1,700 were Catholic. Owen liked the challenge of having some 'primary evangelisation' to do again. Once he got 'dug in' in Kawama East, his colleagues joked that it became the most 'catechetically advanced' outstation in the diocese as he made sure that it had participants at every workshop, seminar, and course held in the diocese. He attended the workshops himself and between them, his sabbatical in Rome, and his perennial serious reading, he was probably the most 'updated' man in the Copperbelt.

Part of Bishop de Jong's post Vatican II vision was to invigorate clergy and laity with the very latest in doctrine, scripture, and pastoral practice. To this end, he invited experts from East and South Africa to give special courses in Ndola. Owen went to them all and was particularly impressed by four: Sr Tomasia Santa Clara Gomez, a Portuguese member of the Grail from Mozambique, who spoke on justice and peace and the need to keep alive the prophetic voice of the church; Fr Tony Dalton omi from South Africa, who gave retreats; Brian Hearne cssp, of the Gaba Institute in Uganda who, Owen said, "had an unrivalled facility in presenting teaching old and new in a simple form"; and Tony Byrne cssp who lectured on Integral Development. Tony Byrne, assisted by Mick O'Malley, the diocesan development officer, carried out an extensive survey of every parish in the diocese with a view of implementing development programmes. The Bishop also initiated the 'Confraternity of Christian Doctrine', an American correspondence course, and appointed Denis Collins sma as its first director.

St Theresa's in the squatter compound of Kawama East, where roads hardly existed, was about three kilometres from the presbytery and took longer to reach than St Mary's. Owen rose early and drove there for Mass and morning prayers. Not many turned up so he allocated a special 'Mass day' to each of the different apostolic groups so that at least there would be a core group present. After *milandu* and *mafundisho* (people's problems and instruction), he returned home for lunch and siesta. Then after a cup of tea and a biscuit, he hurried back and remained 'till darkness began to fall. Looking at the parish's mud-block church he realized that it didn't do much to attract people, not only was it too small, it was in danger of collapsing in the rainy season. He decided to build a new one.

'Kawama' means 'a good little place', but it wasn't good for starting church building. After the mud-walled church was demolished in 1986, Mufulira District Council refused to give permission to build a new one as it was an area marked out for development; any permanent structure would lend support to 'squatter's rights'. The result was that the parish now had no church at all. Stalemate between Owen and the Council ran into weeks and then months. During it, Owen pleaded with God and men and asked the parishioners to do the same. After six months, the Council relented but, with the on-going decrease in the value of the kwacha and rising costs of materials and labour, the delay resulted in a 50% increase in the estimated cost. Owen, worried as to how he would find the extra money, organised special days of intercessory prayer and adoration in the parish's small hall. Shortly afterwards, he received a big donation from the Missionary Sisters of St Peter Claver in England! Feeling it was an answer to prayer and not knowing how to thank them, he began by offering a Novena of Masses for their intentions and promised another one a month later. His letter of thanks was published in their magazine, *Echo from Africa and other Continents.*

He received another generous donation from the archdiocese of Cologne in Germany. In thanking Mgr Michel, the Archbishop's secretary, he admitted that when faced with the shortfall in the amount needed to build the church, "[He had] found it very difficult to follow Christ's teaching regarding being unconcerned about material things". He offered three novenas of Masses for the intentions of the Archdiocese and included it in his monthly Mass for benefactors. With these two donations and some others, he was able to commence building. One positive result of the six-month delay was that when the Council finally gave the 'go ahead', they granted a plot nearly double the size of the one originally requested.

Another setback was that the District Council now began to insist that the new church have electricity and running water. As water pipes and electricity cables would have to be brought a long distance from a residential area called Eastlea, and pass under a railway line, the overall cost would again be greatly increased. Owen managed to raise more money. The parishioners themselves were very generous, each family contributing K100 per month, and giving labour free for clearing and general work. Owen engaged a building contractor, but progress was slow and impeded by many problems, including problems with the builder. Owen "nearly demented" said, "At times, I didn't know whether to blow my brains out or his (if he had any)".

When finally completed in 1988 and blessed by Bishop Dennis on Sunday 13 March, the new St Theresa's church was a fine structure able to accommodate 900 people. Owen was content; on reflection he felt that the sessions of community prayer, and

St. Theresa's, Kawama East, nearing completion

even the setbacks, had helped to promote a good spirit in the parish.

The economic situation in the country continued to deteriorate. The poor, as always, were the first to suffer. To help, Owen distributed a lot of maize seed and fertilizer at the beginning of the rainy season. Most of the people in Kawama had access to small 'gardens'. Unfortunately, the rains failed and drought prevailed until January, by which time the crops were withering in the fields. Ironically, the mosquitoes didn't seem to mind the lack of moisture, "We've had an unholy invasion of them and spraying with insect killer is like giving hormones to cattle. They thrive on it", said Owen.

Feeling the economic pinch, as well as the effects of Owen's mosquito sprays, the community in Kamuchanga tried to remain in good spirits. Sharing house responsibilities, Owen's particular task was to look after the accounts. Noel, with a low income from his two small parishes, appreciated Owen's large-heartedness about money, never once did he mention his small contribution to the house fund. Noel also found him easy to live with and admired the way he related with the cook and the gardener, always treating them with respect (even when they codded him). Not that Owen was always calm and serene. Friendly argument, occasionally threatened to leave the 'demilitarized zone'. One morning as Noel joined him at breakfast, Owen challenged him abruptly, "If it's a fight you're looking for, I'm ready!" Noel never discovered what the matter was, but it certainly spoiled his porridge that morning.

*

Paraic Kelly, in April 1986, nearing the end of his second term as Society superior, was struck down by a very rare type of malaria which nearly claimed his life. Delirious and too weak to be sent home, he was confined to bed in Francisdale where his confrere, Tom Casey[2] and others, did their best to look after him. At the end of three weeks without any signs of improvement, Tom anointed him and brought him to Ndola Central Hospital where he was detained. A friend, the matron of the Arthur Davidson children's hospital, Sr Teresa Murphy, looked after him during the worst nights of the fever.

When Owen in Mufulira heard how seriously ill he was, he went to see him. Always a firm believer in the efficacy of prayer for healing, he prayed over Paraic for a long time. The next day Paraic felt an improvement and a few days later was discharged. When he was strong enough to be flown home, Noel O'Regan, the assistant superior, accompanied him on the flight. Paraic attributed his recovery to Owen's prayers as well as to the hospital's care and Sr Murphy's attention. After recuperating, he was given a home appointment. In Zambia, later in the year, Noel was elected superior.

Working well together, in 1987 Owen and Michael Joyce began building a two-classroom primary school with a teacher's house at a village called "Fourteen Miles". Owen received help from a

Downpatrick group called 'War on Want' and Michael from the Irish Government and his archdiocese. The village was fourteen miles from Mufulira on the road to Ndola, hence the name. In another building venture, Michael continued the building of a church which Owen had begun in an area called Chibolya where there were over 8,000 people but no church. The Archbishop of Tuam, Joseph Cunnane, and other friends of Michael again helped generously with financial support.

The forty miles of road from 'Muf' to Ndola was plagued by armed robbers who set up road blocks, despoiled travellers and disappeared into the bush on the Zairean side. Formerly the Belgian Congo, Zaire is now called the Democratic Republic of Congo. It has been troubled by violence and lawlessness for a long time. In 1983, Pat O'Mahony, parish priest of Kamuchanga, was waylaid on this road, robbed, and left tied to a tree by thieves who made off in his car.

While Owen was on sabbatical, conditions and security in Zambia had declined. On his return, he found severe shortages especially of food and fuel. With the price of copper plummeting, the Zambian economy was in a down-spin. In 1986, faced with the demands of the International Monetary Fund, President Kaunda withdrew subsidies from mealie meal, the Zambians' staple food. Rioting and demonstrations broke out in the Copperbelt towns. Tom Casey, driving near Kitwe, was caught in the midst of a stone-throwing mob. He managed to get away but had to get five stitches in his head and three new windows (in his car). Serious rioting in Kitwe resulted in the destruction of Chimwemwe Post Office, near where the SMA parish priests lived. Bread, sugar, cooking oil, salt, and other essential commodities became scarce and were often unavailable. Food queues grew longer. Owen feared that even 'Irish' potatoes, his staple food, would run out.

Expatriate priests, especially those engaged in building, were presumed to have a lot of money, attacks at night on their houses increased.

Installation of burglar bars, alarms, and the hiring of private security men became big business. Owen and confreres put burglar bars on their windows and reinforced the main door with an iron gate on the inside.

One night, Owen was awakened by shouting and the sound of hammering on the main door. Looking out, he saw a fellow wearing a balaclava helmet run past his window. Others, trying to kick the door down were shouting, "We're coming for you *Basungu* (whites); we're going to get you". Keeping a cool head, Noel O'Regan telephoned the White Fathers in the centre of town asking them to fetch the police and, inspired by stories of Irish monks repelling Viking raiders, yelled to Mick Joyce to start boiling water. Unfortunately, the thieves overheard him and pulled out the electricity wires from the external fuse box. Power was cut off and the whole place was plunged in darkness.

Police response to emergency calls was usually slow. Often they claimed they had no fuel or no transport and couldn't come unless someone came for them! However, the Kamuchanga thieves had overheard Noel on the telephone – it was just inside the main door – and fearing that some trigger-happy officers might come, raised siege and fled. Actually, the iron gate behind the main door was about to give way. The White Fathers escorted by armed police duly arrived and, after the officers ensured that it was safe to do so, advanced on the house. Owen went back to bed and slept well; Michael and Noel didn't. But, in something like delayed shock, Owen suffered later.

After the attempted break-in, all three felt on edge at night and jumped at every unusual sound. When Noel departed for leave in June, Owen got a high security wall built around the house. A new man, thirty-year-old Donal Toal from Dublin, ordained the previous year, came to replace Noel. June and July are cold months in Zambia; Owen was sleeping under three blankets and using a hot water bottle!

During these times of insecurity, people went to bed early or, at least, tried to be home before darkness fell, which in the tropics, falls early and quickly.

The first time the confreres ventured out after dark was to attend a send-off party for two Dominican Sisters who were going home to Germany after more than fifty years in Zambia. Not intending to stay late, Owen travelled on his own. Michael Joyce also went alone in a new vanette. Donal Toal drove with a Zambian deacon in an old Toyota Starlet belonging to Fr Paddy Costello. About 9 pm, Owen returned home. Rather than lock up and go to bed, he waited for Michael Joyce. Pacing up and down inside the wall saying the rosary, he had only two decades said when Michael arrived. Owen opened the gate to let him in; he was surprised to see a man on foot also come in. Perhaps a sick call, Owen thought, but then the man produced a revolver and, pointing it at Owen, told him to do what he was told or he'd be shot, "Naturally, I obeyed", said Owen. The gunman, calling on an accomplice outside to come in, told Owen to move towards the house. Michael, in the garage, parked his car close to the wall, so close that he couldn't get out when the robber ordered him to do so. Angrily, the gunman told him to reverse. As he was doing this, Donal Toal arrived in the Starlet, blocking the gate. The thieves then turned their attention to him and, after ordering him out of the car, drove off in it.

Though shaken, none of the confreres was hurt and the Starlet was not worth as much as either of the other two vehicles. Some time later, they heard that three men had been killed in a car accident near Kabwe; a survivor admitted that two of the deceased had been involved in the robbery at Kamuchanga.

Though most of the news from Northern Ireland had to do with bloodshed and violence, Owen received better news about his nieces, Yvonne and Colette. In the summer of 1988, Yvonne married Noel

McClean in Rome. Mgr Sean Brady, rector of the Irish College, administered the sacrament and, after the ceremony in which twenty-one couples participated, Mgr Brady spoke to Yvonne about Owen whom he had met in Rome. In September, Colette made her final profession as a Nazareth Sister in England. Tom and Sadie who had attended the ceremony, sent him a video. After seeing it, Owen remarked, "Some of the congregation would not get far in a beauty competition!" Like most religious orders at the time, Colette's was an ageing one. Owen hoped that the generation gap would not make things difficult for her.

Though the priests had a good wall around the house in Kamuchanga, they were still very vulnerable when opening the gate to get in. The mission was surrounded by high grass and anthills where thieves could easily hide. On Christmas Eve 1988, Owen helped Michael and Donal to hear confessions in the main church and, when finished, drove home in his blue vanette. Darkness had fallen. When he got out to open the gate, a gun was jabbed in his ribs. Two other men joined the gunman and, leaving Owen standing there, drove off in the vanette. Mick and Donal, returning together, saw the vanette moving off and, seeing that Owen was alright, gave chase. They lost sight of the vanette near the Zairean border. After several hours searching, someone told them he'd seen a blue vanette stuck in mud with *Ba Kabolala* around it. His description of the vehicle fitted Owen's but, before attempting to recover it, Michael and Donal went to a beer hall where they'd seen a few soldiers with guns. After some coaxing, two of the soldiers agreed to go with them. On nearing the place, the soldiers fired shots in the air. The thieves ran off abandoning the car. It was Owen's, but it was deeply bogged down in soft ground. After a further request for help, an army truck came and pulled it out.

As dawn began to break, the rescuers returned to Kamuchanga muddied, but triumphant. Owen opened the gate for them. Great was his relief to see them (and to see his blue vanette!) It was damaged where it had hit a tree during the chase but it was still a runner.

Unfortunately, this wasn't the end of the Kamuchanga confreres' troubles. Not long afterwards, armed men accosted Donal Toal at the gate and took his car. On another occasion, when he was the only Father in the house, thieves broke in, tied him to the bed and ransacked the house.

Incidents didn't always occur at night. One day, when Michael Joyce was saying an open-air Mass in one of his Community sections, a crowd of people, angry over food shortages, began rioting nearby. Police arrived and fired teargas which, infiltrating the Mass area, forced Michael and his congregation to run.

Robberies, insecurity, and food shortages took their toll on all. Compounding financial problems, the kwacha was officially devalued. Parishioners were no longer able to contribute as generously to the upkeep of their pastors as before. Parish expenditure outstripped income. The gloomy mood was reflected in a short note Owen wrote on New Year's day 1989: *1 January, Sunday. A wet, miserable morning. Attendance at Masses in all churches poor. Residents in the house, Michael Joyce … Donal Toal … Owen Maginn".* The same month, following another rise in the price of mealie meal, rioting broke out again.

As if to give himself a real penance for Lent, precisely on Ash Wednesday, Owen fell off the low veranda surrounding the house and fractured his foot. "I suppose I should thank God that it wasn't my neck", he groaned. Confined in plaster and using crutches he felt *hors de combat,* especially as he couldn't drive but, he searched for a chauffeur and before long, disobeying doctor's orders, continued with his work. For four or five months he had occasional pain in his foot but, quickly discarding the crutches, he began walking with a stick (and a limp).

Around the same time, a White Father of Mufulira was caught on the Ndola road, manhandled and robbed. In another incident, a Police car was ambushed and an officer shot dead. In a third incident, a Greek business man, whose driver had tried to break through a road block, was shot and died later in hospital. Eventually, the road was closed and travellers were obliged to make the long detour to Ndola via Kitwe.

1989 Papal visit

Nineteen eighty-nine wasn't all doom and gloom. In May, Pope John Paul II, visited Zambia. On the 2nd he arrived in Lusaka by Concorde from the island of Réunion in the Indian Ocean. After celebrations and meetings in the capital, the following morning he flew to Kitwe. At Old Ndeke Airport where the Pontifical Mass was to be celebrated, he greeted the gathered crowds from his 'popemobile'. The Mass began at 10 a.m. in the presence of some 150,000 people. Kawama East parishioners were well represented; the womenfolk resplendent in the colourful *chitenge* wrappers Owen got for them. Thinking ahead, he brought a six foot locally carved crucifix with him; Michael Joyce brought a block of stone. The Pope blessed these and six church foundation stones at the end of Mass. Owen installed the cross behind the altar of the new church in Kawama East and Michael erected the stone over the main door of the new church in Chibolya. The Pope's Mass was mainly in English, but readings and hymns were in Bemba. John Paul's homily was delivered in English, after it a summary was given in Bemba.

Short as it was, the Pope's visit to the Copperbelt was a wonderful success, due in no small measure to the organizers, prominent among whom were John Horgan[3], Noel O'Regan, Sexton Doran, PJ Gormley, and Fr Tarcisius Mukuka. The event was well publicised in the national media. The *Sunday Times of Zambia* devoted a special supplement to the visit containing a full page colour photograph of the

Pope and the curricula vitae of the nine diocesan bishops of Zambia.

Unknown to John Paul II, thieves nearly succeeded in seriously disrupting his visit to Kitwe. On Sunday evening, less than forty-eight hours before he was due, Noel O'Regan's car and brief case containing the final arrangements and summary of the Pope's homily in Bemba was stolen! The robbery occurred as Noel was on his way home from a papal visit committee meeting in Kitwe. In Ndola, he

Pope John Paul II

stopped to pick up the translation of the Pope's homily. After collecting it, when getting back into his car he heard a shot and was held up by two men. Forcing him out, they made off with the car and the all-important brief case.

The visit organizers spent two sleepless nights frantically re-doing everything – without Noel's typewriter which had also been taken. While the missing documentation was replaced, the car, a new Toyota Hilux twin-cab, recently bought for the Society Superior, was not. Weeks passed without a trace. A sighting was finally reported in Lubumbashi, Zaire. With characteristic grit, Noel and his assistant, Aodhan McCrystal[4], went in pursuit and, after some adventures, recovered it, damaged but able to go. April had been a traumatic time for Noel, he had flown home on the 1st after receiving news that his mother was dying. She died the following day and, after a necessarily brief period of mourning, he got a flight back to Zambia in time to finalize preparations for the papal visit.

Michael Joyce with youth at Mufulira

It would be far from the truth to say that the scares and scarcities of the Eighties, depressed the Kamuchanga team. Michael Joyce, referred to his time in Zambia as "a great grace" and Owen spoke of it as "one of the happiest periods of his priesthood". He and the people of Chibolya honoured Michael in a special way by calling the new church, 'St Michael's'. It was blessed by Bishop Dennis on Sunday 29 August 1990, by which time Fr Joyce, after completing two three-year contracts in Zambia, had returned to Ireland.

After blessing Owen's church in Kawama East, Bishop Dennis asked him would he mind if Sisters took over the running of the parish – a new pastoral trend favoured by Dennis. Owen agreed and a congregation founded by the White Fathers, later called the Missionary Sisters of Our Lady of Africa, took over. Though Owen continued to celebrate Mass and administer the sacraments in the parish, he did not have very much to do but, before he had time to feel redundant, Bishop Dennis asked him to come to Ndola as his private secretary.

1. Pat O'Mahony from West Cork, ordained in 1978, arrived in Zambia in 1979. In 1983, he was assistant Society Superior in Zambia.

2. Tom Casey, thirty-three, from Tipperary, after working in Nigeria, came to Zambia in 1984.

3. John Horgan sma, fifty-five, from Co Cork, worked in Ireland and Nigeria and arrived in Zambia in 1985.

4. Aodhan McCrystal, thirty-six, from Co Tyrone, arrived in Zambia in 1979. He worked mainly in teaching, promoting diocesan vocations, and in school and college chaplaincy work.

Chapter 14

OWEN and BISHOP DENNIS de JONG

The SMA confreres having arrived in 1973 and 1974, and Mgr de Jong, appointed Bishop in 1975, settled into their respective roles in Ndola in much the same period. Dennis entrusted many of them with responsible positions, among them: Sexton Doran, Vicar General; Paraic Kelly, diocesan vocation director; Gerry Hanna diocesan treasurer; Noel O'Regan, head of the catechetical commission and director of the Interdiocesan Pastoral Coordinating Team. As Sexton Doran's time as Vicar General

Bishop Dennis de Jong

(1980-1990) was coming to an end, Dennis appointed Fr Francis Katai, a young diocesan priest, to succeed him but, wishing also to have a private secretary, asked the Irish Provincial Council and the SMA superior in Zambia, Noel O'Regan, if they could suggest a suitable person. Owen Maginn was recommended.

Owen would have liked to spend another tour in Mufulira. He was happy with the new churches at Kawama East and Chibolya and with the parishioners and leaders. Given the opportunity, he felt he could build on the progress made. But, when one's Bishop makes a request he thought it best not to decline. In 1990, he had leave coming to him and three months at home, he felt, would help break his ties with Mufulira.

As always he enjoyed holidaying in Drumaroad, despite the fact that he was limping and still had occasional trouble with his right foot. On his way back to Zambia, his suitcase was ripped as if by a knife, but nothing of value was taken. At Lusaka airport, customs men charged him K4,400 (about £50) duty on a new radio, twice what he'd paid for it! Anyway, he was back and that was something to be grateful for.

By now, Bishop de Jong, no longer resided next to the cathedral but in a private house two kilometres away. The house, a pleasant bungalow, had been the home of an Irish building contractor, Tom Doran. 'Number 46' on quiet tree-lined Kabompo Road, had a good-size plot and another plot next to it on which Tom had begun to build a house but had left Zambia before completing it.

Dennis, six foot four inches tall, was a fine looking man. Speaking at his episcopal ordination, the President of Zambia, Kenneth Kaunda, joked that the ladies would be running after him on the pretext of seeking confession. Despite his size and prestigious office, he remained a humble man, available to everyone. Well-travelled and well-qualified, during his priestly studies in Rome he had gained licentiates in philosophy and theology. As well as speaking excellent English, he spoke Italian, Latin, German and some French. Having been raised in the Eastern Province of Zambia, his mother tongue was Chinyanja.

Owen quickly got to like "Father Bishop", as the Sisters called him, finding him kind, humorous, and prayerful. With just the two of them in the house, they ate and prayed together and, for relaxation, watched television, sharing an interest in the detective series "Inspector Morse" and in sport. When a rat appeared in the kitchen, they tucked their trousers inside their socks and hunted for it. The chase raised their blood pressure and their friendship to new heights. The rodent took refuge in the back of the refrigerator and made good his escape when the 'fridge was removed to the garden.

For the evening meal Mr Sakala, the cook, prepared the food and departed for home, leaving Bishop and secretary to do the wash-up. This domestic chore further cemented their friendship; they found it a good time for having post-mortems on the day's affairs. Writing home in October, Owen said he was getting on fine with the Bishop, the weather was hot and he had already lost some of the weight Sadie's cooking had put on him. October-November, just before the rainy season, is the hottest and about the only humid period in Zambia. Expatriates used to call November the 'suicide month'.

On weekdays at 8 am, Owen and the Bishop travelled together to the diocesan offices near the cathedral. They returned home for lunch and went again at 2.30 pm, continuing to work until 5.30. It was quite a heavy day for a seventy-year-old with health problems. Nevertheless, Owen took on extra pastoral work as well. On weekends, he went to a shanty compound called Nkwazi and, during the week, said Mass for various congregations of Sisters. Whenever asked, he gave retreats. Another task he took on was proof-reading *Speak Out,* a monthly magazine for youth. Founded by Pat Byrne in 1983 to counter prolific 'Born Again' and 'Watchtower' literature, it was now being managed by Sr Connie op, another admirer of Owen.

As Owen got to know him better, his admiration for the Bishop grew. A convert to Catholicism, Dennis had an unusual background. Born in 1931 in a small village near Chipata in the Eastern Province of Zambia, then Northern Rhodesia, he was the first-born of five children. His father, Edwin Adrian de Jong, a motor mechanic, was the son of a Dutch settler. In Chipata, Edwin, a coloured man, married a local woman. Edwin and wife were members of the Dutch Reformed Church and, in his early years, Dennis received a strict Calvinist type of up-bringing. He attended primary school in Chipata from Sub A to Standard VI.

In 1946, when it was time for him to do Standard VII, he could not get a place in Northern Rhodesia where secondary schools were for whites only. Eventually, he managed to get a place in St John's mission school for coloured children in Salisbury, Southern Rhodesia (Harare in Zimbabwe). This school was run by German Dominican Sisters of the same congregation as the Sisters in Ndola. Dennis was one of its most impressive pupils and, on completing secondary in 1950, he remained on as a student-teacher. By this time he had converted to Catholicism and wished to become a priest. Bishops were not keen to accept him for their dioceses as seminaries in Africa then were exclusively for 'whites' or for 'blacks'. Finally, Mgr Francisco Mazzieri of Ndola, influenced by the Dominican Sisters, agreed to take him and sent him to Rome for his studies. He was ordained priest on 20 December 1958 in Rome. Studying for another year in London, he gained a Diploma in Education. On return to Zambia, he was appointed to the staff of Francisdale Minor Seminary of which he became rector. In 1967, Bishop Nicholas Agnozzi, Mazzieri's successor, made him his Vicar General. When the Minor Seminary closed in 1969 for want of teachers, Agnozzi appointed him administrator of the cathedral, a post he kept until he became bishop.

Inevitably, Dennis, a 'coloured' man, often felt 'different' and isolated. He had not shared the camaraderie of seminary life with other Zambian priests and, on taking up pastoral work was virtually a stranger to his colleagues. He had to learn Chibemba as if he were a foreigner, even going to Ilondola to do a short course. Though his Protestant background also made him feel different, there was a positive side to it as Owen noted: he had a convert's zeal, an ecumenical spirit, and a great love for Scripture. Being something of an outsider, Dennis readily empathised with the marginalized, the poor and the handicapped. Commenting on his leadership Owen said, "He was a bishop who tried to put the ideas of the Second Vatican Council into practice and was more of a counsellor than a commander of his flock".

Dennis learned to live with the difficulties minority groups often experience, but being coloured did not make things easy for him. Not long after his episcopal ordination, for instance, he went on a pastoral visit to Tug Argan military camp outside Ndola. At the gate he was refused entry. He felt hurt and embarrassed. However, he might have been over-sensitive. In the Seventies, in neighbouring Southern Rhodesian, the struggle for majority (black) rule was raging. Freedom fighters camped in Zambian territory and the war often spilled over to the Zambian side. Hence, it was a time of tension and strict security. Subsequent to the Bishop's bad experience, a local black priest, Edward Mumbi – the first Zambian Dennis ordained – was appointed to Tug Argan, but he too was denied entry!

In the Seventies, telephones and even fax machines were available in the Bishop's house. Though expensive, Owen occasionally phoned home. Mary Joe Laverty, his feisty cousin in Drumaroad often phoned him. Normally it was the Bishop who answered and, as Zambian time for half of the year is two hours ahead of Irish time, it was usually very late at night when Mary Joe's call rang in the bishop's house. Dennis didn't complain. Owen did, but Mary Joe rang anyway.

The Bishop knew Dromaroad and had met Owen's family and relatives. In the summer of 1978, he had made a courtesy visit to Ireland, to see SMA superiors, the archbishop of Tuam, apostolic groups, and relatives and friends of missionaries working in Ndola. Gerry Hanna, his treasurer, met him in London and escorted him on his four-week tour of Ireland.

Before calling on the Maginns, Gerry let Tom and Sadie know that the Bishop was coming. Nearly panicking at the thought of an unknown African bishop visiting, they went to as much trouble as if it was Owen himself who was coming! At the appointed time, Gerry for 'divilment' left Dennis, who was dressed casually, knock at the door while he hid around the gable end of the house. Sadie was just finishing buttering scones when she heard the knock. On opening the door, she thought the tall stranger with the brown complexion was another travelling salesman come to bother her. She told him to be off, "I'm expecting a black Bishop from Africa". Gerry then appeared and told her who the salesman was. Sadie and Tom entertained him as best they could but weren't really enjoying the experience even though Dennis did his best to put them at ease. To make matters worse, Gerry excused himself and left them alone with him.

*

In 1991, Zambia held its first multi-party presidential and general elections since Independence in 1964. For twenty-seven years, Dr Kenneth Kaunda and his United National Independence Party had ruled the country. This time, he was opposed by Frederick Chiluba, a popular trade union leader, and his Movement for Multi-party Democracy. Election fever rose as 31 October, the day of the election, approached. Violence was feared but, fortunately, was avoided and, as the votes were counted, it became obvious that Chiluba had won a landslide victory. Kaunda stepped down – the first time a country in Africa experienced a peaceful transition from virtual dictatorship to democracy by means of the ballot box.

*

Major changes were also taking place in the Society of African Missions. In December 1991, the Superior General, Fr Paddy Harrington, brought these changes 'home' to the confreres in Zambia. In Ndola, he presided over a meeting in the Regional House on 31st of December. PJ Gormley, Regional Superior of Kenya, Tanzania, Zambia and South Africa, Fergus Conlan, Society Superior in Zambia, eleven confreres, and two Irish students on a year of pastoral experience, attended.

Fr Harrington proposed that the recruitment and training of local men for the SMA begin in Zambia. The idea seemed contrary to the Society's long tradition of working to build up the local church rather than itself. But, first mooted in 1983, the project was already well under way in other African countries, and also in India, the Philippines, and Poland. The decline in vocations in Europe and America dictated that the Society recruit elsewhere or face extinction. Joseph Hardy, a former Superior General, had visited Zambia in 1985 to introduce the project but had received a negative response from the confreres then.

Fr Harrington, giving a brief account of how the existing foundations were doing, said that already six houses of formation were up and running in Africa and currently training ninety-one students. The Zambian confreres, discomfited by this speedy progress, argued that the SMA unit in Zambia was very small and was not long in the country. The local Church in Ndola, still far from being self-reliant needed all the vocations it could get for itself. Countering this, the Superior General said he had already spoken with the Bishop and he was not at all opposed to the project, the Bishop had asked only that the Society would help train local vocations as well as SMA ones. Owen spoke up, and most of the confreres agreed with him when he

Owen and A. McCrystal with D. Toal, N. O'Regan and P. Harrington

said that he would not have a problem accepting Zambian members into the Society, but he did not see how the present small SMA group could spare personnel for recruitment and formation work. PJ Gormley noted that the majority were in favour of the project even if there were still some matters to be clarified. Obviously, Fr Harrington had carried the day, the members reconvened after lunch to select a sub-committee to start the 'African Foundation' in Zambia. Brian O'Kane[1], Donal Toal, and Sexton Doran were chosen.

After the excitement of the Superior General's visit, the confreres settled down to routine again. For Owen, a drawback of living in the Bishop's house was that he missed SMA company. The confreres, especially the leaders had, since the beginning in Francisdale, excelled in hospitality and, no matter how hard-fought discussions were, the welcome, the meals, and camaraderie were always first class. Owen often found himself alone. Dennis had been President of both the Zambian Episcopal Conference and the Association of Member Episcopal Conferences in East Africa and so was frequently away at meetings in Lusaka, Nairobi, and Rome. Also, fund-raising tours often took him abroad frequently. He went especially to "the shrine of St Mark" in Germany. The German diocese of Limburg was particularly supportive.

On leave in the summer of 1992, Owen spent most of it in Drumaroad, but attended two days of Sr Briege McKenna's month of 'Intercession for Priests' in All Hallows College, Dublin. The inspiring Carmelite, subsequent to being cured, apparently

Martin and Jennifer Savage, Clanvaraghan

miraculously, of paralysis, under obedience to her superior had taken on an apostolate of healing and of intercession for priests. She appeared to have uncanny insight into priests' lives. Owen liked the way she and the large group prayed, but he didn't go for a private session with her! Always tending to be analytical, he considered the talks, accompanying Briege's own lively sessions, "ultra-conservative". They were given by a Capuchin, Benedict Groeschel, a leading figure in the renewal of the order in America. "A marvellous communicator", said Owen, "but his theology was basically that of Butler's *Catechism*".

Owen returned to Ndola on the 16th of September in time to say goodbye to Dennis who was departing on the 20th for a hip operation in Vienna. Dennis was not enjoying good health; apart from hip trouble, he had high blood pressure and diabetes. His many responsibilities and frequent travelling probably weren't helping. Saviour Chishala, a young Zambian priest, would live with Owen while the Bishop was away but, after a few days, he was found to be suffering from meningitis and was removed to the Mine Hospital in Luanshya.

When on his own, Owen made a point of going to the SMA Regional House for Sunday lunch. The new Regional House, no longer at Francisdale but on Sheila Dare road in Ndola, was quite near the squatter compound at Nkwazi where he said Sunday Mass. When the Regional Superior, PJ Gormley, was 'on seat' there was plenty of news from the far-flung corners of his extensive region but, with so much ground to cover, he too was often away.

When Owen got to know Nkwazi better he wished he was thirty years younger, there was so much an energetic young man could do. A Sacred Heart sister, Liz Mooney, involved in health care in Nkwazi, asked him to visit a poor woman, Bernadette, who was covered with sores from head to toe and in great pain. Owen asked her, "What can

I do for you?" She replied, "Pray with me". Impressed by her faith, he sat with her on many occasions, praying quietly. Despite her sufferings, praying with Owen brought her great peace and consolation. He was always gentle with the sick and gave them as much time as they wanted. He saw the role of a priest as one who brings the love of God to people and did his best to practise this himself.

In order to help out, in April 1993, he agreed to take St Charles Lwanga parish, Chipulukusu, from the Regional, PJ Gormley. Chipulukusu was a large site-and-service township on the east side of Misundu Road, 6 kilometres from the centre of town but nearer to the new regional house. The lower end of Chipulukusu was a sprawling densely populated shanty town. The whole area had about 20,000 people of whom 2,000 were Catholic. Sexton Doran had built a new church there in 1975. "Kalolo Lwanga", as the people called it, was the first church blessed by the new Bishop. The following year, Mick O'Shea was assigned to it as parish priest. When, in 1980, he was appointed to the national seminary, St Augustine's, near Kabwe, Noel O'Regan and other SMA priests looked after it until Owen took it. Shortly after this, Owen and Bishop Dennis moved into their recently completed house on the plot at 48 Kabompo Road.

Dennis's state of health reminded Owen that he was ageing himself. In October he would be seventy-three and, in December, he would be fifty years a priest. He guessed the confreres would make a fuss, which he didn't want but would have to go through. The Provincial Superior, John Quinlan, invited him to celebrate the Jubilee in Cork with the other seven surviving members of the class of '43. Owen felt the trip home for just one day wasn't justified so he respectfully turned down the offer. Ironically, the first of his class to fall seriously ill and the last to get to Africa, he was also the last remaining there.

Golden Jubilee 1993

The SMA fêted Owen's jubilee in the regional House on the 8th of December, feast of the Immaculate Conception and Foundation day of the Society (1856). Practically all the confreres, even the distant ones in Kabompo and those in another new mission, Zambezi, even farther away, attended.[2] Only Mick Igoe who had fever and a recent arrival, Bob Hales[3], a member of staff of St Augustine's Seminary, were unable to travel. Bishop Dennis was guest of honour. Ambroz, now the 'Custos' or 'Guardian' of the Conventuals, and Ben Henze wf, who 'gate-crashed' on the excuse

Golden Jubilee, with Bishop de Jong

that he was the one who used to put brandy in Owen's coffee when he visited the White Fathers, also attended.

Owen was chief celebrant at the Mass and Sexton Doran, celebrating his own thirtieth anniversary of priesthood, preached. Papal blessings were presented and messages of congratulations were read. A sumptuous six-course lunch preceded some witty speeches which, Owen said, "while not very truthful, weren't very hurtful either".

In his homily, Secky pulled out all the stops in praise of the Golden Jubilarian. "He canonised me thrice over" said Owen. But he excused his Loughinisland neighbour as he, Secky, had just finished preaching a retreat to "the Bishop's widows" (not their real name – a lay group Dennis had founded) and, "as with jet lag, it takes a few days to get back to normal". The Bishop spoke too and, according to Owen, was more truthful. He said, "Since Fr Maginn came to live with me, I have learned to wash dishes!"

The Provincial Superior and the Superior General, both of whom had been students of Owen in Dromantine, sent their best wishes. John Quinlan, recalling Dromantine days said, "Not only did you bring a breath of fresh air to our lives but humanity and humility too. You were real and not just a part of the system. You showed understanding and compassion without ever presenting the soft option. And you had a sense of humour!" Paddy Harrington wrote, "Your personal example of faith, commitment, and enthusiasm for mission spoke much louder than the tomes of theology we were invited to read. We admired your indefatigable energy and ability to get things done. Thirty years later, in different circumstances, we see the same qualities in evidence".

*

Christmas was a busy time for parish priests. Owen, with Chipulukusu and a rural outstation, Chikumbi, on hand, was as busy as anyone. Often the last priest to get home, he never rushed his parishioners; he was there for them and stayed as long as they wanted him. Christmas Eve Mass in Chipulukusu was a long and lively celebration. The church in festive garb glowed with the light of candles and paraffin lamps; the large nativity crib near the altar was animated by a live Madonna with her newborn child. The singing, drumming, and dancing made the wooden pole church vibrate as the packed congregation swayed in time to the music.

Christmas Day was very nearly tragically spoiled, particularly so for Fr Tom Faherty[4]. As he was returning home after saying Mass in Bwana Mkubwa, armed men, attempting to steal his car, fired a shot through the door wounding him seriously in the thigh. Managing to drive on, he got medical assistance from an Irish nurse, Liz Shone. He was

Tom Faherty with Michael Joyce,
Owen in background

detained in hospital for a couple of weeks and after a few months made a full recovery.

On 26 December 1993, Mgr Abdon Potani, the bishop of Solwezi died. Much to the surprise of Noel O'Regan, who was not working in Solwezi diocese, he was appointed Apostolic Administrator. Noel worked in Kabompo, in the diocese of Livingstone, where the SMA began in 1991. There he had learned Luvale, and a little Lunda – languages which were spoken in Solwezi district. While these were a help in getting started as Administrator, he soon realized that he had inherited a huge area with few priests, and a great number of problems.

Thrown in at the deep end, Noel got down to work and persevered. His efforts did not go unnoticed; in 1995 Rome nominated him bishop of Solwezi. His episcopal ordination took place in Solwezi on the 10th of December. The Pro-Nuncio, many bishops, the President Frederick Chiluba, confreres and many other priests and people attended. Two days

10th December, 1995, Solwezi

previously, the new house of the 'African Foundation' near Kabwe, 180 kilometres south of Ndola, was officially opened. Despite the distances (it was about a seven-hour drive from Ndola to Solwezi), Owen travelled to both events.

*

In 1994, Owen went on home leave. He felt physically tired and spiritually needy. In August, he went to the Jesuit retreat centre called 'Manresa' on the shores of Dublin bay. The retreat began with a proposal that the participants individually reflect on God's personal love and care for them. Owen made notes, "God has brought me to where I am despite many sicknesses". He accused himself of, "Failure to appreciate what I had – especially parents and friends". He acknowledged that, despite failures such as being unwilling to accept his weakness, he was loved by people and by Christ. He asked himself, "How strongly did love of God motivate me?" and answered with the words of St Augustine, "God was within me and I sought Him elsewhere". The theme of another day was 'Being loved by God'. "How conscious was I of God's love?" Owen asked himself and, putting his answer in parenthesis, wrote, "Maybe deep down".

He realized that God was continuing to call him – just now to come aside for a while and be with Him and, later, to go out and be with others, sharing their sufferings and endeavouring to bring them to Him. In another talk, the director asked the retreatants to meditate on the words Jesus addressed to his disciples, "What are you looking for?" Owen, unable to meditate calmly, went for a walk in the nearby public 'Rose Garden'. The roses and the grounds were magnificent. After walking, he returned to Manresa and sat on a garden seat. It was a beautiful day, "A sense of God's Presence in nature seized me, I found him there". His favourite religious poem came to mind:

233

I see his blood upon the Rose
And in the stars the glory of his eyes
His body gleams amid eternal snows
His tears fall from the skies.

I see his face in every flower
The thunder and the singing of the birds
Are but his voice – And carven by his power
Rocks are his written words.

All pathways by his feet are worn
His strong heart stirs the ever-beating sea
His crown of thorns is twined with every thorn
His cross is every tree.

Owen loved this poem of Joseph Mary Plunkett, the twenty-eight-year-old patriot executed after the Easter Rising of 1916.

Meditating on the story of Bartimaeus, the blind man in the Gospel who begged Jesus to restore his lost sight, Owen asked himself, "What have I lost?" and answered, "My vision, idealism, innocence, zeal, sense of service, and desire to open the Kingdom to others". Recalling that Jesus said to Bartimaeus, "Your faith has saved you", Owen hoped his own faith would save him, but still he wondered, "In what kind of manner do I follow Him?" Acknowledging that disability can be an excuse for inactivity he admitted, "Often I hide behind it". "Do you want to be made well?" Jesus asked the Bartimaeus. Owen put the same question to himself, "What do I want? Am I afraid of the demands a cure might make on me? Or the price I would have to pay?" His answer he put in parenthesis, "Dying to self".

*

While Owen was on leave, Bishop Dennis appointed a recently ordained priest of the diocese, Alick Banda[5], as his private secretary. Owen accepted graciously his involuntary retirement. He approved of the Bishop's policy of indigenizing important posts and, if he felt a little hurt at being replaced, he didn't say so but, he was pleased by Dennis's request that he remain in the house and continue to be a companion and counsellor.

1. Brian O'Kane, forty-nine, from Omagh, arrived in Zambia in 1986 after working in Nigeria and Ireland.

2. The SMA took on its new mission in Kabompo, Livingstone diocese, over 700 kilometres from Ndola in June 1991.

3. Bob Hales, sixty-five, from West Cork, taught in Mpima Seminary (St Augustine's) from 1993 to 1996.

4. Tom Faherty, thirty-one, from Galway, did a year's pastoral 'stage' in Zambia 1984-5 and returned after ordination in 1988.

5. Alick Banda, born in Mufulira 1963, was ordained priest in August 1994. He served as secretary to the Bishop until 1997 when he was sent to Germany for further studies. After gaining a doctorate in Canon Law in 2002, he returned to Zambia. Parish priest and chancellor of Ndola diocese, in 2007 he was nominated Bishop of Solwezi.

Chapter 15

FINAL YEARS 1994-2006

With Alick Banda installed as confidential secretary, Owen's work was now mainly in the parish of Chipulukusu, and its rural outstation, Chikumbi. As he got to know the parish better, he realized that it had a large population of young people who had neither the benefit of secondary school nor place of employment. Cautiously, he took on youth work and, to his surprise, discovered he was quite good at it. With the help of Zambian Dominican Sisters, he organised events for the young, mainly games and sports, interspersed with some instruction.

At Chipulukusu

In September 1994, a new confrere, Don Burke from Waterford, arrived. He was assigned to learn Chibemba and Zambian pastoral ways with Owen. Don, sixty-one, already had spent twenty-two years in Nigeria and eight in Poland. In Nigeria he learned Yoruba and was nicknamed 'Olufemi', 'God loves me'. In Poland, he learned Polish and changed his name to 'Casimir', the patron saint of Poland on whose feast he was born. In Zambia, finding Chibemba more difficult than Yoruba or Polish, he remained 'Fr Don'.

Penitential Rites, as a new form of 'confession', were becoming popular. Ever ready to try something new, Owen announced that he would hold one in Chipulukusu on the Saturday before Christmas. The parishioners were eager. Though it was the rainy season, it was dry for a week up to the day of the Penitential service. Then the

Chipulukusu children

heaven's opened and torrential rain fell all day. The gravel roads became quagmires, mud block houses collapsed, and all who could stayed indoors. Owen, Don and another priest turned up to hear confessions but, only seven of the two thousand parishioners braved the weather. Unlike the priests, they didn't have cars.

In 1994, Owen again wasn't feeling well. After writing a provisional will pertaining to any money and property he had in Zambia, he went on leave hoping that doctors in Cork might be able to do something for him. The will he wrote before he left indicated his mood and thoughts at the time, it began, "If anything should happen to me during the summer…" Apart from his car which he willed to Bishop Dennis, he left whatever he had to be disposed of by his superior in Zambia.

In Cork he underwent medical tests and treatment but, on return to Zambia, said the doctors hadn't done anything for him. His poor state of health prevailed throughout 1995. Age, as well as old complaints, was beginning to tell. He couldn't do all he wanted to but, apart from the considerable amount he was doing, he was unselfconsciously playing a new role – that of a 'wise elder', who gave good advice or an honest caution to younger confreres and others. Many went to him for guidance and counselling; he was widely regarded as a prayerful, sensible, 'man of God'.

He went on leave in June '95. This time the salubrious air of Co Down and Sadie's 'home-made' soup reinvigorated him. One of the highlights of this leave was meeting old friends, in particular, Gerry Nolan, whom he had known since they were both pupils in the Red High. Now the retired headmaster of a Catholic school in

At Legananny Dolmen with Joe McGowan and Gerry Nolan

England, Gerry was also holidaying in Co Down. Adding to the group of old friends was Mary, Gerry's sister, home on holiday from York, USA, with her husband Joe McGowan. The three men posed for a 'historic' photo taken by Mary at the 5,000 year old Legananny Dolmen high on the mountains near Slieve Croob. His friends asked him why he wouldn't retire into some easier job in Ireland. He answered that he thought he could do more good in Africa, "I'm needed there". The following year he accepted the McGowan's invitation to visit them in America. While there he went on a retreat in Malvern, Pennsylvania, with Joe and his two sons, Dan and Christopher.

Mary said that Owen adopted the McGowan family and when her daughter Rosanne was diagnosed with cancer and had to have successive operations, Owen prayed constantly for her and offered Masses for her recovery. "I am sure that is why she is active today and doing much better", said Mary. "Owen was always there for me and the family. If I had a problem, I'd phone Zambia and he always managed to put things in perspective. He was a priest devoted to family and friends and concerned about their welfare".

On his way back to Zambia in September '95, he stopped off in London to visit his niece, now called Sr Colette Therese, who was working with the elderly in Isleworth. Having met her in Drumaroad during the summer, he felt that she was not too happy in her vocation but she did not seem inclined to talk about it.

At the Bishop's house, he found that Dennis was just back from South Africa where he had been to welcome Pope John Paul. With a chuckle, Dennis mentioned that the Pope seemed a little shocked at the sight of 'topless' dancing girls in an offertory procession. Owen thought it might inspire His Holiness to write an encyclical on liturgical dance.

During 1995, Owen and Don, perturbed by poor attendance at catechetical instruction sessions in Chipulukusu, cancelled the scheduled visit of the Bishop to confer Confirmation. Another problem was simmering over the use of what the parish council called "out-of-date catechetical books". A more serious problem had to do with finance. At a meeting with the parish council, Owen angrily expressed criticism of poor account keeping. His outburst occurred at the first meeting of a newly elected council and, understandably, they took umbrage. The following month he made a formal apology in writing, admitting that he had no right to speak the way he did. However, denying that he had called them "thieves", he explained that if they did not keep proper accounts they would leave themselves open to being called that. Finally, he informed them that the one responsible for the parish was no longer himself but Fr Don. Owen then concentrated on the outstation in Chikumbi.

In November 1995, he gave an eight-day retreat to the Dominican novices in Ndola and, in December, another one to the Little Sisters of Mary Immaculate in Lusaka, "Since my retreats, the Sisters are flying without wings", he joked. Hoping to encourage his niece, Colette, to confide in him, he wrote to her saying he was doing a lot of counselling, adding, "I'm good at it". His premonition about her vocation proved correct. The following year, she left the convent, at first temporarily, but then permanently. Owen wrote advising her that if there was a man in her life she should make up her mind quickly about him as she was no "spring chicken". Before long there was a man in her life, Richard Nuttall, a chartered accountant from North Wales.

Owen took leave a little early to officiate at their wedding in Manchester on 29 May 1999. His nephew, another 'Owen', gave the bride away as Tom, Colette's father, was very ill. Sadie and Richard's parents were there. At the reception, Owen gave the 'father of the bride' speech and congratulated Colette saying, "You got a good one!" "And he did too!" she responded.

*

The Superior General, accepting that the confreres in Zambia didn't have men to spare for formation work, went to the Netherlands in September 1993 and persuaded two retired Dutch confreres that their 'desired future' was waiting for them in the new African Foundation house in Zambia. Wim Jansman and Bernard Wieggers, former missionaries in Ghana, arrived at the beginning of February '94. The new formation house was located in a residential area of Kabwe, called 'Dallas' where a hostel to accommodate sixteen students and a chapel were being built. Dallas was just 8 kilometres from the national major seminary St Augustine's, Mpima where, after their preparatory year, the SMA students would go for philosophy. The first students, Gustave Mukosha and Joseph Banda arrived in March '94. By September '95 there were four more. The house was blessed and officially opened on 8 December '95 by the Pro-Nuncio, Giuseppe Leanza, assisted by the new Superior General, Daniel Cardot, and the

Irish Provincial Superior, John Quinlan. By this time, Bernard Wieggers had returned to Holland and Wim would follow him before Christmas. Mick O'Shea, back in Zambia since October, had taken over the running of the house.

Owen attended the opening at Kabwe and went there again the following March to give a Day of Recollection to the students. That day he was the harbinger of sad news: Brother Brendan Murray sma had died suddenly of a heart

B. Murray (on right) with J. Dunne, W. Jansman, J. Banda, M. McCabe and G. Mukosha

attack the day before in Ndola, 7 March '96. He had suffered heart trouble in Nigeria where he had worked for nineteen years. He expired on the way to Dr Eileen Keane's house, where Don Burke, with whom he was living, was bringing him. Owen, a friend of Dr Eileen and her community, the Holy Rosary Sisters, was at the house when Don and Brendan arrived. Brendan, fifty-eight, from Dublin came to Zambia in 1994 and worked especially with youth and handicapped children in Chipulukusu and Kansenshi. He was the first of the confreres to die in Zambia. His requiem Mass was celebrated in the cathedral by Bishop Dennis and, afterwards, he was buried in Francisdale cemetery.

Following his Day of Recollection, Owen began a faithful association with the formation house in Kabwe, returning every year up to 2001 to give the students their annual week-long retreat. His timetable was always much the same: two talks in the morning followed by interviews with each student about vocation and prayer. He expected them to do at least two hours daily private prayer. Mass was at 5 pm and, after supper, he led a Holy Hour. Private confessions, or a penitential service, were held towards the end of the week.

Always interested in the progress of the young Dominicans and Franciscan Conventuals, he gave them courses in spirituality as well as retreats. In the Franciscan Centre there was an international group of sixteen young novices aspiring to the Franciscan priesthood or brotherhood. Owen spoke to them on vocation, discipleship, and the kingdom of God. He stressed companionship with Christ and a filial relationship with God the Father.

Silver Jubilee of the SMA in Zambia, 1998

On 27 January 1998, in the new regional house, on Kuomboka Avenue not far from the Bishop's house, the confreres celebrated the Silver Jubilee of the pioneer confreres' arrival in 1973 with a special Mass and get-together. Bishops Dennis de Jong and Noel O'Regan, and all the confreres attended. Of the thirteen pioneers of the first year, five still worked in the country, Secky, Mick Igoe, PJ, Mick O'Shea, and Noel. Seven had departed; Paraic Kelly, invalided home in '86, was in a home appointment for the time being. The Provincial Superior of the Dutch Province, Ton Storcken, was present – a number of Dutch confreres and an associate priest member from Ghana, John Affun, were working in the country. Among other guests were Frs Tiziano and Miha from the Franciscan Centre, Ben Henze wf, and Sr La Salette shjm.

For the occasion, Owen was asked to give a commemorative talk. In it, he praised Sexton Doran, the first leader, and Mick Igoe his assistant, for the high quality of their leadership, dedication, example, hospitality and humour. He thanked Bishop Agnozzi, who received the SMA, and Bishop de Jong who put such trust in them. He praised

Jubilee 1998: D. Toal, T. Storcken, Bishops de Jong and O'Regan, M. Igoe,
Standing: O. Noonan, M. O'Shea, PJ Gormley, Owen, Secky, J. Smele (NL),
J. Horgan, D. Burke, P. Monahan, W. Zijlstra (NL), F. Conlan

the other congregations in the diocese with whom they worked:
Franciscans, White Fathers, Dominicans, Sisters of the Sacred Hearts
of Jesus and Mary, Holy Rosary, and Charity Sisters. He did not forget
the many teachers, nurses, builders and business people, many of them
Irish, who had befriended and helped the confreres in the early years.
The four priests from the archdiocese of Tuam received a special word
of praise for their generous and fruitful collaboration. And, ever
grateful to the major hosts – the people of Zambia – he said that in the
past twenty-five years, the country had remained free of serious
political conflicts and wars, in fact it had been "an island of
tranquillity" in a very troubled region. "Here we have been free to
preach the Gospel without hindrance".

Warming to his subject, Owen said the SMA had contributed greatly
to the diocesan building programme, listing the many churches, halls,
and extensions they had built. Even more important was their
contribution to the recruitment and formation of diocesan priests to

whom they had duly handed over parishes. He gave the example of Kabushi where in the Seventies the confreres had worked, not only in Holy Cross, the main parish, but in other centres like Ndeke, Lubuto, and Mushili, all of which were now busy parishes run by Zambian priests. Likewise, the confreres had helped build up lay and religious communities by retreats, seminars, vocation clubs, prayer groups, and development activities.

He regretted that the early apostolate of full-time teaching in secondary schools had almost disappeared. Of the early teachers, only PJ Gormley had continued. Aodhan McCrystal before his departure had been involved in school and chaplaincy work; Sexton Doran was currently teaching religious knowledge and doing secondary and post secondary chaplaincy work in Luanshya. Otherwise the teachers had either left, been transferred or, had embarked on the, apparently, more attractive field of pastoral work. Owen paid tribute to Fergus Conlan, from Barr near Dromantine who, since his arrival in 1986, had made a tremendous contribution to the apostolate of youth, justice and peace.

Believing that "our faith demands that we be optimists", Owen stressed the positive in the SMA's first quarter century in Zambia. The highpoint of achievement, he said, was reached by 1989, the year John Paul II visited Zambia. After that, departures of confreres and diversification to North Western Province (Kabompo-Zambezi) depleted the team in Ndola diocese so much that Chimwemwe parish in Kitwe and Kamuchanga in Mufulira had to be handed back to the Bishop and, apart from Sexton Doran in Luanshya, the confreres were once again working only in Ndola town and in Francisdale.

Disclaiming that he was a prophet, Owen said that the future lay with the 'African Foundation' but, loathe to relinquish totally his critical bent, he asked, "Is the traditional seminary type of formation really preparing priests for the needs of today?" He thought the answer was

"No", though the recently introduced 'spiritual year' for diocesan students and the period of pastoral work before ordination were, steps in the right direction. Finally, he appealed to the members who might still be around for the second twenty-five years, "Be united in your convictions and united in your love, with a common purpose and a common aim" (St Paul to the Philippians 2,1).

Chikumbi

Shortly after Mick O'Shea began working in Chipulukusu, he took on four outstations in rural Ndola. The nearest one was called 'Martyrs of Uganda', Chikumbi. There, he and the parishioners built a permanent church to replace the existing small mud-block chapel. In 1991, Noel O'Regan, then in charge, began the construction of a medical clinic, a felt-need in an area far from hospitals and lacking public transport. Serving a large hinterland, including villages on the Congo side of the border, the clinic would cater for a scattered rural

Chikumbi church

population of over 10,000 people. When Owen began working there in '93, the number of parishioners had increased considerably and he thought the church should be enlarged but, first, he turned his attention to the clinic, work on which had come to a standstill since Noel's departure.

Owen began to look for financial assistance from the fundraising agency 'Misereor' in Germany and from other sources. From '93 to '96, the work proceeded at a snail's pace. Nineteen-ninety-six was a particularly bad year for building. During the rainy season, the roads to Chikumbi became impassable, lorries bringing materials got bogged down, and work on the site was impossible. Owen, frustrated, grumbled, "Like the Temple in Jerusalem, it could take another forty years to finish".

He described Chikumbi as, "Something like Drumaroad, only flatter, dustier, poorer and more religious (if possible)". He got to like the parishioners, most of whom were subsistence farmers. Poor as they were, they were generous in giving their labour free of charge and supporting the priest with the produce of their gardens. Owen appreciated this but was often driven to distraction by delays in the construction work, "I've been suffering from fits of madness bordering on insanity, sleeplessness, and temptations to murder".

Resident in the area were two men who were very active in Zambian public life, David Mulenga, a land clearing agent and building contractor and Ben Kapita, a farmer. In 1994, Mr Mulenga was Mayor of Ndola and, in 1996, Member of Parliament for Chifubu. Ben Kapita was leader of a farmers' party, called the 'Lima Party' and, though it did not get into power, he became Minister for Agriculture and Fisheries in President Levi Mwanawasa's government. David Mulenga had been Chikumbi Parish Council Chairman in Mick O'Shea's time and he still was in Owen's time with Mrs Kasama and Ben taking over for interim periods. Now, Ben was the Chikumbi clinic 'Project Chairman'.

The drive from Ndola to Chikumbi, about 20 kilometres, took one over high ground, appropriately called North Rise, to Misundu affording a panoramic view over the low-lying swampy hinterland of Chipulukusu and the arable land of Chikumbi–Lubendo. Not far beyond in a northerly direction, was 'bush' and forest where the Zambian border with the 'Democratic Republic of Congo' lay. On leaving Ndola, the road was tarred for a few kilometres but pitted and pock-marked with pot-holes of elephantine dimensions. Further on, it became a gravel road liable to flooding in the rainy season.

On his way to Chikumbi one day, Owen witnessed a sensational electric storm and waxed eloquent when writing about it to his friends the Cochranes in Clanvaraghan, "On the 8th of December, I went out to the parish for an evening Mass. On the way I thought I was in Heaven. The sun was shining over a wide area and on the horizon on every side there were dark clouds pouring rain. In the middle of Mass, a terrific storm arose – thunder, lightning and a ferocious wind. It blew open the main door of the church and whipped up a large strip of linoleum and laid it at the foot of the altar. I couldn't even hear the choir singing and that says something for they have mighty strong voices. The storm partially passed after half an hour but we had to curtail our celebration. The roads on the way home were a foot deep in water. The storm had swept towards the Congo but fire balls were darting out from the flashes of lightning".

He was lucky to get home without mishap that day. On Christmas Eve, another year, he got stuck on the same flooded road and the engine cut out. Fortunately, the first person to come along was a mechanic. He got Owen going again and the Christmas Vigil Mass, though late, was able to proceed. After the long celebration, final blessings, and seasonal greetings all round, Ben Kapita, worried about Owen's safety on the bad road home at night, kindly offered to accompany him. Owen wouldn't hear of it and drove off 'in high doh'. Ben followed in his car at a discreet distance. Owen drove fast; Ben had difficulty keeping him in sight. Owen negotiated the flooded section, taking care not to let his engine stall. Once out of it, he increased speed. Ben, wondering what was making him drive like a hornet, kept after him until Owen stopped at the gate of the Bishop's house. Ben rolled down his window and bade him a cheery 'Happy Christmas'. "Well, you d____ fool", retorted Owen angrily, "I thought it was thieves who were following me! Go off home now and if you get stuck, don't call me!"

The spectacular display the heavens put on the day Owen was caught in the storm moved him to write a poem. Though a lover of poetry, like many shy dabblers, he was not keen to expose his talent; this is the only poem of his that has come to light. Sr Connie, for whom he was proof-reading the magazine *Speak Out,* came across it. The typescript is headed, "A poem by Fr Owen Maginn on a silk-painting by Sr Judith Johanning" (superior of the Dominican Convent).

> *A rainbow clasps a world chaotic*
> *Violent colours on a silken background running*
> *Trespassing on each other*
> *Disfigure the sign of promise*
> *String out branches*
> *Bear life holding leaves*
> *Aimlessly stretched unentwined*
> *While life-giving waters flow to nowhere*
> *Encircled by decreasing coloured rings*
> *A white host broken*
> *Symbol of Christ's body*
> *Like a ray of light*
> *Bends earth and heaven*
> *Bespeaking peace and hope*

The poem contains the themes of nature and religion and climaxes in the great animators of Owen's life, the Eucharist and Christ. While plateau-top Zambia is not especially noted for landscape, its 'skyscapes' are often spectacular: rich azure depths, brazen sunsets, starry heavens, racing storm clouds and enormous double or even triple ringed rainbows. The Misundu Road is an advantageous location for witnessing the vaulted beauty of sky and distant horizons.

While skyscapes inspired him on the road to Chikumbi, more mundane affairs affected him in the Bishop's House. A new domestic help, unaccustomed to electric irons, left a red hot one on the seat of his best Downpatrick trousers, "Sorry to say, there's no seat in it anymore", he reported. The laundress did something similar with his only smart shirt, rendering it 'armless'. Another time, the cook saved wash-up liquid in a water jug on the draining board. Returning tired from a long Sunday Mass, Owen made tea with it! "I was belching all afternoon and thought I'd be blowing bubbles by supper time".

He wrote home about a fellow parish priest's attempt to dramatize Jesus's entry into Jerusalem on Palm Sunday. The innovative pastor rode a donkey in the triumphant procession. All went well until near the church door something unsettled the donkey. Bucking vigorously, it threw the would-be messiah on the ground and galloped into the church. The priest, limping, had to be carried in, while the donkey, braying, had to be carried out.

Chikumbi clinic was finally completed in 1997. For a while it was the jewel of rural clinics with ten beds, running water, electricity, and four good staff houses. On the 27th of November it was officially opened and handed over to the Ministry of Health. The list of invited dignitaries was long and included Bishops Dennis de Jong and Noel O'Regan, David Mulenga MP, Senior Chief Chiwala (who had granted the land), Dr Nkanda Luo,

The new clinic

deputy minister of health, and many more. Owen had hoped that he would be on leave when the opening took place but, delays in completing arrangements meant he was back in time. Such affairs were not his cup of tea, "They largely consist of Government ministers taking credit for things they didn't even know existed". Ben Kapita, giving the welcome address, thanked the VIPs for coming, the funding agency Misereor for their support, and the parishioners for their work and contributions. He thanked Owen for taking on the work and for his "great sense of humour which kept spirits burning through the times of difficulty and frustration".

With the clinic completed, Owen turned his attention to the church. His plan was to knock the walls around the sanctuary, build two sizeable transepts and enlarge the sacristy. The extension would nearly double seating capacity and provide an office and meeting rooms. David Mulenga's firm did the building and, with few delays, the work was completed by April 1998.

Difficult times in Zambia continued through the late Nineties. In nineteen-ninety-eight, the rains failed completely, drought and starvation affected 135 districts in the country according to official reports. On top of this, eighty-four percent of the people were living in poverty, malnutrition was widespread, and infant mortality was very high. AIDs, malaria, and tuberculosis were rampant. At this time, Pope John Paul honoured Zambia by making Archbishop Adam Kozlowiecki a Cardinal. Adam, a Polish Jesuit who had arrived in Northern Rhodesia in 1948, was the first bishop of Lusaka. Owen, forgetting his own age, said that as the new Cardinal was an octogenarian and a survivor of Dachau and Auschwitz, "he probably won't do much harm".

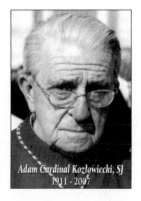

Adam Cardinal Kozlowiecki, SJ
1911 - 2007

Actually, Adam was still quite active in a rural mission near Kabwe, while Owen, though active, was still quite ill. Nevertheless, Owen pushed himself to perform the Christmas 1998 and New Year ceremonies and, joking about the state of the country and his own decrepitude said, "The next life can't be much worse".

Like many other dioceses in the country, Ndola was suffering from serious financial problems; Bishop Dennis wondered how he might stem rising debts. "He worries a lot about money", said Owen, "It is the main topic of conversation at dinner and supper and sometimes at breakfast too!" Dennis went on a two-month fund-raising campaign overseas, especially in Germany.

In November 1999, Owen and confreres enjoyed a retreat given by Fr Tony Butler sma who travelled from Ireland to direct the Zambian bishops' annual retreat and give some seminars. Owen noted with particular glee some of Tony's witty sayings: "Religion is for those who are afraid of going to Hell; spirituality is for those who have been there". One Tony didn't share with the Bishops was about Church leaders, saying they might better be described as "crooks with their staffs rather than as shepherds with their sheep". Recommending giving voice to all members of a community, including 'senior citizens', Tony quoted an elderly missionary who, on being asked, "Are you being retired?" answered, "No, re-threaded".

In December, the Vicar General of the Society, Kieran O'Reilly came from Rome and presided over the two-day Regional Assembly in Ndola. Owen found his talk on 'Mission in the 21st century' absorbing. After question time, subjects like the new foundations, Society structures and, as Owen put it, the "unpredictable future" were discussed. At the time, Owen, still 'home alone' in the Bishop's house, was glad to share in the camaraderie of the Assembly. The confreres' Christmas Dinner, enjoyed on the 8th of December, was a beautiful meal cooked by a recently arrived confrere, Kevin Mulhern from Derry city, a former chef.

At the Assembly: K. O'Reilly, Owen, D. Toal, J. Horgan
Standing: S. Doran, T. Butler, Rathnam, PJ Gormley, D. Burke, TT Simon,
J. Smele, P. Monahan, K. Mulhern, TJ Anthony, F. Conlan, M. Igoe, M. O'Shea

In the millennium year of 2000, Ndola experienced bad storms. The Bishop's phone and fax machine were hit by lightning and remained out of action for months. Owen felt 'cut off' more than ever. Apart from this, he suffered from a bad septic throat which took a long time to heal. It also took him a long time to live down the aftermath of an 'apparition' in his parish. Having been informed that a communion host had appeared miraculously on the wall of a private house, he went to investigate. Parishioners on their knees were praying quietly when he arrived. Impressed, he prayed with them for some time. At lunch, he told the Bishop what he had seen and heard. The Bishop was not at all pleased and reprimanded Owen for lending credence to such phenomena. Dennis was proved right in this case as it was later discovered that someone had glued the host to the wall!

Naturally, Owen and Dennis didn't always see eye to eye on everything; some of their discussions devolved into protracted arguments even in the presence of secretaries. Usually it was Dennis who gave in or let the matter go. However, the Bishop 'used' Owen in his own way, not only to sound out ideas, but to do awkward tasks for him. One day, the Bishop was asked to cast out an evil spirit from a man who was acting strangely in the cathedral. Dennis passed the buck to Owen. Owen entered the church through the sacristy, collecting stole, holy water, candle and book on the way. Standing in front of the altar was an agitated man with a crazed look in his eyes. Owen prayed over him and blessed him with holy water. As soon as the water touched his skin, the man leapt high in the air, fell to the ground and started rolling at great speed down the main aisle to the other end of the church. On hitting the door he reversed and rolled rapidly back to the front. Owen prayed some more and, avoiding sprinkling water on him, blessed him, calmed him somewhat and sent him off.

In February 2001, on his way to give the SMA students in Kabwe their annual retreat, Owen, once more found himself in high water. Eighteen kilometres north of Kabwe, the Mulungushi River was flooding over the only bridge to the south. Earlier, a mini-bus had been swept away and two passengers drowned. Cars were piled up on either side. When Owen got there, the rain had ceased and the water level was going down. He waited saying the sorrowful mysteries of the rosary. A big car on the other side edged onto the bridge and succeeded in crossing. Other cars began to move. Not to be outdone, Owen started his car and swung out but, concentrating on the bridge, he didn't notice the big Zimbabwean truck just about to pass him. He 'brushed' into it, slightly denting its mudguard. The driver insisted that they go to the police otherwise he'd be blamed for the damage. The nearest police post was in Kabwe.

At the formation house in Kabwe, Mick O'Shea was very worried. Owen was long overdue. Mick had telephoned the Bishop's house and was told that Owen had left after lunch "without even taking siesta" and should have been in Kabwe long ago. Mick had two 'scouts' on the main road to check for Owen's approach as, on previous occasions, he had overshot the turn-off to the house. The two students, Edmund

Mick and Owen at Dallas

and Simeo, eventually saw a charcoal grey Toyota approach with the black-berried retreat master behind the wheel. As they flagged him down, they wondered why a big truck pulled in behind him.

The students accompanied Owen and the truck to the Central Police station. There, the police told Owen, "No problem, all you have to do is sign this form admitting dangerous driving, pay a fine, and you can go". Owen, outraged at the idea that he had been driving dangerously, refused to sign. The officers sighed and explained that if "Sir" would not sign, then he'd have to be detained and await trial. As darkness had fallen and the cells didn't look inviting, Owen finally gave in.

It was nearly 8.30 pm when he arrived at the formation house. The first thing he said to Mick was, "What time does the retreat start?" "Normally at 8.30", said Mick, "but you can start tomorrow morning". "We'll start as usual" said Owen with that determined look which brooked no opposition. After a talk which lasted nearly an hour, he returned to the Fathers' house, admitted he was a bit tired and agreed to have a cup of tea, but first he'd like a hot whiskey.

With the dying

Dr Eileen Keane, a Holy Rosary sister from Limerick, came to work in Zambia in 1991. One of the first she met in Ndola was Owen who took her on a tour of his pastoral areas. After visiting her convent, he agreed to say a weekly evening Mass for the Sisters. These Masses were always followed by a cup of tea and a chat. On the first occasion, Dr Eileen remarked that he shouldn't take so much sugar in his tea, "four spoons are too much!" Owen added a fifth and stirred it noisily. A friendly, combative relationship developed between them. Eileen, quickly realizing that no matter what she said, Owen would oppose it, began to start conversations with the opposite point of view from what she really believed. Discussions became minefields but, both of them enjoyed the tussle.

Eileen was a consultant doctor in Ndola Central Hospital where Owen often went visiting the sick or bringing ill parishioners. Even the seriously ill were frequently turned away from the hospital, or were kept only overnight, because of overcrowding and shortage of beds. Owen brought one sick man five times, only to bring him home again each time. Eileen told him that Ndola's greatest medical need was a hospice where the dying could receive palliative care. She ardently wished to found such a hospice herself. In 1996, she made a start, setting up the 'Ndola Ecumenical Hospice Association' with herself as secretary and Sr Philomena, a Dominican, as chairperson.

She established a board of trustees of which Ben Kapita was a prominent member. Owen joined the Association and gave it every support he could. Meetings were sometimes stormy, Ben often appealed to Owen, "What does my friend say on this?" Owen, as long as he wasn't the one who started the row, was quite good at diffusing tension among others.

Ben Kapita

Fund-raising received a significant boost when the Lions Club of Ndola made a large donation which, added to funds Eileen had collected from home, enabled her to make a start. An old dilapidated beer hall in Lubuto was bought, and re-constructed with male and female wards for twenty-five patients. On 'opening day', 8 Sept 1999, Owen said Mass in 'Cicetekelo' (Trust) Hospice as it was named, and blessed it. After Mass, he anointed the hospice's first patient, Theresa, who died four hours later.

Beginning the hospice

First Mass at the Hospice

As Sr Eileen and her staff got into a routine, Owen offered to visit and say a weekly Mass for the patients and staff. Apart from Eileen, Sr Alice (an Irish Sister of Charity), a driver and a nurse, there were thirty-seven voluntary caregivers. Every Friday, after early morning shopping for the Bishop's house, Owen went to say 10 o'clock Mass at Cicetekelo. Usually, the first person he met on entering was the nurse, Mrs Stephanie Mpabulwani RN. He discovered that she was the wife of the young man, Patrick Mpabulwani, who had re-written his Baptism Register in Twapia a long time back. Patrick was now a Ndola District Councillor. On

Friday mornings, Owen greeted Stephanie with a smile and asked her, "What's Sister-Doctor Keane's mood like today?"

Patients and their carers gathered in the hospice chapel for Mass. Most of the caregivers, practically all women, belonged to the organisation known as 'Home Based Care'. Caring for the extremely ill patients was difficult work. Often the carers had to put in long hours as most of the patients needed twenty-four hour attention. Yet the caregivers were not paid. Owen said, "I see Christ in them and in what they are doing, more than in what I'm doing". He raised some funds to give them a small stipend and a monthly bag of mealie-meal. Later, Dr Eileen managed to give them some training and a small subsistence wage.

By Friday morning, Owen had already prepared his Sunday homily for Chikumbi, so he liked to try it out in the hospice. Eileen, knowing how little stamina her patients had, told him his sermons were too long; Owen wouldn't shorten them. After Mass, he went around

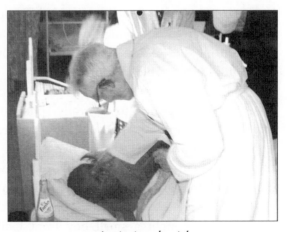

Anointing the sick

the wards, praying with individual patients, anointing those who needed the sacrament of the sick, baptising those who requested baptism, and hearing confessions. After this, he gave the thirty-seven caregivers a catechism class.

Sr Alice (Maguire) first arrived in 'Northern Rhodesia' in 1957. In 2001, after many years in Southern Province and in North Western Province, she was appointed to Ndola. Among other duties as 'pastoral caregiver' in the hospice, she prepared patients for reception of the sacraments. She instructed those who wanted baptism as best she could, but Owen sometimes complained, "They don't know their prayers". Alice smiled, "They're dying, how can you expect them to remember prayers?" Often, after Owen left, she and Eileen baptised those whom they knew were dying and had requested the sacrament.

Owen, declining in strength himself, used to say Mass at the hospice sitting on a chair. It reminded Alice of the old Dutch chaplain at Maheba refugee camp in North Western Province who used to say, "Jesus sat at his first Mass so why shouldn't I?" Owen's voice was becoming weaker and he found it difficult to swallow, even the sacramental bread and wine. Sometimes during Mass he'd have to stop. During these pauses, the sympathetic congregation would sing a hymn until he was able to continue.

Whenever he appeared to be really spun out, Alice would ask the driver to take him home. Owen always refused and, gathering energy from God knows where, would drive himself. "He had a Rolls Royce engine in a Tin Lizzie body", said Alice, giving a very appropriate description, though she wasn't aware of his Ford-Detroit background.

One day he brought a small boy from Chikumbi to the hospice. 'Masuso', about eight years of age, had an open wound on his back which would not heal. He adopted Dr Eileen as mother and Owen as father. Despite the sore, he was cheerful, attended the local primary school and learned to speak English quite well. Eileen persevered in her efforts to heal his back and eventually succeeded. He was then 'transferred' to the school Sr Philomena had founded in Twapia.

Owen also had a 'joking' relationship with Philomena.   From Germany, she had learned her English in Westminster while cooking for three successive Cardinals: Godfrey, Heenan, and Hume. A feisty woman, she was well able to exchange repartee with Owen and wasn't at all fazed by his "holy temper". Speaking of his concern for children, she mentioned, Joyce, a seven-year-old girl who had club feet. Owen took her for medical attention and agreed to pay for a remedial operation. After surgery, she began to walk and, over the following months, made great progress until eventually she was able to walk, even without a limp. The surgeon waived his fee.

Death of Bishop de Jong

In the summer of 2003, two Tuam priests, Paddy Williams and Paddy Costello, who had been working in the Copperbelt in the Eighties made a short return visit to the diocese and spent some time with Owen.   In reply to a letter of thanks from Paddy Williams, Owen wrote to him in September. It was a significant letter because in it he spoke of Bishop Dennis whom he had found dead the previous week.

"Dear Paddy, You probably know by now that Bishop Dennis is dead. I found him lying in his bed when I returned from Mass at 7.30 am on the morning of 17 September. The two of us normally went out for Mass at 6 am on Tuesday mornings. He didn't go on that day but I thought that he might be taking a rest as he had a meeting in Lusaka that morning. When I came back and saw the driver sitting outside, I suspected something. I rushed to his room, called his name and shook him gently. There was no response. He was lying like a child asleep. I phoned Sr La Salette to come immediately and the Cathedral to get a doctor. The word spread like wildfire and within twenty minutes we were swamped with callers.

The family and the Bethany Sisters took over the house. It became one centre for a *cililo* (wake). The Cathedral became the centre for the 'hoi polloi'. People came in their thousands. There were continual prayers going on in the Cathedral.

It would take ages to recount what went on. I will mention only two things. Firstly, the body had been brought to Ibenga Hospital. On the way back to the Cathedral on Friday evening, the streets of Luanshya were lined with people. There were groups all along the route, particularly round Twapia, crying 'Our Father has been taken from us! The Shepherd of the Poor has gone!'

Secondly, Ndola was impassable that evening. There was an all-night vigil with a Mass celebrated by Archbishop Medardo Mazombwe of Lusaka. I was sick in bed but I went to the funeral Mass on Saturday morning. It was held in an open field behind the Dominican Convent. Some of our men reckon that there were over 100,000 people there. The Nuncio was chief celebrant. Everything ran smoothly. No pushing, no screaming. Great reverence. It was very moving. I can't praise the Zambian Fathers highly enough for the work they did, or the people for the respect and love that they showed.

Dennis was a great man. It is only now when he is gone that we realise it. The people did. And Paddy, I miss him very much."

Dennis, the bishop of one of the most important dioceses in Zambia, up to his death remained a simple, humble man with neither a personal bank account nor possessions of any value. In his will, made in 1990, he left his pension fund to the community of widows he had founded, his vestments to the cathedral, his episcopal insignia to his successor, his books to the diocese and his personal clothing to the poor. In a postscript, he asked to be buried in Francisdale cemetery in a simple, poor man's coffin without a concrete slab. (In the event, after his sudden death, the interim diocesan administration decided to bury him next to the cathedral beneath an engraved memorial slab.)

As he sat alone the evening of the funeral, Owen recalled that the night before Dennis's death, they had watched football together on TV until quite late. Now the house felt very empty, a 'Bishop's house' without a bishop. Fr Patrick Chilambwe, the Apostolic Administrator, did not reside in 'number 48' but next door in 'number 46'.

Speculation arose as to who would be the next bishop. Chilambwe was a strong possibility but he wasn't the only one. Dennis didn't have a coadjutor or auxiliary bishop and hadn't appeared to be grooming any one in particular for the office. Thinking of his own situation, Owen wondered whether he should remain in the Bishop's house. As no one else seemed anxious to move in, he thought it best to stay to keep an eye on things, at least until the new bishop was appointed.

Sixty years of priesthood

Owen celebrated the diamond jubilee of his ordination on the 19th of December 2003. Sharing in the celebration that evening in the Regional House, Fr Doran celebrated his 40th anniversary. Flanked by Secky and Sr Charity Nkandu, a Franciscan, Owen cut his jubilee cake. A good number of clergy and religious attended. Ambroz came from overseas and local lay friends including Ben Kapita and wife were present. Fergus Conlan, the regional superior, preached. During the after-dinner speeches, Owen was once more the focus of praise. "A lot of nonsense" he said and, in his own few words, he simply thanked God for a long and happy life as a priest. At midnight, feeling he'd 'suffered' enough for the sake of fellowship, he made to depart, only to find that his car had a flat tyre – a deflating experience after so much praise!

No one came to live with him. A neighbour from Co Down, Colette McCartney, a nurse working with the FMDM Sisters[1] in Chingola took to visiting him. She tended his ingrown toenails, and tried a bit of reflexology on him. Owen thought the latter great fun but, if Fr

Chilambwe came in, he would quickly pull his socks up! Noticing that he found it difficult to swallow, Colette regularly made jelly for him. From Hilltown, near Dromaroad, she had plenty of 'local' chat. On a few occasions, she accompanied him to Chikumbi and Twapia. In Chingola, with the Sisters, she worked for the 'under fives' and helped establish a care centre for orphans.

Owen always took good care of his car. He kept it well groomed and got it serviced at Mr Desai's garage, possibly the best and, probably, the most expensive in town. Owen got the car insured overseas and, as windscreens are vulnerable on gravel roads, he took out extra insurance on his windscreen. However it was rear windows that were Owen's nemesis. On New Year's Day 2004, returning from Mass at Chikumbi with two passengers on board, he passed a fast-moving cyclist. As he did, one of his passengers shouted, "Stop! Let me off here!" Owen braked hard. The cyclist (who hadn't had his brakes serviced by Mr Desai), came through the back window head first. He suffered a gash on his head and was bleeding pretty badly. Owen took off his own raincoat, a good one, wrapped it around the man, and took him to Casualty at the Central Hospital where he was detained.

Owen reported the accident to the Police who required him to bring an officer to the scene of the accident for on the spot investigations. Next morning, Sr Alice who had heard of Owen's 'accident' went to the Police station asking where he was. Four policemen shook their heads sorrowfully, "He parked illegally, Sister, he's in the cells!" Seeing how upset she became, they relented, "No, don't worry, he's at home. We won't be locking up your friend this time!" Relieved, she raced to the Bishop's house where she found Owen drinking tea. When she told him she'd been to the police he asked dryly, "Did they have my raincoat?" Earlier in the morning, he had gone to the hospital to visit the patient but found he'd been discharged, "He was gone and so was my raincoat!"

Things had gone reasonably well for Owen in 2003 but, his New Year's Day accident of '04 began what he called an '*annus horribilis*'. While waiting for a new back window to be installed in his car, he borrowed an old one. On its 'maiden voyage' – to Desai's to get it checked – it broke down and subsequently gave him numerous problems including six punctures!

Tired and feeling the burden of his eighty-three years, he was not looking forward to the heavy Holy Week ceremonies at Chikumbi. But, to his relief they went well, "Thanks be to God, I enjoyed every minute of them including the four kilometre walk to the church on Palm Sunday when the people turned out in large numbers".

After Easter, he felt the emptiness of the Bishop's house getting in on him. Someone told him that the reason others didn't want to reside there was because the Bishop's spirit might resent it. At first he thought this was nonsense, but with his New Year accident and the punctures, he began to think there might be something in it. While parish affairs continued on a good note, news from home was not good, his brother Tom was seriously ill and in decline. Owen, hoping to have the summer with him, planned going on leave after the ordinations of two new Zambian members of the SMA, Peter Makasa and Benedictus Nshikita on the 19th of June '04. Peter and Benedictus were the next two Zambian members of the SMA after the 'pioneer' Gustave Mukosha who had been ordained in 2002.

Once at home in Dromaroad, Owen spent all the time he could with Tom who had been moved downstairs into Owen's parlour. He was weak but patient and resigned. Owen was very grateful to Sadie and the family and to a neighbour Maureen King for the care they bestowed on Tom. He appreciated too the frequent visits of Fr Moley the parish priest, and many others who were so good to Tom. "The best brother one could ever have" died in Owen's presence on 21 September, a few days short of his eightieth birthday. While missing him greatly, Owen felt relieved that Tom's sufferings were over.

At Tom's requiem Mass, Owen chose for the Gospel reading, the Sermon on the Mount explaining, in his homily, that the Beatitudes summed up Tom's spirit and each one of them found an echo in his heart. He had failings like everyone else but, "Even his failings leaned to virtue's side" said Owen quoting Oliver Goldsmith's *Deserted Village*. Tom was buried next to Mark, Annie, and his sixth child Martin, in Drumaroad cemetery.

*

Owen was no sooner back in Zambia in October than, ending much speculation, Rome, transferring Bishop Noel O'Regan from Solwezi, appointed him as the new bishop of Ndola. More populous than Solwezi, Ndola diocese from many points of view was a more onerous responsibility. As a successor in Solwezi had not been named, Noel had to administer both dioceses. He was officially installed in Ndola's cathedral of Christ the King on 13 November 2004 in the presence of a large congregation including nearly all the Ndola diocesan priests as well as members of the African Missions. When he took up residence in 48 Kabompo Road, he assured Owen that he wished him to continue living there.

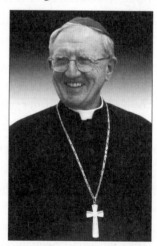

Bishop Noel O'Regan sma

Now eighty-four years of age, Owen found that many things took him longer to accomplish – even siesta. After lunch, he retired to his room, switched on the radio quite loudly to listen to the news and promptly fell asleep. When Noel installed satellite TV, Owen took to watching it after lunch until 3 pm, and only then did he go for siesta. The new bishop greatly appreciated being able to discuss problems with him and valued his advice. Noel observed that Owen never asked for any special consideration either for his age or health but, even if a bit slower, was as keen as ever to be doing something useful.

Owen took on a new role in Ndola Convent as occasional invitee for the senior pupils in a faith sharing exchange. Sr Judith, the Convent superior, observed that in his "earlier years" he could be a stickler about doctrine but, in later years, he mellowed and was able to admit that there were other ways of looking at things besides his own. He said Mass in the Convent every Tuesday morning and occasionally took the first teaching period with Sr Rosemarie and other teachers of the senior Catholic pupils. Always obliging and open to new things, he fell in with whatever they wanted – Mass, 'creative' Penitential Services, or discussions. In the convent proper, he conducted regular sessions of praying with and anointing the sick.

In the Kabompo Road house, the new bishop was struck by Owen's prayerfulness. Besides regular spiritual exercises in the oratory, he spent a lot of time walking up and down outside praying the rosary, "He struck me as being in close union with God". They recited the Office together as Owen used to do with Bishop Dennis. When it was Owen's turn to choose a hymn for Night Prayer, he favoured Gerard Manly Hopkins' *Pied Beauty* or *God's Grandeur*, Cardinal Newman's, *Lead, kindly Light*, or Francis Lyte's *Abide with me*. Noel and Owen got on very well together and Owen was glad to have someone in the house again, especially at night. But, as Noel was dividing his time between Solwezi and Ndola, he was often away.

Noel, needing exercise, had a small swimming pool dug in his garden. Game for anything, Owen was one of the first to try it. He pumped up the old car tube which had given him such trouble in the New Year and used it to keep afloat in the deep end. But, the infernal tube still managed to trouble him, poking him painfully in his not too well protected ribs. Finding it difficult to get out of the tube and then out of the pool, he didn't take to the waters again.

2005

Communication between Ndola and Drumaroad in the New Year of 2005 was difficult. The bishop's telephone was again out of order. Owen heard that Sadie was very down after Tom's death. To make matters worse she suffered an unfortunate accident in her own back yard when a car, reversing, knocked her down. Detained for a few weeks in the Royal Victoria Hospital in Belfast, on being discharged she telephoned Owen. This time the phone worked. To his surprise she was in very good form. Though she was the only Catholic in the ward, she said she had had a great time and made many new friends. "Just the therapy she needed", thought Owen, wondering whether something similar would work for himself. He was feeling exhausted and seriously thought he would have to throw in the towel and leave Zambia.

After Easter, he got a bad eye infection and was put on a course of antibiotics. Despite the way he felt, he decided not to go home in the summer fearing, that if he did, his superiors would not allow him to return to Zambia. He determined to persevere on the mission as long as he could drive. If he became too dependent on others he would leave.

In June, Bishop Noel undertook a few improvements in the house, including the installation of an *en suite* bathroom for Owen. Before the construction work was completed, Owen, alone in the house one night, was sitting on a chair in his room tidying some builder's rubbish on the floor. In the process, he slipped awkwardly off the chair hurting his collar bone, fracturing a rib, and knocking himself unconscious. It was after 3 am when he regained consciousness. Too early to telephone for help, he crawled painfully to bed and waited until morning to seek medical assistance. For a few days he could scarcely move.

Ironically, the day he fell, a South Down youth group, founded by Frances McNally in Castlewellan, arrived in Zambia. Owen's niece, Yvonne, one of its first committee members was treasurer; her daughter Aine was due to come with a second group in July. Owen

Yvonne McClean at Chikumbi

had been looking forward to showing them around, but now he wasn't able to.

He was somewhat improved by the time the second group arrived, which included his grand niece and Fr Sean Cahill, parish priest of Castlewellan. On telephone to Yvonne, he told her not to worry about anything as <u>he</u> was looking after everything. Yvonne's three children, Aine, Niamh and Aoife, in years past, had taken over their mother's role as Owen's Ludo and Snakes and Ladders opponents. In Zambia, he was more like a good friend of Aine than a 'grand uncle'. He managed to bring her and the group to Cicetekela Hospice where they were very moved by the Mass and anointing of the sick. On Sunday, he took her and Fr Sean to Chikumbi.

Another North of Ireland group familiar to Owen was 'The Friends of Africa', founded by Anthony Kelly[2] in Dromantine in 1998. 'FOA' volunteers, with experience ranging from construction work to computer skills came, one or two at a time, to work with the SMA for a year or more. As well as teaching and building they helped care for orphans and vulnerable children. Among them, were Suzanne Bradley, Angela Dougan, Louise Haigney, Conor McKay (the 'Singing Brickie' from Dromara, Co Down), and Rory Mullan. For all of them Owen was a friend and father figure with whom they found it easy to relate.

A cheering bit of news Owen received from the South Down Group was that a baby 'Joseph Owen', whom he had baptised at home the year before was doing well. The infant son of Cathal Steele of Clanvaraghan and his wife Clare had been named 'Joseph' after Cathal's father and

Clare, Cathal and baby 'Joseph Owen' Steele

'Owen' after 'Fr Maginn'. So pleased was Owen to have someone named after him that he usually reversed the baby's names to "Owen Joseph", his own names as written in his SMA file. Cathal Steele had spent two summers doing voluntary work in Kavu clinic near Francisdale, the first time as a medical student, the second as a qualified doctor. His wife was also a doctor. Their second child, Isabel, was found to have serious medical problems shortly after birth. Informed by Mary Steele, Isabel's grandmother, Owen offered Masses and prayers for the baby. Isabel made a speedy recovery against the odds, "a miracle baby" some said. And, though Owen was by no means the only one interceding for her, his prayers were particularly valued by the Steeles.

In 2005, Bishop O'Regan turned the Francisdale pastoral centre, which in years of straitened circumstances had been running at a loss, into a place of preparation for his diocesan seminarians. The first group of fifteen students began their 'preparatory year' in August under Frs Martin Bwalya and Evaristo Chisenga, assisted by a number of voluntary teachers including Owen. Rejuvenated when working with the young, Owen drove there twice a week, ignoring pot holes and corrugations on the dirt road which hadn't been graded since President Chiluba had driven that way to open the new Kavu clinic.

Students like Richard Mwila, Chanshi Oregan and Benjamin Muhongo[3] who had Owen as a teacher in Francisdale said they enjoyed his classes, "He was a cheerful man who laughed a lot; in fact he laughed at his own jokes more than we did!" He taught spirituality which he described as "a movement towards God" and prayers, like the *Memorare* "which became my favourite prayer", said Benjamin. "He got us to learn a poem which, he said, was very special to him, *I see his blood upon the rose / And in the stars the glory of his eyes*".

"His voice was weak but he used a loudspeaker. If he forgot it, he'd ask us to draw near so we could hear him. No matter what the weather was like, even when others failed to show, he would come. We asked him why he didn't get someone to drive him and he said 'I trust in God. He's looking after me. Whenever I'm to die, I'll die whether I'm driving or not'. If we had two classes with him, he'd take a break in the middle and have a cup of tea with the SMA Fathers, Reginald and Thyago[4] in the parish house. We found him good to talk to and he listened to our problems. After awhile we realized that the fastest way to get a problem to the Bishop was to tell Fr Maginn".

*

The 18th of October was Owen's eighty-fifth birthday. He celebrated Mass in the Dominican convent. Afterwards, the Sisters treated him to a birthday meal. During it, he stood to say a word of thanks. Recalling home and parents, he wept when he spoke of Mark.

Owen's 85ᵗʰ birthday with Dominicans, Regina and Laetifica

One Friday evening in November in Kabompo Road, watching television with Bishop Noel, Owen said, "There's something wrong with my left hand". Without realizing it, he had had a mild stroke. The following Monday, he suffered a more severe one. Doctors gave little hope of being able to restore strength to his arm. Unable to drive, he was compelled to let others chauffeur him. He wasn't happy with this and, when the Regional Superior, Fergus Conlan, suggested that he go home, at least for medical attention, he did not argue. Fergus booked a flight for him departing Lusaka on 27 December.

Paraic Kelly, since his return to Zambia in 2002 was the spiritual director of St Augustine's Major Seminary. On a Christmas break in Ndola, he drove Owen to Dola Hill, to celebrate the Christmas Masses. As always there was a big congregation for the vigil Mass. The ceremony was long, made longer by the parishioners' dramatisation of the nativity. Owen sat quietly through it all. Paraic led the concelebrated Mass. Afterwards, Owen said goodbye to the people. On Christmas morning they concelebrated Mass there again. The congregation was smaller, the elderly and the very young being the main participants. When all was over, Owen, standing at the entrance to the church, bade them farewell shaking hands with each one.

Owen with Hamish Cameron Smith

On leaving Dola Hill, Owen asked Paraic to drive him to the other side of town where a dear friend was very low, Hamish Cameron Smith, the architect who had designed the Twapia church extension. Since Hamish had become bedridden, Owen brought him Communion every Sunday on his way home from Mass in Chikumbi. After Hamish received the host, both men remained in silent thanksgiving for a long period.

Originally from Scotland and a non-Catholic, Hamish was a World War Two veteran and prisoner of war of the Japanese. In his earlier conversations with Owen he had become interested in the Catholic faith and eventually asked Owen to baptize him. On Christmas day 2005, the old soldier, now very weak, and the departing missionary bade one another farewell; there was little chance they'd meet again in this world. Ben Henze, had already agreed to take over Owen's weekly visit, but Hamish did not survive Owen's departure long; he died on New Year's Day.

Packing was always a major task for Owen. In Drumaroad, Sadie or his nieces did it. In Kuomboka, he instructed Mr Sakala, the cook, to do it but, when Sr Liz Mooney dropped by, he asked her to check the suitcase. "Is my family photo album in it?" he asked. Liz, finding a new empty one said, "Why are you bringing this home?" "Ah, that's not the one I want; my family album is an old brown one; try the wardrobe". She found it and passed it to him. He leafed through the pages, pointing out people and places. He paused at a photograph of Mark, "I loved that man", he said quietly. Liz returned the album to the suitcase noticing, beneath where she put it, a Christmas card from Hamish.

Though Owen's arrival in Zambia thirty-one years previously had been a pleasant experience, his final departure was difficult. 'Zambia Airways', under-booked for its early morning flight to Lusaka on the 27th of December, cancelled it. Owen would have to be driven the 350 kilometres to Lusaka to catch the BA flight to London departing at 9 am. Fergus Conlan and Tom Casey drove, leaving Ndola at 3 in the morning. Despite the inconvenience of the cancelled flight, Owen was in good form. Arriving in Lusaka at dawn, they called on the Holy Rosary Sisters for some breakfast. Dr Eileen Keane was there. Owen, able to move his left hand slightly, told her he thought he was getting better; as usual she didn't agree with him!

Fr Paddy Barry[5] accompanied him on the homeward flight. At Heathrow, Owen, in a wheelchair, was told he could wait in the first class lounge until his onward flight to Cork was called but his companion would have to wait outside. "Unless we can both go in", said Owen firmly, "We'll both wait outside". They arrived safely in Cork; unfortunately, somewhere, his cherished family album disappeared.

St Theresa's, Cork

The African Missions Society has a medical unit called St Theresa's at its Provincial headquarters in Cork where Sr Margaret Kiely and assistants look after seriously ill and incapacitated missionaries. As it has only thirteen bed units, new arrivals often have to wait in the larger retirement house until a bed becomes vacant. When Owen arrived the unit was almost full. He was given the last vacant bed in a two-bed room, which already had one occupant. After a day or two he wrote to Ndola to thank Fergus and the others for their assistance with his departure and to wish them a happy New Year. Always including a bit of news, he spoke humorously of his new circumstances: his room mate "snored like a volcano, the only chance I get of unbroken sleep is during Mass"; "another confrere, suffering from Alzheimer's disease, has jumped into my bed and is currently beating off the best efforts of three nurses and an ex-rugby player to remove him". The reception parlour was fitted out as a temporary bedroom for Owen.

2006

In January, he was seen by a specialist who put him on medication and physiotherapy. At the end of the month, he was admitted to the Bon Secours hospital where he came under the attention of Dr Nolan. After tests, the doctor confirmed, more or less what Owen knew already: loss of power in his left hand, a pain in his left shoulder, a history of hypertension and TB. An MRI scan indicated 'cerebrovascular accident'. The doctor judged that his 'chest pains' were of 'musculoskeletal' origin rather than cardiac. Overall, Dr Nolan thought he was doing alright and could be discharged.

Back in St Theresa's, he still had no power in his left arm, but was able to move about with the aid of a stick. He joined the larger Blackrock Road community for liturgy, meals and other activities, a favourite one being the Sunday evening get-together called a *Gaudeamus*, meaning 'Let us rejoice'. At it, he joined his Cambridge colleague, Jim McCarthy, and others for a 'happy hour' with a drink on the house. Jim and Owen were the last survivors of the class of '43. Jim, still in good spirits, was using a wheel chair for moving about but, unfortunately, was losing his eyesight.

As the New Year wore on, Owen relaxed more and even turned his (right) hand to some practical matters like applying for the non-contributory pension and procuring a new driving licence. His pension, backdated to January, came through in April and he received a new driving licence valid 'till 2008. Looking at his passport, which would expire in March, he decided to postpone renewing it for the time being. In his will, after disposing of his worldly goods (not many), he asked that <u>one</u> Mass be said for his intentions.

Archbishop Michael Francis of Monrovia, Liberia who, while campaigning for peace in his country, had become paralysed by a stroke was occupying a room in St Theresa's. When sufficiently recovered, accompanied by Sr Margaret and the vice superior of the house, Lee Cahill, a long-time missionary in Liberia, he was flown home to a state reception. Subsequently, Owen was given his room.

Winter was cold, but the house was well heated. Nevertheless Owen rarely left off his anorak even during a Holy Hour. For walking the long corridors of the house, he wore the anorak and his familiar black beret. Spring was the season he liked best, "When the countryside showed signs of new life and everything is so fresh and tender". Though the view from his window in St Theresa's could not compare with that of his parlour in Dromaroad, the sight of snow drops on the lawn reminded him of his walks around Shanbally when the hawthorn blossoms were in bloom.

In April, he was officially posted as "Retired in Blackrock Road". The Provincial archivist, Eddie Hogan, came to interview him. Owen, giving a cogent account of his life, work, and hopes for Zambia, accepted that he was retired but also said, "If I manage to get more power back I may be able to do some work. I couldn't imagine myself sitting quietly in my room for the rest of my life. I feel I am improving".

At a mid-week morning sing-song in St Theresa's organised by the house superior Damian Bresnahan, Owen, instead of singing, recited a long poem he had learned in primary school, *Barbara Fritchie*:

...Up the street came the rebel tread, Stonewall Jackson riding ahead,
Shoot if you must this old grey head, but spare your country's flag she said.

When he faltered, memories of Dan Fitzpatrick, or his cane, inspired him to continue and, skipping a verse or two, he continued to the end. By May he felt much better, but still had little use of his left hand. Four of the retired men in the house had died since the New Year, including his fellow parishioner, Jim Lee and another man from Co Down, John McCreanor. Hoping that his improvement would continue, he joined the confreres' annual retreat in Dromantine in July. The long journey from Cork by road took more out of him than he expected. Once the retreat was over he went to Drumaroad intending to spend some time there but, that very evening, as Sadie was climbing the stairs to her room, she missed her footing near the top and fell heavily. Badly hurt, she was moved to hospital where her right leg was set in plaster. Unable to be of any assistance, Owen returned to Cork the following day.

In Cork, he maintained a strong interest in world news, the Middle-East, the war in Lebanon, and anything to do with Zambia. He wrote to Bishop Noel, contributing some money for a project and enquiring about the cook and others. His handwriting was as good as ever. He got news of Zambia from Sexton Doran and Don Burke who were on leave. Ben Henze visited in August. On handing Owen a well-wrapped brown paper parcel, Ben saw the old smile light up on Owen's face as he recognized the four-cornered shape of a bottle of Bushmills.

Some 'Zambians' were already in the house, Willie Cusack[6], the former guest master of the regional house in Ndola and Mick O'Shea, who was temporarily at home finishing a book for the Society's 150th anniversary of foundation. Owen kindly read the proof copies of the book, *Bishop Kelly of Western Nigeria,* and made many useful comments. After it was launched in August, Mick returned to

Zambia. On the morning of his departure, Owen, in a wheelchair, came to bid him goodbye. Mick wondered if they'd meet again. Owen seemed to have the same thought.

Family and friends from Co Down and elsewhere came in great numbers to visit him. He grumbled if they arrived at an inopportune time, but then kept them for hours in conversation. Mary McGowan, Gerry Nolan's sister, visited him in August. Resident in America, she was on a short holiday in Co Down when she heard that Owen was ill in Cork. Accompanied by her niece, Maire, she flew to Cork. What a surprise she got on arrival at the airport to find Owen with Paddy Jennings of Castlewellan waiting for them. They had a pleasant day of reminiscing. Sadly, her brother, Gerry, had passed away in 1998 and her husband, Joe, in 2001.

Ironically, it was on the 18th of October, Owen's 86th birthday, that he became seriously ill. Nurse Colette McCartney from Hilltown and Dr Eileen Keane from Limerick had come to celebrate with him but, for once, he was in no form for company. That evening he was moved to the Mercy Hospital.

Dr Eileen continued to call on him. On her last visit, she found him reading, *A Different Journey,* the autobiography of Fr Brian D'Arcy, a Passionist priest, well known in Ireland. "Why are you reading that?" she asked. "I want to find out more about him", he replied. Owen's voice was weak, but his mind was as sharp as ever. "Look I've marked this bit where he talks about Jesus 'choosing life through death'. He says, 'I should not be afraid of death, because for the Christian, there is no other way to life'". The two argued a bit about life, vocations, and death. When it was time for her to leave Owen said, "I'm not afraid of dying but", he lifted his right arm and described a big question mark in the air, "My question is, WHO IS GOD?" Eileen, feeling a bit unprepared, hazarded an answer, "He is the one who has been looking after you all your life and has seen you through everything". Owen's face split in a grin and, chuckling, he blurted out, "That's the first true thing you've said to me as long as I've known you!" She left him, laughing his way to God.

Shortly after this, Owen sank into a state of unconsciousness which continued for nine days. Confreres and family members kept a twenty-four hour vigil at his bedside. On Sunday morning, 3 December, at 8 am, he died peacefully in the presence of his niece, Colette, and the Provincial Superior, Fachtna O'Driscoll.

Born on the feast of St Luke the Evangelist, dying on the feast of Francis Xavier the patron of missionaries, Owen was buried on the 5th of December, three days before the 150th anniversary of the foundation of the SMA. His requiem Mass was led by the Provincial Superior assisted by Edwin Mulandu (Ndola), Sean Cahill (Castlewellan), Zambian missionaries, PJ Gormley, Willie Cusack, Denis Collins, and thirty-seven confreres. Among the clergy present in the congregation were Fr Moley PP of Drumaroad and Clanvaraghan, Fr Tony Owens[7] from Lindisfarne, and many religious brothers and sisters including Sr Christine, a Zambian Dominican. A great number came by plane, bus, and train from Co Down. In the words of Ann Fitzpatrick, the headmaster's daughter, "We were there, not to grieve but, to celebrate the life of our fellow parishioner and friend, Fr Owen, the meditative priest we knew".

Captain Barry Studdart of the UN in Egypt and his wife Frances were there too.

Fachtna O'Driscoll preached, highlighting special characteristics of Owen: his contagious laughter, his genuine interest in people, and his ability to form friendships. "A unique and gracious character, in his near sixty-three years on mission, he brought many people to the love and knowledge of God. His death was peaceful, the mirror image of a life well lived. His epitaph might well be written, *He was one nice, decent, wholesome human being*".

1. Franciscan Missionaries of the Divine Motherhood, an international group, specialising in medical work.

2. Fr Anthony Kelly, Co Galway, the present Regional Superior, arrived in Zambia, after working in Ghana and Ireland, in 2000 aged forty-eight.

3. Richard Mwila, Benjamin Muhongo and Chanshi <u>Oregan</u> (called 'Oregan' after Noel O'Regan who baptised him), interviewed at St Augustine's Seminary in 2008.

4. Fr Reginald Nwachukwu sma from Nigeria, ordained in 2000, arrived in Zambia in 2003; Fr Thyagu Arputhnam sma from India, ordained in 2004 arrived November '04. Both departed for other missions in 2008.

5. Fr Paddy Barry, fifty-five, Cork city, after working in Nigeria and Ireland arrived in Zambia in 2003.

6. Fr Willie Cusack, sixty-six, from Dublin, missionary in Nigeria, arrived in Zambia in 2002.

7. Fr Tony Owens, a native of Drumaroad, is working in the English ministry; as a young man he was greatly encouraged in his vocation by Owen.

EPILOGUE

In his primary and secondary education, Owen profited from good schools. After six years of philosophy, theology, and seminary formation, he was sent to one of the best universities in the world. Subsequently, he was appointed to educational work in Egypt, and to lecturing and formation work in Ireland. In the 'second part' of his life, he opted for change – pastoral work in Zambia but, on taking a sabbatical, chose studies in a Roman university. Despite the high quality of all these, mainly academic, type of opportunities, he chose none of them when, towards the end of his life, he was asked what did he consider to have been the most formative influence upon him. Without hesitation, he clearly answered that it was the four years he spent in hospital with tuberculosis.

In the sanatorium, struggling to come to terms with his own cross, he became aware of the crosses of others. When undergoing tonsure at twenty years of age, he had sincerely dedicated his life to the Lord "my portion and cup". But, the "cup of the Lord" took on a form which, in the seminary, he never imagined would be his – the cup, or better the cross, of illness and weakness. In coming to terms with this, he became the priest he wanted to be – one who, despite signs to the contrary, felt and believed in God's love for him and for others.

Though a firm believer in the divine godhead, it was Christ Owen related to. In hospital he responded to a love affair with Christ; the suffering Christ captivated him.

At home, over the mantelpiece of his sitting room in Drumaroad, he hung a large copy of Salvador Dali's painting of the crucified one. In his bedroom, he hung a large reproduction of the crucifixion by Tintoretto and, near it, a woodcut of Christ in Gethsemane. The 'Crucifixions' stand out in his two rooms which contain few other pictures (an 'Assumption of Mary' by Tiziano and a couple of Zambian paintings).

Owen didn't wallow in suffering, go on about his own health or, in preaching or teaching dwell on Christ's sufferings. He enjoyed life, was interested in people, politics, world affairs, and sport. He lived an appropriately simple lifestyle but, loved a laugh, liked a drink, and had an infectious sense of humour. Christ, for him, was one who spread joy not sorrow. On earth, He *had* made a difference; Owen believed He still could through others.

Grateful that he was raised in the country, he remained a countryman at heart and retained a strong regard for nature and animals. Once, when he was home on leave, a worried farmer of Slieveniskey, whose cattle were dying of 'black leg' disease (five had already died), sought out the parish priest. Discovering that Fr Parke was away, he sought out Fr Maginn. Owen told him to gather the cattle in his corner field. Owen prayed over them and blessed each one in turn, marking them with the sign of the cross. No more died.

Owen's concern and healing prayer for people have already been mentioned, there are other cases and, without drawing any particular type of conclusions, they help us to understand the kind of priest he was and what he meant to people. Ill and worried people sought him out, asking for prayers and blessings. If they were unable to travel, he would go to them. Many attested that in some way he helped them.

Leontia, the six-year-old daughter of Mary and Dermot Maginn, Owen's nephew, was seriously ill. Doctors, thinking she might have leukaemia seemed unable to help her. During Mass at home in Drumaroad one day, in the presence of the little girl's parents and others, Owen prayed over her. She reported that she felt heat flowing from his hands. After a few days, she began to feel better; the doctors couldn't account for her great improvement.

In 2007, Ben Kapita, Minister for Agriculture and Fisheries, became afflicted with cancer of the spine and was unable to stand or even sit up. He was flown to South Africa, but doctors there did not hold out hope for him. Ben, a man of deep faith, insisted that he would recover, telling Dr Eileen Keane, "The doctors have given up on me, but I'm putting my trust in God and in Fr Maginn". He did improve and, since August 2008, though in a wheelchair, is back in State House as presidential aide for special projects.

A sociable man, Owen preferred community living to a solitary life. Feeling befriended by Christ, he wished to make Him known, or better known, wherever he worked and with whomsoever he lived. A simple Christmas card produced in the Mission Press, Ndola, made good sense to him. It consisted mainly of a quotation from Meister Eckhart, the Rhineland mystic, "What good is it to me if Mary gave birth to the Son of God fourteen hundred years ago, and I do not also give birth to Him in my time and in my culture".

Christ's gift of friendship, gave Owen a deep-felt motive and purpose in life, "To make a return for all he has done for me". St Paul's 'Caritas Christi urget nos', 'the love of Christ impels us', was Owen's inspiration. He impressed on young men preparing for priesthood, "If the love of Christ is not your motive, then you're going into the wrong vocation" and, "Your personal motivation should be to make Him known".

Younger confreres were sometimes surprised by Owen's liberal views for example on marriage for priests, "There were married priests before the twelfth century, why not again". Neither was he opposed to the ordination of women. For him, priesthood should not be tied to celibacy or gender but to the desire and need people have for the Eucharist. The Eucharist, for him, was the source and fountain of all priestly activity and the summit to which all his (or her) activities converge. Priesthood was not about authority but about service, the highpoint being the task and privilege of worthily serving people with the Eucharist.

Salient in his experiences as a young priest was the giving of Communion to a dying man on Good Friday 1944. The reverence with which the man received the sacrament impressed and affected Owen deeply and permanently. He had similar experiences throughout his priestly life and especially when tending the dying in Ndola. The reverence and gratitude with which extremely ill people received Communion constantly reminded him of Christ's presence, "The heart of my faith is belief in the Eucharist".

He nourished this faith by quiet time in prayer, "I feel the presence of Christ in adoration before the Blessed Sacrament. At times I feel his presence very strongly". At other times, he felt His "absence" and, like Jesus in Gethsemane, he then "prayed prayers of loneliness". Prayer was "essentially listening and waiting" even when, or perhaps especially when one is "uncomfortable and fidgety". Prayer is an "expression of yearning to be re-made in Christ's image".

Always and in all things, Owen was a man of deep gratitude. One thinks he may even have come to have been grateful for the terrible illness which made him weak (the weakness which made him 'strong in Christ'). He hadn't expected to live long, "I thought I wouldn't see forty; I've more than doubled that! I'm grateful. Death doesn't worry me. I haven't excluded Christ from my life. I see no reason why He shouldn't welcome me".

In 2009, the Society of African Missions commemorated the 150th anniversary of the death of the Founder on the coast of West Africa, 25 June 1859. Owen, without consciously 'imitating the Founder', reproduced in his own mission work some of Marion Brésillac's cherished aims and desires: 'primary evangelisation', mission to the 'most abandoned', and promotion of the local church. In Egypt, Owen's ministerial possibilities were limited but he did what he could, showing special care for those who suffered. In Zambia, in his parish appointments, he preferred small, less developed places to more developed ones and was especially concerned to start something for the un-evangelized. In his long service as secretary and counsellor-companion to two bishops in Ndola, and in his teaching Zambian Franciscan and Dominican novices and seminarians in Francisdale, he worked for the local Church. No matter where he was, he

The founder of the SMA

showed special concern for the poor and the sick. Appropriately, the parishes where he worked in Ndola were named after saints beatified for suffering in witness to faith in Christ: Twapia was called "St Stephen's" after the first martyr; Chipulukusu, "St Charles Lwanga" – the leader of the Uganda martyrs; and Chikumbi, "The Martyrs of Uganda". His parish in Kawama East, St Theresa's, was called after the young saint who died of tuberculosis.

De Marion Brésillac was surprised by death on the coast of Sierra Leone at the age of forty-six, forty-one days after arrival. Owen Maginn, after forty-six years in Africa, was surprised that he, Maginn, had lived so long.

Some sayings about Owen:

"A holy priest and educator, a courageous worker of charity and a tireless self-effacing servant of God, he merits the title 'saint' more than any other person I ever met". Ray Hazboun, Egypt and California.

"He was always ready with a smile to help someone in need. He walked with dignity as if an angel led his steps. Everyone's friend, he was a truly saintly man". Madeleine Hazboun, Egypt and California.

"I'm sure he doesn't need my prayers. He was just a saint". Rosaleen Laverty, Dunturk, Drumaroad.

"Nature's gentleman", Captain Joe Fallon, UN officer, Egypt.

"A holy man, a saint", Lily Russell, Clanvaraghan.

"When he blessed you, you knew you were blessed", Ann Valentine, Clanvaraghan.

"I am sure I was not alone in feeling that he was someone who had a real knowledge of and love for God", Siobhan Fitzpatrick, Drumaroad.

In 2008, Jacob Nuttall taking 'Owen' as his Confirmation name asked his Mum, "Who is St Owen?" She replied, "Your great uncle".

"He never neglected us in life, I'm sure he will remember us from his heavenly home", Mary McGowan, York, USA.

"When things are difficult, I turn to Fr Owen". Lily Cochrane, Clanvaraghan.

"He was an academic who had the common touch", Benedictus Nshikita, headmaster, Kamuchanga Primary School, Mufulira.

"A frail old man he may have looked, but he was not; even in his mid-eighties he was young at heart and strong willed", Susanne Bradley, Ndola.

"A thoughtful man; letter-writing was one of his gifts", David Mulenga MP, Chikumbi.

"He loved a tough debate", Fr Francis Katai, Ndola.

"He made friends, even among the most unlikely people", Anthony Kelly, regional superior, at Owen's Memorial Mass, Ndola, 2007

"He was one of the all-time greats. I don't think there is anybody in the Society of African Missions that he has not touched. I owe my presence here today to his fatherly care. In the seminary he looked so frail we thought he wouldn't last too long – that was forty years ago". Bishop John Moore sma of Bauchi, Nigeria, 4 December 2006.

"Sage and prophet, he reflected the love of Christ to us all", Tom Casey sma, Ndola.

ACKNOWLEDGEMENTS AND SOURCES

My gratitude is due to the Maginn family, especially Sadie (Owen's sister-in-law) and Yvonne and Colette, his nieces, who shared with me their knowledge of and affection for Owen, his home background, and allowed me to see his parlour and books. Yvonne, searching the internet, found many items which were of great use, including Irish and Detroit censuses, information on old Kilcoo, and on the RMS *Baltic,* its passenger manifest; and the book *Pioneers of the Faith* by Lt.Col. FJ Bowen (1935). She procured other useful books such as, *History of a County Down Townland, Drumaroad,* by Patrick J. Clarke (2004), and "Drumaroad and Clanvaraghan", by Rev Gerald Park PP (unpubd. 1985). On a few visits to Dromaroad and Clanvaraghan, I was kindly treated by Fr Peter Donnelly PP, parishioners, neighbours, and friends of Owen. Many shared with me their knowledge of Owen and the letters they received from him.

I am greatly indebted to Fr Tom Casey, Ndola radio producer, for allowing me to use the excellent set of six taped interviews he made with Owen in 2002. They covered Owen's life from earliest memories to final aspirations.

While a keen correspondent, Owen wasn't given to autobiographical writing or diary keeping but, in response to a general request for accounts from Zambian confreres of their lives and missions, he wrote a 'Brief History' (6-page typescript, Ndola, 2005).

Anthony Kelly, SMA Regional Superior, Ndola, following the Society's 150th anniversary of foundation in 2006 asked me to write a history of the SMA in Zambia, and facilitated me with documentation in the regional house. After initial work I decided to concentrate first on the 'grand old man of the Zambian mission', Owen Maginn.

Bishop Noel O'Regan kindly gave me access to Ndola diocesan records and Edmund Hogan, SMA Provincial archivist, Cork, facilitated me with archival material there; I also used his "Short Lives" of the Irish confreres and the 18-page transcript of his interview with Owen in 2006. I gratefully acknowledge the kindness of the Master and Fellows of Downing College, Cambridge University, and its assistant archivist, for facilitating me with the Cambridge file on Owen.

My SMA confreres "at home and abroad" narrated many a story about Owen with obvious relish and delight. Significant among the senior ones were Jim McCarthy, his room-mate in Dromantine and colleague in Cambridge, and John Creaven, a massive presence in the Irish Province throughout Owen's time. Jim, the last of the class of '43, and John, both died in 2008. Among other confreres were Jean-Marie Guillaume, Mossie Kelleher, Peter Thompson, Joe Maguire, Tom Fenlon, John O'Keeffe and Tuam men Paddy Williams and Michael Joyce.

Thanks to all my Zambian confreres, Ndola diocesan workers, lay and clerical, Dr Eileen Keane, Sr Carla, Sr Judith and many more Sisters of different congregations. Having known Owen myself since he was acting superior in Cloughballymore during my 'novitiate' in 1963, I have fond memories of him and, like many others, miss him a lot.

For relating their stories of Owen and other information, I'd like to thank: Ray and Madeleine Hazboun, Mary McGowan, Lily Cochrane, the Steeles, Malachy Magorrian, the Irish UN officers, Fr Michael Moloney and James O'Shea. A number of people made photographs available to me, among them the Maginn family, Colette McCartney (the cover photo of Owen with parishioners at Chikumbi is hers), Tom Casey (cover background photo), Fionnbarra O'Cuilleanain, Don Burke, the Hazbouns, and the SMA archives, Cork. Sincere thanks to

St Patrick's High School for the photograph of the opening 1934 and to Ann Fitzpatrick for the 1933 photo of Drumaroad Primary School.

I am most grateful to Paddy Jennings, Castlewellan, Sexton Doran, Loughinisland, Paraic Kelly, Cornamona, and Fachtna O'Driscoll for reading all or parts of my typescript. Thanks to Shanway Press, Belfast for their care and patience in printing the book and to Ann Fitzpatrick, Yvonne McClean and colleagues for help with launching it. Finally, thanks to the Irish Provincial Council of the SMA for their generous support and encouragement.

Michael O'Shea sma

25 June 2009 - 150th anniversary of the death of the Founder of the Society of African Missions, Melchior de Marion Brésillac in Freetown, Sierra Leone.

michael.oshea@sma.ie

Address in Africa:
St Augustine's Major Seminary,
Box 81011 Kabwe, Zambia
(or c/o Provincial Superior, African Missions,
Blackrock Road, Cork, Ireland).